HAPPY VALLEY

HAPPY VALLEY

THE STORY OF THE ENGLISH IN KENYA

Nicholas Best

First published in hardback by Martin Secker & Warburg and in paperback by
Marlborough Editions.

This edition first published in 2013 by:

Thistle Publishing
36 Great Smith Street
London
SW1P 3BU
ISBN 13: 978-1-909869-19-6

CONTENTS

ILLUSTRATIONS

ACKNOWLEDGMENTS

The author wishes to thank the following for their help: the Duke of Portland, the Duke of Manchester, David Allen, Charles Douglas-Home, Haydon Warren Gash, Eustace Gitonga, Ian Hardy, Randle Meinertzhagen, J. L. Warui and Brian Yonge.

He acknowledges his extensive use of the following books: *No Picnic on Mount Kenya* by Felice Benuzzi; *The murder of Lord Erroll* by Rupert Furneaux; *The hunt for Kimathi* by Ian Henderson and Philip Goodhart; *White man's country* by Elspeth Huxley; *Kenya diary 1902–6* and *Army diary 1899–1926* by Richard Meinertzhagen.

The author and his publishers wish to thank the following for their permission to quote: William Blackwood & Sons Ltd: *Confessions of a rum runner* by James Barbican (1927); Chatto and Windus Ltd: *White man's country* by Elspeth Huxley (1935); Hamish Hamilton Limited: *The hunt for Kimathi* by Ian Henderson and Philip Goodhart (1958); Michael Joseph Ltd: *My sister, Isak Dinesen* by Thomas Dinesen (1975); William Kimber and Company Ltd: *No picnic on Mount Kenya* by Felice Benuzzi (1952); Oxford University Press Eastern African Branch: *'Mau Mau' detainee* by J. M. Kariuki (1963); A. D. Peters & Co. Ltd: *Men at arms* by Evelyn Waugh (Chapman and Hall Ltd, 1952); Mrs Theresa Searight: *Kenya diary 1902–6* (Oliver & Boyd, 1957) and *Army diary 1899–1926* (Oliver & Boyd, 1960) by Richard Meinertzhagen; Anthony Sheil Associates Limited: *The iron snake* by Ronald Hardy (William Collins Sons and Co. Ltd, 1965); Auberon Waugh and George Weidenfeld & Nicolson Limited: *The diaries of Evelyn Waugh* (1976).

CHAPTER ONE
THE DREADED MASAI COUNTRY

Surrounded by a Masai war party intent on cutting him to pieces, the Scots explorer Joseph Thomson did the only thing possible to save his life. He took out his false teeth and flashed them at the advancing warriors.

The Masai drew the obvious conclusion. Clearly the twenty-five-year-old white man, the first they had ever seen, was a sorcerer and caster of spells. Abandoning all thoughts of murder, they turned to run and were only persuaded to creep back after Thomson had discreetly replaced his teeth and tapped them with his knuckles to show how firm they were.

'As they thought I could do the same thing with my nose or eyes,' he recalled, 'they hailed me as a veritable *lybon n'ebor* [white medicine-man].'

But being a medicine-man worked both ways, as Thomson was soon to find out. An epidemic of rinderpest was ballooning outwards across the Kenya highlands in 1883. It was killing Masai cattle in tens of thousands and rotting the flesh of the unfortunate creatures which still remained alive.

As he continued on his journey, word quickly went ahead that the white man with the strange hair was responsible for this devastating disease and the famine which followed on its heels. He would shortly catch up with his reputation.

Thomson was in Kenya, then known as Masai Land, at the behest of the Royal Geographical Society. He was looking for a practical short cut from the ports of the East African coast to Lake Victoria and the central African kingdom of Buganda.

Instead of taking the comparatively safe but long and unhealthy southern route, the short cut was to push straight through territory dominated by the most warlike tribe south of the Sahara. The territory was the last truly mysterious part of Africa since the identification by John Hanning Speke of Lake Victoria as the probable source of the river Nile in 1862.

The society was mean with money. At first it was prepared to put up only £2,000 to finance Thomson's expedition, when experienced Africa hands were agreed that a caravan through Masai country could not be properly equipped and fitted out with fighting men for less than double that amount. That was why the youthful Thomson was in command. No one else wanted to know.

Yet Thomson was not in the least put out. Already the veteran of two African expeditions, he firmly believed in the lucky star which had been with him all his life – and besides, exploring was the only work he knew.

At the age of eleven he had volunteered for Stanley's expedition to find Livingstone, only to have the scheme vetoed by his mother. He was driven forward by an obsession, a never-ending desire to see over the next horizon, to climb the highest mountain and cross the widest desert.

That he might end up spitted on the spear of a Masai *moran* in the process never seriously entered his head. As well as immense self-confidence, he possessed an abundance of the quality which, above all else, had served to bring one quarter of the world under British domination: a total inability to appreciate the gravity of the danger lying ahead.

To be fair, Thomson fully realised that testing the viability of the short route to the central lake would be no easy task. He found out as soon as he arrived on the slave trade island of Zanzibar to begin recruiting porters for a caravan to the interior:

'The very idea of going to the dreaded Masai country was sufficient to take their breath away,' he remembered. The only porters willing to risk their lives with him, and then only after he had promised to ask no questions about their past activities, were 'the blind and the lame, the very refuse of Zanzibar rascaldom, beachcombers, thieves, murderers, runaway slaves, most of them literally rotten with a life of debauchery'. Even these intended to desert with three months' advance pay as soon as they had gone a couple of days' march up-country.

Fortunately, Thomson had been to Zanzibar before and was wise to their game. Backed by an illiterate Maltese sail maker named James Martin, who had begged to join the party, he took elaborate precautions to make sure no one should escape until they reached the Masai. Camp was always pitched in an open spot, and Thomson ostentatiously gave his sentries orders to shoot anyone attempting to sneak out at night.

Once among the Masai, he calculated that desertion would cease to be much of a problem. With warrior *morans* prowling around the camp perimeter, thirsting for the slightest excuse to blood their spears, nobody in his right mind would ever drop behind.

After several weeks of preparation, during which Thomson sometimes wondered whether it would ever get under way at all, the expedition finally left the Mombasa mission station that was the gateway to Africa on 15 March 1883. Somehow he had managed to scrape together more than a hundred porters for the venture.

Twenty-nine carried beads – not then a cliché – to distribute to the natives. Thirty-four carried iron, brass or copper wire, fourteen cloth, fifteen personal stores, nine clothes, boots and books of poetry, five ammunition and six scientific apparatus or photographic equipment. There were also two donkeys, Nil Desperandum and Excelsior, who answered when in the mood to Dick and Billy.

Thomson stayed to chat with Mrs Shaw, the missionary's wife, while the caravan filed past him on the outward leg of a journey that was to cover thousands of miles over the next fourteen months. Not until the last man had shouldered his load did he take leave of the English couple.

'I shook hands with my pleasant hostess,' he wrote, 'lifted my hat, and set my face towards the setting sun.' A quarter of an hour later, he was in the unknown.

The following day, though still far away from Masai country, the caravan had its first glimpse of what a marauding war party could do in the form of hundreds of skulls strewn across the ground where *morans* had slaughtered three hundred Nyika tribesmen. That night, in spite of Thomson spreading false rumours that the Masai were already in their rear, two men managed to desert.

For the most part, however, the tribes lying in the expedition's immediate path were not only friendly but obligingly anxious to please. At Ndara, for instance, about ninety miles inland across the waterless Taru desert, the caravan received an enthusiastic welcome from the women of the Teita tribe, who ran to greet it with curious stares and excited laughter.

From underneath his pith helmet, Thomson surreptitiously noticed that the girls had 'pendant breasts flapping against their bosoms like half-empty, loosely-attached leather bottles'.

'In a short time,' he went on, 'we found ourselves camped under a shady sycamore, drinking deep draughts of clear water from a cool rill which splashed and tumbled down the rugged face of Ndara, and invited us by its merry music to the luxury of a bath.'

Sadly, though itching to tear off his clothes and plunge straight in, Thomson could not bring himself to do so. The man who had explored a thousand horizons was suddenly bashful. He found himself unable to strip naked before the interested gaze of the natives.

Only after the bottle-breasted girls had wended their way home towards nightfall, with many a wistful backward glance, did the great white god at length unbutton his clothes and surrender himself to the welcoming stream. Even then he made sure first that no one was peeking from the bushes.

As the expedition advanced towards the beginnings of Masai country proper, rumours began to expand and multiply at an alarming rate. There was peace, there was war, there was famine in the land ahead. The last caravan to venture among the Masai had reportedly been responsible for the killing of a girl – an unheard-of occurrence in a society where women constituted a source of wealth, and a clear breach of the rules.

The whole country was said to be screaming for revenge. If rumours were to be believed, thousands of warriors were ready and waiting for Thomson's inadequately armed party to step into their territory. Prospects of a peaceful passage to Lake Victoria seemed doubtful in the extreme.

Yet when at last it came, the expedition's first contact with the Masai was nothing like as traumatic as conjecture had led Thomson to expect. Indeed, compared with the build-up, it was something of an anti-climax.

News reached the caravan by way of a group of Masai women, themselves returning from a food-buying expedition, that the European's presence had been reported to the tribal elders. They were even now considering what to do about it. In view of the killing of the girl by the previous caravan, opinion was heavily divided as to Thomson's future.

Some were for annihilating him on the spot. Others were curious to see a man of whom they had heard such interesting descriptions. After much discussion therefore, they had compromised by agreeing to send a deputation to interview Thomson the following day. On the result of that meeting would his future depend.

Understandably, Thomson was apprehensive next morning as he waited to learn his fate. Privately he was determined to press on and enter Masai Land come what may – but he would naturally prefer to make the crossing in peace, with the active blessing of the inhabitants. By mid-afternoon he had reached the height of nervousness when loud chanting from the forest told him his hosts had arrived.

'Seizing a tuft of grass in one hand, and our guns in the other, in token that we meant peace, but were prepared to fight, we proceeded outside to hear our fate,' he reported. 'Passing through the forest, we soon set our eyes upon the dreaded warriors that had been so long the subject of my waking dreams, and I could not but involuntarily exclaim "What splendid fellows!" as I surveyed a band of the most peculiar race of men to be found in all Africa.'

Splendid indeed. Six foot tall, daubed in oil and clay, armed with shovel-headed spears and shields of bullock hide, they carried themselves with the aristocratic dignity of men who reigned unchallenged throughout the length and breadth of their world, and knew it. The Masai were afraid of no one, least of all a white man. Because they were not afraid, and could afford to be magnanimous, they had agreed among themselves to let the caravan pass in peace.

This was wonderful news. Thomson promptly invited the warriors to spend the night at his camp. They duly did, looking around inquisitively and examining everything he showed them with the combination of curiosity and aloofness that was a major characteristic of their tribe.

Taking great care not to favour one more than any other, Thomson ceremoniously presented a gift to each warrior from his stores. He was not a fighting man. He intended to prove that it was possible to cross Masai Land without firing so much as a single shot in anger. To this end his caravan contained sixty thousand specially prepared sets of coloured beads so that, if anything did go wrong, he would always be able to buy his way out of trouble.

Trouble was coming, though, and not the kind that could be met with generous handouts of wire, beads or cloth. Thomson was about to be betrayed. Though the Masai elders were in favour of the white man's passing, it seemed the younger men could not bear to let the opportunity for such sport slip through their fingers.

Their impatience had prevailed over wiser counsel. Having nothing better to do, warriors for miles around were gathering together in organised groups, savouring the imminent prospect of a massacre. It wouldn't be long before they attacked.

Learning that the raid was planned for next morning, Thomson frantically pondered his options. To press on in the face of impossibly superior numbers – as many as two thousand warriors might be coming for him – was clearly out of the question. Though no coward, he was not looking for 'sensationalism and adventure'. His was a scientific expedition, with definite geographical goals which would not be served by unnecessary slaughter.

If he could not go forward, therefore, he would have to go back. The whole idea of retreat was repugnant to him, but there was no sensible alternative that he could see.

Conceding to the inevitable, Thomson gave orders for camp to be struck that night, secretly after dark, so that the lurking *morans* would know nothing about it until the withdrawal was well under way.

Not a sound broke the stillness as the porters carefully packed their loads and shouldered their equipment. As soon as the caravan was ready to move, extra wood was heaped onto the camp fire to build up a strong blaze as the porters tiptoed silently into the outer darkness.

They knew the first half mile would be the most dangerous, because the column had to pass within a whisker of the warriors' camp. Every man in the expedition prayed that Dick and Billy, the two donkeys, would not choose this particular moment to start braying. Their prayers were answered. It was not the donkeys that broke the silence but the surrounding hyenas, whose scalp-prickling laughter mocked the unhappy porters and hastened them in their flight.

Once safely past the warrior camp, the men quickly picked up speed, anxious to put a good distance between themselves and the long-legged Masai while they still had the chance. The night was heavy with tropical rain, punctuated by thunder and lightning, but nothing could deflect the terrified porters.

Driven now by headlong panic, they pushed on for most of the night, cold, wet and exhausted, until at length they reached shelter just before dawn and threw themselves down to rest. Now, at last, they thought, the expedition would be abandoned. Now, at last, they would be returning to the peace and tranquillity of the coast.

Unfortunately for them, Thomson was not a man to give up without a struggle, particularly now that he had had his first exhilarating taste of the Masai. He shared the general gloom for a day or two, but not for longer. It was obvious that what he needed were reinforcements — both of men and trading goods — such as could only be obtained from the coast.

Oblivious to the cursing and complaining which now broke out behind his back, he ordered the 'insolent and mutinous' porters to set up camp where they were, under the command of James Martin. He himself would make a lightning trip on foot to Mombasa — a small matter of two hundred miles there and another two hundred back - to recruit the extra men he was obviously going to need.

In just over a month Thomson was back up-country, having obtained the necessary porters cum fighting men through a combination of press gang-ing and force of his powerful personality. With them came an additional twenty-one loads of wire, ten of cloth and five of beads to grease the ever-outstretched palms of the Masai.

Gunfire and loud cheering greeted his return. In spite of themselves, the men of the expedition were beginning to warm to Thomson, a man far removed from the missionaries of the coast who summed up their experience of white men. And now that he had rejoined them, the lucky star in which he placed such faith was about to shine on him once more.

He met up with a one-eyed slave trader named Juma, a half-Arab, half-negro Swahili who made a living transporting slaves and ivory to the coast for export to Arabia. Juma was a hard man and a seasoned traveller. More important, he commanded a large caravan about to enter Masai Land. He was prepared to let the white man's column come along too.

This was all Thomson needed. Together, the two caravans added up to a force of several hundred armed men, more than a match for even the most numerous Masai war party. This time there would be no going back. On 11 August 1883, filled with renewed confidence and rising expectations, Joseph Thomson re-entered Masai Land for the last time.

By early September, after a lengthy trek dogged every foot of the way by *morans* eager for blood but settling for beads and cloth, the convoy arrived in the cloud-covered uplands of Kenya. They were approaching the Great Rift Valley which splits Africa from Egypt all the way to Mozambique.

The route had taken them across an enormous plain beside which ran the cold waters of a river known to the Masai as Uaso Nairobi. At the head of the plain lay a thickly wooded region occupied by the Masai's ancient enemies, the Kikuyu, a wily tribe of forest dwellers.

As the caravan progressed towards the Rift Valley, the Kikuyu made several attempts from the protection of the trees to stampede Thomson's cattle. When that failed, they sent their women to trade with his porters – or rather to rob them by the not particularly subtle method of luring them into the woods where Kikuyu warriors were waiting with heavy clubs.

Nobody was happier than Thomson to leave the Kikuyu behind at length and descend 2,000 feet onto the volcano-strewn floor of the Rift Valley. So far as penetrating Masai Land was concerned, the major part of the expedition was coming to an end. Northwards, the remainder of the journey to Lake Victoria and Buganda would lead through relatively peaceful country.

Despite the initial setbacks, and there had been many, the expedition was undoubtedly a success. Though not yet free of the Masai, Thomson could afford a pause for rest and recuperation.

On 30 September, therefore, he pushed his way through thousands of zebra to pitch camp along the luxurious shores of Lake Naivasha. The lake lay some 360 miles and six months from his starting point at the coast. By measuring the temperature at which water came to the boil, he calculated the altitude at 6,200 feet above sea level, which explained the coolness of the evenings.

To the east rose up a distant chain of mountains, perhaps forty miles long, their summits hedged in cloud. The local Masai had no collective name for these mountains, but other people called the area Nyandarua. Unaware of this, Thomson decided to christen them the Aberdare range after Lord

Aberdare, president of the Royal Geographical Society and sponsor of the expedition.

Yet although the highest peak in the Aberdares stands at an impressive 13,120 feet, it was not that which held Thomson's attention as he turned his face towards the rising sun. He was far more interested in something else, something which might or might not lie beyond the Aberdares. He was interested in investigating a thirty-four-year-old claim that somewhere in the plain behind, almost straddling the Equator, lay an enormous mountain covered in snow.

The claim had been made by a bespectacled German missionary carrying an umbrella and burdened with the unmelodious name of Ludwig Krapf. On 3 December 1849, while unsuccessfully attempting to convert the Wakamba tribe to Christianity on behalf of Great Britain's Church Missionary Society, Krapf had noticed a gap in the rain-swollen clouds north west of him.

Through the gap he claimed to have seen 'two large horns or pillars, as it were, rising over an enormous mountain ... covered with a white substance'. This was the first recorded sighting by a European of the mountain known to the Africans by many names, and to the Kikuyu as Kirinyaga, the mountain of whiteness. It was usually abbreviated to Kenya.

In his own day, Krapf's report had been widely ridiculed by geographers in far-away London, unwilling to accept that the received wisdom could be confounded by the existence of snow on the Equator. They talked instead of chalk or white stones littering the summit, anything but snow. Krapf, they argued, was no scientist but a missionary blinded by religious zeal. He was probably off his head after too long in the tropics. Mistakes were easily made in heavy cloud.

Nor were they impressed by one of Krapf's colleagues, Johann Rebmann, who had already recorded the existence of another snow-topped mountain further south, a mountain called Kilima Njaro. One geographer, who had never set foot in East Africa, sneered openly at Rebmann's claim. He called it 'a most delightful mental recognition only, not supported by the evidence of his senses'. In other words, anyone who said there was snow on the Equator was a liar.[1]

But Thomson had climbed the lower slopes of Kilimanjaro on his way up-country and had seen snow with his own eyes. If one report was true, why not the other?

Sitting in his tent at Lake Naivasha, with the main purpose of his mission well on the way to completion, he had time to contemplate the secondary reason for his journey. This was to check out Krapf's report and make an attempt to pinpoint Mount Kenya exact location.

Juma's men would soon be going north in search of ivory. There was no reason why Thomson should follow at once. He decided instead to take a small party on a flying visit in search of the mysterious second mountain.

His Swahili companions were horrified. 'On mooting my scheme,' he remembered, 'it was received with laughter and incredulity, which changed to remonstrance and profound astonishment when it was seen that I was serious.

'"What!" said they; "do you think you can penetrate a district with a few men, which we should be afraid to attempt with several hundreds? ... Do you know that a few years ago a caravan of two hundred was totally annihilated in that very district?" ...

'My only reply was that Mount Kenya *had to be reached somehow*, as all my countrymen wanted to know the truth about it; moreover, I had now learned something of the ways of the Masai, and thought I might rely upon my character as a *lybon* (medicine-man), where men and guns were of little use.'

He got his way, of course, as he so often did. Taking thirty of his best men, plus a similar number of Swahili traders who appear to have followed him everywhere out of the curiosity of sane men for a lunatic, Thomson set out towards the east on 6 October. He was armed with little more than a rifle and a set of false dentures.

Almost immediately, while on his way around the northernmost shoulder of the Aberdare range, he was intercepted by a group of Masai. They insisted that he should use his magic powers to turn back the rinderpest that was decimating their livestock.

Thomson thought fast. The rinderpest would certainly stop, he promised, but only ten days after he had left the neighbourhood. This idea gained a mixed reception from the warriors. It was only after considerable argument among themselves that they reluctantly agreed to let him continue his journey unmolested towards the north east.

He was now in an enchanted green land of wild fig trees, podo and cedar-like junipers. The trees were often a hundred feet tall, mingled with clumps of yellow cassia and maidenhair ferns clustered along the banks of the mountain streams which trickled down towards the plains.

The altitude was so high that the grass outside Thomson's tent was unmistakably covered in hoar frost in the mornings. He greeted this phenomenon by dancing a Scotch reel in his overcoat – to the consternation of his shivering porters, for whom the highlands held no charm. Coast-bred every one, they longed only to return to the life-giving warmth of the open plain, far below the mist-drenched country that now enveloped them.

To cheer them up, Thomson waited a couple of hours after daylight for the sun to take the chill off the air, then took his rifle into the nearby bush in search of wild game for the pot. Full stomachs all round would do wonders for morale, particularly as the Masai pestering of the past few days had made it impossible for the party to cook any food. They had been living off mealie cobs prepared before they set out.

As luck would have it, the first animal he came across was not a candidate for the cooking pot at all, but a fully grown leopard, concealed in a patch of grass near the top of a steep slope. It growled as Thomson approached, then retreated into heavier undergrowth before he could get a shot in. Undeterred, Thomson plunged in after it. A leopard wasn't edible, but it would look good in his trophy book if he could bring it down.

Crashing headlong through the scrub, he climbed rapidly towards the crest of the ridge. He intended to get a good view of the leopard's movements from the top. He got a view, all right, but not the one he had been expecting:

'Through a rugged and picturesque depression in the range rose a gleaming snow-white peak with sparkling facets, which scintillated with the superb beauty of a colossal diamond. It was, in fact, the very image of a great crystal or sugar-loaf. At the base of this beautiful peak were two small excrescences like supporters to a monument.

'From there, at a very slight angle, shaded away a long glittering white line, seen above the dark mass of the Aberdare range like the silver lining of a dark storm-cloud. This peak and silvery line formed the central culminating point of Mount Kenia.'

The mountain was a good sixty-five miles away, but looked much closer because of the thin highland air. Entranced, all idea of hunting forgotten, Thomson simply stood and stared. Even as he watched, soft clouds came hurrying in from nowhere to gather protectively round the summit, like nuns defending the Mother Superior from rape.

Yet Thomson had already seen more than enough to lure him onwards. His eyes filled with unaccustomed moisture. He had become the first of many Europeans who would weep for Mount Kenya.

To his everlasting regret, though he went on to reach the base of the mountain, he was prevented from climbing it by the Masai, more than ever convinced by now that he was behind the rinderpest blackening their land. The party had run out of beads to distribute.

Although Thomson had been removing his teeth at least once every hour for the benefit of his onlookers, this was no longer enough for the *morans*. The teeth caper was wearing thin. They wanted to see him take out his eyes and nose. Failing that, they would kill him.

So there was nothing for it but yet another retreat after dark, in several groups this time so as to reduce tracks through the scrub. Because of the excessively cold mornings, the Masai could be relied upon not to leave their huts until long after daybreak, by which time Thomson and his men were already far away.

Instead of retracing their steps, they headed north west out of Masai Land towards a prearranged rendezvous alongside Lake Baringo. A few days' forced march across a plateau in which 'buffaloes, zebras, elephants and rhinoceroses were in astonishing numbers' then brought them to safety and a cheerful reunion with the rest of the caravan.

The reunion celebrations did not last long, however. Thomson's bottomless fund of energy soon took him west towards Uganda and the great inland sea of Lake Victoria, while the Swahili traders continued north in their hunt for ivory. Thomson considered pressing right on to the Nile, but eventually decided against it. For him, the high spot of the expedition was already over.

His thoughts lingered long on Mount Kenya and the Aberdare region, a marvellously temperate land to which he had so readily adapted because it 'roused stirring memories of home scenes, so distinctly European-like was the aspect of the crags'. It was his considered opinion that 'a more charming region is probably not to be found in all Africa'.

Of the return trip to Mombasa he remembered little, because a serious attack of dysentery – which would have killed a lesser man and, indeed, almost killed him – left a blank of many weeks in his mind. Having walked on his own two feet all the way to Lake Victoria, he was now carried back towards the coast by his porters. They had come to believe that no disaster could possibly strike the expedition while its leader remained alive.

From their point of view, this was correct. Although Thomson personally disapproved of the practice, it was customary then for porters to forfeit their wages if by any mischance the expedition leader died on them.

He arrived back at the Mombasa mission station on 24 May 1884 – Queen Victoria's birthday – having not seen another white face for almost a year. He had penetrated Masai country, and he had confirmed the existence of Mount Kenya. More than that, he had neither fired a shot in anger nor hanged a porter during the entire period. That made him unique in the annals of African exploration.

On the debit side, his health had been ruined by a prolonged round of fever which he himself recognised would shorten his life by several years. Even the return sea voyage failed to restore his strength. When he got back to England, having travelled via Zanzibar and Bombay, he half-jokingly described himself as 'a sad wreck – only a few planks, as it were, holding together'. And the ordeal was not yet over.

On 3 November 1884, after a lengthy convalescence, Thomson was well enough to present himself at the University of London theatre in Burlington House for a meeting of the Royal Geographical Society at which he had been awarded star billing.

The meeting was a personal triumph on a large scale. Some of the more sensational aspects of the journey had been judiciously leaked in advance, with the result that geographers from all over the country had gathered to hear him speak.

Proceedings were opened by Lord Aberdare, proud patron of a new mountain range, who spoke in glowing terms of the great difficulties and danger Thomson had faced. *The Times* reported it thus: 'In his expedition Mr Thomson had marched about 3000 miles, of which 1200 lay through wholly new countries (Cheers).' For the fifth son of a stonemason, he had indeed come a long way.

Thomson's book *Through Masai Land* came out in January 1885. It was an immediate best seller. The irresistible combination of volcanoes, mountain ranges, wild animals and wilder men – not to mention occasional glimpses of naked black women seven feet tall – guaranteed it a wide circulation in Victorian England and won for its author an instant entrée to high society.

Thomson found this adulation overpowering. It meant that his time was no longer his own. Wherever he went he had to fight off requests for interviews, lectures, articles and after-dinner speeches, all of which served to tie him down and box him in. The wilds of unknown Africa were where he wanted to be. London he could live without.

One of the first to read *Through Masai Land* was an ambitious young lawyer named Henry Rider Haggard, who had only that year been called to the Bar. As a youth, Haggard had been sent to South Africa to make his fortune but had come to the conclusion, between the Boers and the Zulus, that there was no future in it.

He had returned to England to set up house in West Kensington. While doors all over London were being opened to Thomson, Haggard's one aim in life was to write a better adventure novel than one published two years previously: R. L. Stevenson's *Treasure Island*. In Joseph Thomson he found his plot.

Imagination fired by the Masai expedition, Haggard sat down in his dining room early in 1885 and wrote *King Solomon's Mines* in six weeks. He placed the 'Kukuanaland' of the story firmly in what is now Zimbabwe, but cheerfully stole many of his ideas from Thomson (fearing an action for plagiarism, he later denied it in a letter to *The Athenaeum*). Haggard already had an interest in East Africa because his kinsman, D. C. Haggard, was British vice-consul on Lamu, the Arab island off the Kenya coast.

King Solomon's Mines is narrated by the white hunter Allan Quatermain, who leads two European companions, Sir Henry Curtis and Captain John Good, across unknown wasteland in search of a legendary diamond mine. Stumbling across an arid desert – such as the Taru, standing between Mombasa and the Kenya highlands – they come eventually to a range of mountains perhaps forty or fifty miles away:

'There, straight before us, were two enormous mountains, the like of which are not, I believe, to be seen in Africa, if, indeed, there are any other such in the world, measuring each at least fifteen thousand feet in height, standing not more than a dozen miles apart, connected by a precipitous cliff of rock, and towering up in awful white solemnity straight into the sky.

'These mountains standing thus, like the pillars of a gigantic gateway, are shaped exactly like a woman's breasts. Their bases swelled gently up from the plain, looking, at that distance, perfectly round and smooth; and on the top of each was a vast round hillock covered with snow.'

Allowing for artistic licence – Mount Kenya is 17,058 feet, Kilimanjaro 19,340 feet, and they are separated by just over two hundred miles – Haggard stuck closely to Thomson's original story. No more so than when the three explorers have their first meeting with the warlike Kukuana tribe:

' "What does that beggar say?" asked Good.

"He says we are going to be scragged," I answered grimly.

"Oh Lord," groaned Good; and, as was his way when perplexed, put his hand to his false teeth, dragging the top set down and allowing them to fly back to his jaw with a snap. It was a most fortunate move, for next second the dignified crowd of Kukuanas gave a simultaneous yell of horror and bolted back some yards ...'

King Solomon's Mines was published just nine months after *Through Masai Land*. Within a few weeks it had sold more than five thousand copies, little short of miraculous for an unknown writer of boys' stories. Thomson was so annoyed by its success that he wrote a novel of his own about the Masai, only to discover that fiction was not his forte.

King Solomon's Mines, on the other hand, went on to sell in tens of thousands, for Haggard had put his finger on the new mood of the British public. The nineteenth-century upsurge in education – combined with a growing awareness of Britain's imperial role, fuelled by greater access to library books and newspapers – had given the masses a taste for mystery and romance which Africa filled to perfection.

Men like Thomson inked in the blank spots on the globe. People at home loved them for it. Here was the heady thrill of adventure, the lifeblood of the *Boys' Own Paper*, to be read below desk lids or by candle in the dorm after lights out – and by many of those adults whom Thomson customarily referred to as 'easy-chair geographers'.

Yet there was more to it than adventure, much more. Although Thomson had been prepared to wander through Masai Land simply for the hell of it, the hard-nosed businessmen of the Royal Geographical Society who had put up the cash for his expedition were far more interested in what might come of it in the way of trade. Trade, and ensuing profit for the motherland, was the only reason for the existence of the British Empire.

The great powers of Europe were beginning to look towards Africa as a massive counter in the absorbing game of politics. Thomson's journey raised the question of just how much profit could be squeezed from this vast new territory, at present under no country's sphere of influence.

Thomson himself, a romantic pure and simple, vigorously opposed the idea of opening up the area to commerce. He did not see himself as the representative of Mammon. So far as he was concerned, he told the *Pall Mall Gazette*: 'You cannot trade in that region unless the Masai allow you, and at present they would rather have your head than the present of a linendraper's warehouse.'

Others agreed with him. At a time when budgets were things that balanced, powerful forces in Parliament, notably Lord Salisbury, were convinced that British involvement in East Africa could only lead to financial disaster.

Some people talked fondly of building a railway along Thomson's route from the coast to the flourishing kingdom of Buganda. The Foreign Office's view was that the five hundred miles in between constituted a sterile region of which nothing could be made. On the face of it, even the most optimistic had to admit that the prospects for trade did not look at all good.

Yet there were other, more important considerations to be taken into account. Germany, newest and most obstreperous power in Europe, was making hesitant but unmistakable attempts to muscle in on the new territory.

Inch by inch, peering over their shoulders all the while, the Germans were edging towards Uganda and the headwaters of the river Nile. They were determined to secure a foothold in the area while the parsimonious British were occupied elsewhere.

This was not a threat that London could ignore for long. Control of the Nile meant effective domination of the agrarian economy of Egypt, whose Suez Canal provided the short cut to India.

General Gordon had pointed this out while Governor-General of the Sudan. His plan for subduing the Masai and securing the Nile for Britain had been turned down by a Government ruled by Little Englanders for whom any colonial involvement was a sin.

Whether the Government liked it or not, though, Germany was already on the march. Behind the Germans would come the French and the Italians. There was really no way now that the British could avoid becoming involved in the scramble for Africa.

1. The missionaries' claims to be taken seriously were not helped by their incompetence in recording their sightings. Krapf made no attempt to get an astronomical bearing on Mount Kenya. Subsequent efforts by English geographers to establish its whereabouts had to be based on an abstruse calculation of how much distance he might have covered in each day's march from the coast.

Using this method, E. G. Ravenstein of the Royal Geographical Society placed Mount Kenya in the empty plain south west of Lake Naivasha. Thomson only had to look over his shoulder to see no mountain there. Krapf's own map put the mountain in the Tanzanian sector of Lake Victoria. Native reports must have convinced Thomson that east of the Aberdares was the place to look.

Curiously, very little notice was taken at the time of a Captain Short, who also claimed to have seen a snow mountain in 1849. On Krapf's map, Short's mountain lay slightly north of the Equator, between Archer's Post and the Lorian Swamp – much closer to Mount Kenya's true position.

CHAPTER TWO

THE LUNATIC EXPRESS

The first Britons to reach East Africa had been sailors stocking up with food and water for the long voyage across the ocean to India. They followed the route taken by Vasco da Gama, whose arrival at the port of Mombasa in 1498 had touched off more than two centuries of intermittent Portuguese colonisation along the coast.

The Portuguese never succeeded in taking root however. When an Arab army finally drove them away from Mombasa in 1729, they left behind little more than the stronghold of Fort Jesus, which straddles Mvita, the island of war. The fort still dominates the seaward approaches to the old harbour.

British involvement in Kenya really began in 1824, when two Royal Navy ships, HMS *Barracouta* and HMS *Leven*, while charting the coast for the Admiralty, found themselves drawn into a local squabble over who should rule Mombasa. From Muscat and Oman, at the head of the Persian Gulf, the Imam of Muscat claimed the East African coast as part of his empire. A local family of Arab sheikhs, the Mazruis, disputed his claim. Both sides looked to Britain for support.

The sailors lining the rail of HMS *Barracouta* knew little of this as they sailed into Mombasa harbour on 4 December 1823. As always when they entered port, they were far more interested in the experiences of their sister ship, HMS *Leven*.

The *Leven's* captain had earlier observed of another island: 'The *ladies* of this place, and in fact all others on the island of Madagascar, have full licence in the indulgence of their fancies or affections, and as in point of number the fair sex muster about three to one, they were ready to embark by *hundreds* whenever we anchored.'

To the seamen's disappointment, no women surrounded the *Barracouta* when she dropped anchor. Instead, a delegation of Mazrui sheikhs came on board to demand British protection against the Omanis, three of whose dhows could be seen blockading the entrance to the harbour.

Unfortunately for the sheikhs, Britain had a longstanding treaty of friendship with Oman. The *Barracouta's* commander very properly refused to give any such undertaking.

The Mazrui family remained undeterred. If the British declined to raise their flag over Fort Jesus, then it could easily be done for them. The Mazruis waited only until the *Barracouta* had put to sea again before breaking out a home-made Union Jack over the battlements. The sight was not wasted on the Omani admiral watching from beyond the reef.

When Captain William Owen, senior officer of the two survey vessels, subsequently entered Mombasa in HMS *Leven* on 7 February 1824, he viewed the flag with astonishment. His first impulse was to tear it down and punish the offenders for their temerity. On reflection, however, he decided that the situation could be turned to Britain's advantage.

A man of his times, he detested with religious zeal the trade in black slaves to Arabia which was the corner stone of Mazrui power and prosperity. In Owen's eyes, Britons could never be slaves, and no one else should be either. Now here were the Mazruis offering not only to abolish slavery on the spot, but to cede Mombasa and two hundred miles of coastline to King George IV in return for support in their struggle against Oman.

Taking them at their word, Captain Owen graciously accepted the gift of Mombasa on behalf of His Majesty and sailed away again, leaving behind five men under Lieutenant Reitz to oversee the ending of slavery along the coast. Reitz and two others promptly died of fever. The governorship of Great Britain's newest territory thereupon passed to a teenaged midshipman, George Phillips. He was left holding the fort, as it were.

Phillips must have been surprised at the turn of events. He had been staying with his elder brother at Lisbon two years earlier when the *Leven* put in for a few days en route to the Cape. For a lark, he asked Owen to take him on as a midshipman, and was accepted. His subsequent elevation to colonial governor had been nothing if not rapid.

The slave trade, of course, remained as prevalent as ever, and the British Government recognised a bad deal when it saw one. A millstone like Mombasa was the last thing the British needed around their neck.

When Owen's report reached London, the Cabinet immediately rescinded his annexation and ordered the Union Jack to be hauled down again from Fort Jesus. The Mazruis were left to be crushed decisively by their enemies from Oman. Another half century would pass before Britain again became entangled on the East African mainland.

Meantime, merchant ships of another nation became increasingly active along the coast, seeking to monopolise a lucrative trade in copal, gum and ivory one way and cheap, unbleached cotton cloth the other. Operating mainly from the rival ports of Boston and Salem, American vessels visited the east coast in ever-growing numbers after Charles Millet, captain of the brig *Ann*, first dropped anchor in Mombasa in 1827.

As well as merchant ships came whalers and the occasional slaver, trying its luck a long way from home. At one stage the traffic was so enormous that there was even fantastic talk, much exaggerated by English alarmists, of the Americans setting up a colony for themselves in East Africa.

Their energy was boundless. Of the island port of Lamu, an English sea captain wrote: 'Few have visited it except the enterprising Americans whose star-spangled banner may be seen streaming in the wind where other nations, not excepting even my own country, would not deign to traffic.' A legacy of this trade, which lasted until the American Civil War, is the Swahili word *merikani*, meaning coarse cloth.

What ultimately forced the British to take notice of East Africa was the setting up in 1885 of a German charter company to exploit treaties negotiated with a number of illiterate native chiefs in what is now Tanzania. The chiefs ceded to Germany some 2,500 square miles of land nominally owned by the Sultan of Zanzibar, who had inherited the Omani mantle.

To gain the Sultan's blessing for this arrangement, the Germans casually sidled five warships into Zanzibar harbour, guns plainly visible, and assured him of their goodwill at all times. The race for Africa was about to begin. No major nation could afford to be out of it.

In 1888 a Scots businessman, Sir William Mackinnon, formed the Imperial British East Africa Company to administer and develop the British sphere of influence in that unknown and still undefined stretch of land separating the Germans from Uganda.

Under Royal charter, IBEA's brief was to govern the country in all but name. It was also to administer the coastal strip on behalf of the Sultan of Zanzibar, in return for a fifty-year lease granting the company virtual sovereignty over a two-hundred-mile stretch.

One of the first projects IBEA undertook was the much-heralded construction of a 'Central African Railway' from Mombasa to Lake Victoria. The railway could hardly be described as an unqualified success. It penetrated just seven miles from Mombasa, more than five hundred short of its destination, before being abandoned for lack of funds and skilled labour.

Worse was to follow. In return for the North Sea naval base of Heligoland, Germany grudgingly recognised Uganda in 1890 as a British sphere of influence. Instead of taking the source of the Nile under its own wing, the British Government happily lumbered IBEA with the task – with inevitable consequences.

Unsupported by public money, IBEA staggered under the weight of Uganda for a few difficult months and then declared itself unequal to the struggle. Faced with the need to show a profit for its shareholders, it proposed nothing less than total withdrawal from Uganda.

This, of course, was unthinkable to the British. Jingoism was at its height in Britain. Public opinion would not stand for imperial retreat on any front, particularly not in an area where the slave trade still flourished.

Especially incensed was Queen Victoria, who had been following the debate in the papers. She made it clear to the Prime Minister that she would take any withdrawal as a personal insult. So, in 1893, Uganda was officially declared a British protectorate.

Two years later the IBEA directors wound up their company and handed the poisoned chalice of East African administration to the body which should have accepted it in the first place: the British Government.

By this time the exact sphere of influence in East Africa had been precisely determined. Under the Heligoland treaty, someone in London drew a line straight through the Masai tribe and called one side of it British East Africa and the other side German East Africa.

With Queen Victoria's blessing, the line was kinked around Kilimanjaro to make Kaiser Wilhelm a birthday present of Africa's highest mountain. Unwelcome neighbour the Kaiser may have been, but, so far as the old lady was concerned, he was still family.

Bowing to the inevitable, the Cabinet turned its attention somewhat belatedly to East African affairs. With public money behind it, the old IBEA idea of a railway to Uganda could now be given a fresh airing, particularly since Germany was also known to be planning a railway from the port of Tanga to Lake Victoria.

An extensive survey of the proposed route had already been carried out by Captain J. R. L. Macdonald of the Royal Engineers, following the trail originally taken by Joseph Thomson. Early in 1896 construction began at last on the first few yards of a 582-mile line that was to take countless lives and more than five years to build.

Public money was one thing, but skilled labour proved to be quite another. Few of the African tribesmen around Mombasa, where the line was to begin, had the knowledge or the expertise to work on a railway line. None of them wanted to anyway, not even for the bright rupee which had recently been introduced as the protectorate's official currency.

Indeed the full significance of money had yet to dawn on them. European missionaries liked to talk of beating swords into ploughshares. In the tribesmen's experience, the reverse did not hold true at all. Weapons forged from melted-down rupees were so soft that they invariably crumbled in the hand.

Furthermore, the population density along the railroad's right of way averaged just two adult natives per square mile. With thousands of labourers needed to carry the line forward, it became increasingly clear that the work force would have to be imported from abroad.

The obvious answer was to recruit from India. The sub-continent's vast railway network had created a solid nucleus of stone cutters, smiths, carpenters and other craftsmen well versed in the technique of railway building. India also had a plentiful supply of lower grade and unemployed workmen who would jump at the chance of a job overseas.

From India, too, would come European engineers and surveyors accustomed to working with coolies and already inured to the harsh climate of the tropics. The newly formed Railway Committee acted at once. It recruited from India as many coolies as could be persuaded to immigrate to Kenya on a three-year contract. In so doing it unwittingly fired the opening shot of a bitter racial war that was to last well over seventy years before finally being resolved.

During 1896 and 1897, Indian coolies descended on Mombasa by the boatload. Many were low caste untouchables. Almost all were illiterate, unable to find regular work in their own country. To get higher wages, a good number had passed themselves off as experienced stonemasons, only to be unmasked once they had been issued with a hammer and chisel.

Beset by financial worries and an unrealistic work schedule, the Railway Committee could not afford to be choosy. It admitted unqualified Indians to the new country in hundreds at first and then in thousands as the need for workers grew. The Indians brought unfamiliar diseases with them, probably including venereal disease. It spread rapidly to the African women who flocked to the railway camps to sell themselves for food or brightly-coloured bolts of cloth.

Reaction to this invasion varied considerably from tribe to tribe among those who found themselves in the railway's path. The line passed through Wakamba country, for instance, at a time of great famine. The warriors raised no objection to their women living with the coolies in return for food and shelter.

Indeed, once the famine had passed and children began to be born in the railhead camps, the Wakamba announced that the Indians could keep the women as long as they liked, provided they returned the miscegenated offspring to the tribe.

But the Nandi – one of the most belligerent of Kenya's forty-two-odd tribes – took great exception to the prostituting of their womenfolk at the hands of the brown men who poured into their territory. Particularly corrupt was the railway camp at Fort Ternan, a dismal place in which local women and children were nightly subjected to appalling sexual mistreatment.

The Indians' behaviour did not go unnoticed by the Nandi. From beyond the defences of Fort Ternan, their warriors began to plan a bloody reprisal.

They watched and waited for the right moment to massacre the Indians and take their women back.

Fortunately for the coolies, the railway authorities were alive to the danger and moved to head it off while there was still time. An order went out for Fort Ternan to be cleared of local women. Under the command of Robert Turk, a squad of railway police moved into the camp in the middle of the morning, when the coolies were out at work.

What happened next was recorded by Turk in his diary: 'We went through that place with a comb, tent to tent, rousing out the whores, I never saw such a harem of whores – from coffee to black as coal and done up to the nines ...

'The Indos got mad when they saw their tickly going and some of them got rough and we had to clobber a few. We leave them the muck, some eighty or ninety first-class Coast and Masai whores, and we take Nandi girls and some Lumbwa and Wa-kamasie and a whole lot of little boys and girls the Indos had been at, it made you cry to see them.'

Turk's men went back to the camp in strength that evening, prepared for a mutiny from the returning coolies who had been so unceremoniously robbed of their pleasures. But there was no mutiny. To Turk's surprise, the Indians took their loss philosophically. 'They did not want trouble, only women,' he commented in disgust. 'If the whores don't go round they have plenty of mules to fall back on ...'

And the Masai? How did they react to the sudden appearance of the railway in their midst? Amazingly, the warriors seem to have accepted it with hardly a murmur, according to contemporary accounts.

Why they did so has never been satisfactorily explained. One theory is that the railway was fulfilling an ancient tribal prophecy that an iron snake would one day cross their land from the lake of salt to the lands of the Great Lake.

A similar prophecy has been attributed to the Kikuyu. It sounds too good to be true, more the vision of a hack journalist than a witch doctor. Or perhaps it was the invention of a railway PR man, attempting to smooth a path across hostile terrain by filling the warriors' heads with a lot of guff about prophecies – which could be instantly fulfilled as soon as the first engine came puffing over the skyline.

Another theory argues that the Masai already had enough troubles of their own with outbreaks of smallpox, rinderpest and clan warfare occupying their full attention at the time of the railroad's appearance.

As always, the Masai's chief interest in life was cattle raiding. But the British had no cattle to steal. Nor, wisely, did the protectorate authorities attempt to prevent the *morans* from carrying out raids in areas where the white man as yet held no sway. The success of the railway depended entirely on the goodwill of the Masai. Both sides were fully aware of it.

Indeed a bond was established between the British and the Masai in the last years of the nineteenth century which was to survive throughout the long decades of colonial occupation. The bond was based on mutual respect for each other's qualities – both sides recognised each other as good fighting men – and a shared contempt for the less warlike tribes on the plains. It had its origins in the aftermath of the Kedong massacre of 1895.

The Kedong valley forms a small part of the larger geographical fault known as the Rift Valley. Passing through it one afternoon at the head of a large caravan carrying supplies for the British, a Swahili leader foolishly abused the hospitality of the local *morans* by kidnapping two Masai girls for his own amusement. His pleasure was short-lived. Later that same night, a band of warriors dropped round and killed 650 of his porters.

Since the Swahili caravan was clearly in the wrong, the matter might have rested there but for the impulsiveness of an English trader named Andrew Dick. He got it into his head that *Pax Britannica* had been violated. Against Government advice, he took it upon himself to see that the Masai were punished for what had happened.

Quickly recruiting three Frenchmen who happened to be on a hunting trip nearby, Dick led a punitive expedition against the Masai. He confiscated a large number of their cattle and set out to drive them back towards his own base.

Naturally the Masai came after Dick in great force. Exactly what took place when they caught up with him has never been established for certain, because the chief character in the drama did not survive to talk about it. Armed with a Remington, it seems Dick put up a strong fight and killed a great many warriors – estimates vary from seventeen to more than a hundred – before his rifle jammed.

For a few desperate minutes thereafter he continued to jab the useless weapon at the advancing *morans*, until eventually they closed in on him and cut him down. Then they withdrew, taking their dead and wounded with them.

The Kedong incident drove home two lessons to the Masai. It taught them that spears and shields were no use against bullets. And it taught them that British justice need not necessarily work against the black man. The Kenya administration imposed only a token fine on the tribe for destroying Government property and killing a white man, in recognition of the fact that the warriors had been excessively provoked.

By soft pedalling the massacre, the Government ensured peace and harmony for many years to come. From that time onwards, Lenana – leader and chief *laibon* of the Masai – was to remain a loyal and true friend of the British until the day of his death in 1911.

For their part, Europeans also learned to treat the Masai with respect. The site of the massacre was a salutary reminder. Several years afterwards, Kedong could still be identified from a distance by what looked like a large pile of ostrich eggs heaped on the ground. These proved, on closer inspection, to be the skulls of the 650 dead porters.

For all the Masai cared, then, railwaymen were free to come and go across their land whenever they wanted, provided the warriors were left in peace to carry on life as they pleased. The main threat to the railway's existence came not from hostile tribesmen, nor even from Opposition politicians in London bickering about the expense.

It came from the sheer size of a project that all but defeated the hapless engineers and administrators assigned to undertake it. Everything had to be begun from scratch, from the building of a wooden jetty at Mombasa to the construction of workshops and accommodation, to the digging of a rainwater reservoir supplementing the coast's inadequate drinking supply.

Kilindini, Mombasa's 'place of deep water', had to be expanded from nothing into a busy port capable of handling the phalanx of 30-ton locomotives, steel girders, fishplates, tenders, brake vans and sleepers by the million which would be hoisted onto dry land by a mobile steam crane, itself an import, operating along the new jetty.

Because Mombasa is an island, construction of the railway proper could not begin until completion of the Macupa Bridge linking it to the mainland. The bridge could not be completed without vast quantities of wood. There was plenty of suitable wood in Kenya, but it was 400 miles up-country on the slopes of the Rift Valley.

The only way the wood could be transported to Mombasa was by the railway, which had not yet been built. So timber had to be imported from England instead, leading to a delay of eight months in an already tight schedule.

By the end of 1896, the railway had advanced exactly twenty-three miles from Mombasa. Mathematically-inclined humorists were making arrangements for an end-of-line celebration to be held on the shores of Lake Victoria in 1924 or thereabouts. To make matters worse, more than five hundred workers had already gone sick with malaria, amoebic dysentery, jungle sores or pneumonia. A month later, one half of the entire work force was unfit for duty.

There were, in any case, no duties to perform. November 1896 had seen an official rainfall figure of 27½ inches. For more than three weeks the rail gangs were unable to move from their tents for fear of being washed away in the flooded rivers or subsiding culverts which were collapsing by the dozen.

Later, when suffering from acute dehydration in the desolate sterility of the waterless Taru desert, the coolies were to recall those November rains with bitter irony.

Fourteen months further on, in January 1898, the line had cleared another hundred miles between railhead and Mombasa, and the situation was looking a little less bleak. In their monthly progress report, the engineers allowed themselves a cautious note of optimism.

The Taru desert, far the most intractable stretch of the whole route – except perhaps the Kikuyu escarpment – was safely behind them. Survey parties reported that the land immediately ahead would not present any major engineering problems.

Though neither on schedule nor within budget, the Uganda railway – its enemies called it the lunatic express – was beginning to take a step closer to reality. If the recent rate of progress could be kept up during the coming year, the authorities could afford to be reasonably satisfied with their efforts. It seemed as if everything in the garden was going to be rosy at last.

Until the line reached Tsavo.

Tsavo is the Wakamba word for slaughter. It was, and is, an unremarkable piece of bush through which flowed the first important water obstacle to the railway since the Macupa Bridge, some 132 miles back down the line. The river had been spanned with a temporary bridge on a diversion, enabling the tracks to push ahead with all speed while a rear party got on with the lengthy job of building a permanent structure.

Construction of the permanent bridge was scheduled to take four months. In fact it took very nearly a year, thanks to the efforts of two maverick lions. Their activities achieved a mention in a Prime Minister's speech in the House of Lords and gained them long-lasting notoriety as J. H. Patterson's *The man-eaters of Tsavo*.

The statistics are clear enough. Before being hunted down, the two lions consumed between them twenty-eight Indian coolies and untold scores of Africans, of whom no official record was kept.

The lions' skill at evading detection was so great that they won a widespread reputation as poltergeists. They stampeded an entire railway camp, attracted large numbers of sportsmen and bounty hunters to East Africa, and made Patterson so famous around the world that he sold out twelve impressions of his book in five years.

Patterson was a lieutenant-colonel in the Indian Army, an experienced engineer with considerable knowledge of both railways and coolies. He had been given the job of overseeing construction of the permanent Tsavo bridge. Once completed it remained his personal monument to East Africa until the Germans blew it up during the Great War.

Patterson was typical of all that was best and worst in the British imperial officer of that time. A brave man, but also a harsh one, who treated the coolies as if they were subject to Queen's Regulations instead of being an indentured work force. A martinet as hard on himself as on his men, who brooked no nonsense from anyone. A man who was later to burn down the plague-ridden Indian quarter of Nairobi on his own initiative because, as he afterwards explained, he did not like the look of it.

For the moment, however, Patterson was just an engineer with a job to do. He was determined to see it done properly. In his opinion, he knew all about Indians. He thought them workshy and dishonest, but responsive to treatment if handled properly, as only a lieutenant-colonel of the Indian army could handle them.

Whenever he walked among the coolies, Patterson took with him his little book. In it he recorded every crime, great or small, committed by the train gangs, from insubordination to theft to – worst of all – slacking. When a mason named Karim Bux claimed that he was dying, and was therefore too ill to work, Patterson lit a fire under the invalid's bed, promising him that he would soon be up and about again – as indeed he was.

Ghastly as a public school prefect or a Sandhurst under-officer, Patterson prowled his empire continually, making a note of every minor transgression and ensuring that the offenders were dealt with at the daily punishment parade. No sin was too small for his hated book. Nothing ever escaped his attention.

It wasn't long before the work force decided to kill him.

The plan was to murder Patterson during his daily inspection of a quarry, and then to throw his body into the jungle, where it would swiftly be eaten. That way, the railway police would not be able to pin anything on the coolies. Or so they thought.

Unfortunately for them, one of their number covered his back by tipping off Patterson about the plot. The colonel was not impressed.

'I thanked him for his information, but determined to go to the quarry in the morning all the same, as at this stage of affairs I really did not believe that they were capable of carrying out such a diabolical scheme, and was rather inclined to think that the informant had been sent merely to frighten me.'

Strolling down to the quarry next day, Patterson observed the unease among the men. This did not deter him from taking out his pocket book in his usual manner and writing down the names of two mutinous coolies. Under the circumstances, it was not the most tactful thing he could have done.

'Immediately a yell of rage was raised by the whole body of some sixty men, answered by a similar shout from those I had first passed, and who numbered about a hundred. Both groups of men, carrying crowbars and flourishing their heavy hammers, then closed in on me in the narrow part of the ravine.

'I stood still, waiting for them to act, and one man rushed at me, seizing both my wrists and shouting out that he was going to "be hung and shot for me" – rather a curious way of putting it, but that was his exact expression. I easily wrenched my arms free, and threw him from me; but by this time I was closely hemmed in, and everywhere I looked I could see nothing but evil and murderous-looking faces.

'One burly brute, afraid to be the first to deal a blow, hurled the man next him at me; and if he had succeeded in knocking me down, I am certain that I should never have got up again alive. As it was, however, I stepped quickly aside, and the man intended to knock me down was himself thrown violently against a rock, over which he fell heavily.'

After that, it was simply a case of climbing on top of the rock and haranguing the mob in Hindustani until they had been wholly subdued. Provided the coolies were willing to return to work, Patterson promised, he was prepared to overlook the attempt on his life.

He called for a show of hands. Every man present voted to go back to work. Then Patterson came down from the mountain, dusted himself off, and calmly carried on his rounds as if nothing had ever happened.

Staring down a mutinous work force was all in a day's work to him, but coping with a pair of man-eating lions was decidedly more of a problem. The lions seemed to be everywhere and nowhere, all at once. In the opinion of the coolies, the lions had the luck of the devil – or at the very least, they possessed the souls of two long-dead native chiefs. There were times when Patterson almost agreed with them.

Even before he took over the camp, there had been isolated cases of coolies disappearing without trace. He had been inclined to blame this on other coolies, not above murdering a comrade for his money. What changed his mind, a few days after his arrival at Tsavo, was the abduction from a crowded tent of a *jemadar* named Unghan Singh.

Singh had been sharing the tent with half a dozen other workmen. His bed was nearest the open door. At about midnight one warm evening, a lion put its head through the opening, seized him by the throat and dragged him outside before the others even knew he had gone. He never had a chance.

Next day, Patterson and another European followed up the lion's spoor and quickly arrived at the spot where the unhappy Sikh had been eaten. 'A dreadful spectacle presented itself,' wrote Patterson.

'The ground all round was covered with blood and morsels of flesh and bones, but the unfortunate *jemadar's* head had been left intact, save for the holes made by the lion's tusks on seizing him, and lay a short distance away from the other remains, the eyes staring wide open with a startled, horrified look in them.'

Never the most sensitive of men, Patterson picked up the head and carried it back to camp for identification by the medical officer, a sight which can hardly have done anything for Indian morale. That night he took a rifle and sat up in a tree close to Unghan Singh's tent, waiting for the man-eaters to reappear.

With him perched a number of terrified coolies, weighing down the boughs like ripe fruit. The men were unwilling to act as live bait for Patterson's trap by remaining in their beds on the ground below. They need not have worried. The lions did indeed strike again that night, but not in the same place.

The first Patterson knew about it was an outbreak of roaring, followed later by a tremendous hullabaloo in another camp half a mile away, indicating that another coolie had suffered the fate of the dead *jemadar*. By the time Patterson reached the place, the lions were already long gone.

So began a reign of terror that was to last the best part of 1898 and at one point brought all work on the bridge to a halt for twenty-one days. Sometimes the lions carried out raids on the rail camps almost nightly. Sometimes they stayed away for weeks at a time. Wherever Patterson placed his increasingly ingenious traps, the lions were sure to be somewhere else. Not even a massive influx of bounty hunters, lured by the offer of a large reward, could deter them.

In fact they grew bolder as time went on. With no fear of human beings, they thought nothing of promenading openly along Tsavo's station platform, while the station master and signalman locked themselves with bulging eyes in the ticket office.

A similar incident later took place at Kima, whose Asian station master frantically telegrammed for help: '*Pumping-engine employee wickedly assassinated by fractious carnivore. I unable pacify it. Situation perilous. Implore you alleviate my predicament.'*

What could anyone do? Although the coolies were given time off from plate-laying to strengthen the stockades around their sleeping quarters, the lions simply vaulted over the top. Sometimes they came so close at night that Patterson could hear them crunching bones in the darkness. The coolies took to sleeping in trees, cages and railway carriages rather than their tents, anywhere where they thought they might be safe.

One man even bedded down in a water tank. He calculated that its opening was big enough to admit a human being, but not a lion. The man was right, but only just. He spent a miserable night shrunk against the far end of the tank, desperately trying to elude the paw that was groping for him all around the aperture.

Casualties began to mount, and with them the flow of remains and belongings to be sent back to the men's families in India. A set of teeth, much prized by certain castes, was boxed up and posted to Mombasa. So were silver rings and other trinkets undigested by the lions.

A solemn debate was held over what to do with a solitary foot. It was all that remained of a sergeant of *askaris* who had left two wives behind at Kilifi. Eventually the foot was interred beside the Tsavo river, while six comrades fired a volley over it.

December 1898 saw lion hysteria at its height. By now the coolies had had more than they could take. On the first day of the month, hundreds of them threw down their tools and declared that they would not work on the bridge another minute.

'They would not remain at Tsavo any longer for anything or anybody,' they told Patterson. 'They had come from India on an agreement to work for the Government, not to supply food for either lions or "devils".'

Patterson was trying to calm them down when he heard the toot toot of an approaching train. As one man, the coolies raced to the track and flung themselves onto the rails in front of the train. Sparks flew as the driver slammed on the brakes. When next he picked up speed, the train was heavier by several hundred frightened Indians and a lonely empire-builder was gaping after it open-mouthed with his work schedule in ruins.

Nevertheless, even a man-eating lion's luck has to run out sooner or later. Barely a week after the train incident, word reached Patterson that one of the predators, having failed to catch a man, had killed and partly eaten a donkey close to the river.

The lion had been chased off the kill almost before it had begun to eat. All things being equal, it was a reasonable bet that the hungry animal would return to complete its meal later that night.

Since there were no trees near the dead donkey, Patterson ordered a twelve-foot-high *machan* to be built close by. The *machan* consisted of four poles topped by a plank on which he settled himself as the night shadows began to close in.

His foresight was rewarded. After a lengthy wait, a deep long-drawn sigh, sure sign of a hungry lion, came from the bushes. The man-eater began its approach through the darkness, though not quite in the way Patterson had anticipated:

'Matters quickly took an unexpected turn. The hunter became the hunted; and instead of either making off or coming for the bait prepared for him, the lion began stealthily to stalk *me*! For about two hours he horrified me by slowly creeping round and round my crazy structure, gradually edging his way nearer and nearer.

'Every moment I expected him to rush it; and the staging had not been constructed with an eye to such a possibility. If one of the rather flimsy poles should break, or if the lion could spring the twelve feet which separated me from the ground ...'

Tense and nervous, 'trembling with excitement', Patterson watched helplessly as the lion continued its stalk. The crouching body was too indistinct for him to risk a shot. He wanted to scream instead. Then, suddenly, something struck him hard on the back of the head.

Gibbering with fright, he almost fell out of the *machan*, convinced the lion had somehow jumped him from behind. He took a moment or two to recover his wits. When he turned round, he saw that he had been hit by nothing more dangerous than an owl, which had unwisely mistaken him for a tree.

By now the lion had abandoned caution and was close enough for Patterson to make out its shape against the white backdrop of undergrowth. With unsteady fingers Patterson took aim and fired.

The shot was followed immediately by a terrific roar as the lion began to thrash around in the bushes. Though he had lost sight of it, Patterson kept firing in the general direction until the lion's howls gave way to deep sighs and eventually to absolute silence.

Even then, the cautious colonel declined to search for the body until daylight burst at length over the treetops. It revealed nine feet eight inches of dead man-eater lying stone cold on the ground.

This was triumph indeed, and more was to follow. On 29 December, Patterson met up with the other man-eater in almost identical circumstances, hastily swinging his legs up into a tree a second or two before the lion arrived at the foot of it. If the animal's hind leg had not been shattered by an earlier shot, he would certainly have been a dead man.

Seizing a rifle from his gun bearer, he aimed once more and watched with satisfaction as the beast toppled over. Even then it was not finished. It staggered to its feet again as he jumped down, attempting a final desperate charge – and died just five yards from him with another two bullets in the head and chest, biting savagely at a branch which had fallen to the ground.

When it was carried back to camp, it was found to have six bullet holes in it. The coolies had to be forcibly restrained from tearing the body to pieces. At long last, the spirits of Tsavo had been laid.

The railway, meanwhile, had been continuing its erratic progress up-country, thrusting ever onward in the frantic race to reach Lake Victoria before the Germans. Though the German line from Tanga had already got as far as Kilimanjaro, the Kaiser's men had been visibly shaken by an official visit they had paid to inspect the British effort.

Their own railway was advancing at the rate of perhaps five hundred yards a day. Yet with their own eyes they had seen the British lay down a mile of track in a single day and link it together with parade-ground precision before the sun went down. The Germans went home much impressed. They didn't realise that the coolies had been rehearsing their performance for weeks and were on double pay for the big occasion.

By September 1899, railhead had reached the lip of the Kikuyu escarpment, overlooking the Rift Valley some two thousand feet below. In places the escarpment wall sloped at an angle of forty-five degrees. It presented a major engineering problem to the railwaymen. Their locomotives were not designed to cope with a gradient of more than two and a half degrees.

Having come this far, however, the engineers were not going to be defeated now. Until permanent viaducts could be completed, all essential traffic was laboriously shunted up and down the hill in specially built cable cars of the kind that carry tourists to the first stage of the Eiffel Tower in Paris.

Altogether the railway took another two years to complete. The final key in the last rail at the Lake port of Kisumu – then part of Uganda – was not driven home until 21 December 1901, a good five and a half years after the project had begun.

The occasion was marked by a thundering editorial in *The Times* and other British newspapers. The press were glad of an opportunity to praise the latest of Britain's imperial achievements at a time when the activities of a few Boer commandos further south on the Dark Continent were making a considerable dent in national pride.

On a less elevated plane, the *South African Railway Magazine* also waxed lyrical:

'Never was there such a railway since the world began ... It starts from a windswept island in the blue Indian Ocean and it ends by the wooded shore of the largest lake in Africa.

'It passes through jungle, swamp and desert; zig-zags across plains where elephant roam by day and lions roar by night; corkscrews up the sides of outlandish snow-capped mountains; circles round the base of volcanic cone-shaped hills; meanders by the *shambas* and cultivated patches of rude inland tribes; strikes athwart treacherous swamps, and ploughs through the darkness of primeval forests, until it emerges, calm and triumphant, from under the flat-topped mimosas by the shelving shores of the shimmering inland sea ... On its way it samples every climate; touches every degree of temperature; experiences every extreme.'

Never indeed had there been such a marvellous railway. It was a 582-mile-long monument in shining steel to the imperial glory that was Queen Victoria's England. That it was a tremendous achievement, nobody could ever deny.

Yet what was it *for*, this lunatic express? Sir Charles Eliot, appointed HM Commissioner to British East Africa in January 1901, readily confessed that he had no idea. As it stood, the railway appeared to have little practical significance. Wandering through the Kenya uplands, it crossed enormous tracts of unoccupied land standing spare and unutilised as far as the eye could see, linking nothing to nothing.

The land was empty because the altitude made it too cold for many tribes, and because disease had wiped out many of the nomads who grazed it part of the time. Yet it was good land, arable land, land that could be made highly productive if only someone would take the trouble to cultivate it scientifically.

Eliot was a fine scholar and a gifted administrator. He was keen to ensure that the protectorate paid its own way, rather than depend for ever on handouts from Whitehall. The railway ate up easily the largest share of the administration's annual budget.

To his precise mind, the line should be made to show a profit. It could never do so unless it carried regular loads of agricultural produce to the coast for sale abroad.

In short, what the economy needed was an infusion of large-scale, efficient farmers. It needed Anglo-Saxons with the capital and the knowhow to make good use of those neglected but healthy highlands.

Sir Charles Eliot put his plan to London. London agreed. Soon after completion of the railway, a call went out to all corners of the Empire for men of courage and enterprise to come and settle in the empty highlands of Kenya.

CHAPTER THREE

THE FIRST SETTLERS

The most influential of the early settlers had already arrived. His name was Hugh Cholmondeley, third Baron Delamere. He first entered Kenya by camel from the north, while on a hunting trip from Somaliland. The year was 1897, and he was twenty-seven years old.

'Never in all a very varied life have I seen such disorder, wanton waste, selfishness and utter want of self-control as these young men daily and hourly show,' complained a white hunter of an earlier trip to Somaliland made by Delamere and a party of useless friends. 'D is by far the best in many respects, but the waste and wilful prodigality is beyond description – and may very likely lead to serious consequences for us all.'

It was fair comment. Arrogant, feckless, reckless and rich – as the world counted riches – the youthful Delamere conformed closely to the unattractive pattern of behaviour often seen in young bucks of his type and class.

His father died when he was seventeen, leaving him a title, an estate in Cheshire and an uncontrollable temper that knew nothing yet of self-discipline or good behaviour or consideration for others. An idle and stupid schoolboy, his main achievement at Eton had been to wreck a boot shop in Windsor and throw the boots all over the High Street.

He left at sixteen to go to a crammers for entry into the army, but quickly gave up the idea of soldiering when he came into his estate. Instead he became a keen racing man and a rash horseman. He once dropped £3,000 in a single bet at Chester races – £3,000 he could not afford to lose. Delamere had style, no doubt about it, but he was still a long way from learning moderation.

Happily, Kenya was to be the making of him – and he, perhaps, of it – although his first experience of the country could not be described as encouraging. While camping near Lake Baringo, having not seen another white man outside his own party for the last thousand miles, he was approached by a native runner who curtly presented him with a letter bearing neither name nor address:

'Sir,' it said, 'Please take notice that you are now on British soil. Any act of aggression on your part will be sternly resisted.' The letter was signed with a barely decipherable 'J. Martin'.

This was James Martin, the Government's man in the Baringo area. He was the same Maltese ex-sail maker who had accompanied Joseph Thomson on his epic trek through Masai Land. After a very diverse career, including a spell as second-in-command of the Zanzibar army, Martin still could not read or write. He had learned to sign his name, but that was as far as he went. The rest of the note had been penned by his Goanese clerk.

Curious to find out what he had done to warrant such a hostile reception, Delamere rode over to meet Martin at Eldama Ravine. On the way he set eyes on the Kenya highlands for the first time. When he reached Ravine, he found the place in a state of siege. A deep trench was being dug around the administration *boma*, and the timber palisade was being hurriedly reinforced and strengthened.

The explanation was simple. News of Delamere's arrival over the frontier had gone before him, but had been slightly exaggerated in the telling. As Martin understood it, an Abyssinian army of at least a thousand camels was on its way to rape, pillage and burn everything that lay in its path. Hence his stiff note.

Once that misunderstanding had been cleared up, Delamere was free to continue his expedition south and east into the heart of the highlands. After the dust and desert of northern Kenya, the temperate parklands and tinkling Aberdare waterfalls came as a revelation, a complete turnabout from the thorn, scrub and lava of the frontier district. Although he did not at once realise it, the noble lord had reached his journey's end.

In fact several years were to pass before Delamere decided that East Africa could be anything more than just a spectacular playground for sportsmen. It was not enough that he had fallen in love with the new country. The feudal system ran deep in his blood. He had always accepted that seigneurial obligations would one day summon him back to England to play an active part in administering his estate.

Dutifully, therefore, he took himself back to Cheshire. There, for a long time, he fretted, torn between old ties and new horizons, ancient privilege and the powerful attraction of virgin soil.

Only after marriage to the Earl of Enniskillen's daughter and a fruitless attempt to settle down to the tedium of a country landowner's existence did he at length cut his ties with England. It wasn't until December 1902 that Lord Delamere set sail for a permanent home in Kenya.

Five months later, in May 1903, he put in a formal application for a parcel of sheep-grazing land on the Laikipia plateau between Mount Kenya and the Aberdares. The request was turned down by Sir Charles Eliot on the grounds that the land was too far away from the railway and the Government's administrative posts.

A second application, for 100,000 acres on the other side of the Aberdares next to Lake Naivasha, was also rejected, this time because its annexation might cause hardship to the Masai. But with his third attempt, Delamere struck lucky.

He asked for a block of land near Njoro, unoccupied pasture that had never been grazed by the nomadic *morans*. He was granted a ninety-nine-year lease for an annual rent of £200 and a written undertaking to spend at least £5,000 on the property within five years.

Delamere immediately launched himself into the project with all the restless energy that was his to command. A barrage of letters was fired off to the manager of his English estate, ordering him to buy quantities of top quality livestock to be shipped out to the new farm, which Delamere had christened Equator Ranch.

A pedigree Hereford bull and a Shorthorn from a milking herd were to be cross-bred with local cattle to produce an upgraded strain that, with luck, would not be prone to tropical disease. Six Ryeland rams, two Lincoln rams, two Border Leicesters and a pair of Romney Marshes were also on the shopping list because, as Delamere explained:

'I am in process of buying native ewes at 2s 6d or so apiece. I hope to get up a stock of three or four thousand native ewes. I propose, as was done in

South Africa in the early days, to put woolled rams to these ewes and again to the progeny, and so on until a woolled type is fixed.'

Besides writing off to English markets, Delamere also sent an agent to New Zealand, where conditions were said to be broadly similar to Kenya, to bring back five hundred purebred merino ewes. After a long sea voyage the ewes reached Mombasa at the end of 1904.

Their new owner awaited their arrival up-country with impatience. Soon after turning in the gate of Equator Ranch, four hundred of them dropped dead, unable to adapt to the rich damp pastureland of Njoro.

The cattle fared little better. Using the half-bred heifer progeny of his Shorthorn bull as a solid foundation, Lord Delamere had scoured the countryside for the best Boran cattle he could find, until he had scraped together a herd 1,500 strong. At the same time, he acquired a batch of oxen from Kavirondo country to be broken in for the plough.

Unfortunately, the oxen brought pleuro-pneumonia with them. Before Delamere had time to blink, a large part of his herd, including all the imported Herefords, lay dead.

Most died from pleuro-pneumonia, some from East Coast or Texas fever carried by ticks, some from rinderpest and others simply because the land at Equator Ranch was not suitable for grazing. The grass lacked iron and other essential minerals. That was why the Masai had never used it.

Delamere did not allow this setback to deter him. He was too stubborn to admit defeat. He reasoned that land unsuitable for livestock must surely be good for something else. Why not wheat? The altitude was right. The soil was undeniably good.

Delamere sent to Australia for a ten-furrow disc plough. It duly turned up at Njoro to much acclaim from passers-by. The locals were growing accustomed by now to an endless procession of strange and wondrous sights on the road to Equator Ranch.

'Don't waste time turning,' Delamere briskly ordered his ploughman on the first day of ploughing. 'Just go straight on.'

The ploughman did exactly what he was told. The first furrow of Lord Delamere's wheat-field was three miles long across the open plain. It might have been twice as much again if the ploughman had not begun to feel lonely out there all on his own.

The first wheat planted was an Australian variety which took four or five months to ripen and yielded an initial harvest of some twenty bushels an acre. The yield was not far short of miraculous for newly broken virgin soil.

Delamere was delighted. The earlier experiments with sheep and cattle had very nearly broken the bank, but here evidently would be his reward at long last. From the saddle of his mule, he shaded his eyes and proudly surveyed the fruits of his enterprise.

Then, dismounting with sudden urgency, he bent to look closer. The stems and leaves of each plant were slowly turning black. In a matter of days, the wheat began to wither and die, eaten away by black stem-rust, probably the most virulent of all the funguses to which wheat is susceptible.

So it went on. By trial and error, writing his own rules as he went along, Delamere and others like him painstakingly built up a storehouse of knowledge from which the foundations of an agricultural economy could be laid.

Delamere soon discovered that an Italian wheat called Rietti was the only variety resistant to black stem-rust – but it took eight months to ripen, and was particularly prone to attack by an aphis. Everything had to be learned by trial and error, mostly error. And errors cost money.

The brunt of Delamere's early mistakes was borne by his English estate, but inevitably there had to come a time when the well ran dry. It happened in 1909.

In a single field that year, Delamere had planted more than 1,200 acres of wheat, gabbling a hurried prayer that the anticipated crop would wipe out his overdraft, meet his debts and pay for the new thresher he had ordered on tick. Instead the crop failed. It was obliterated by yellow rust and Delamere was left with next to nothing.

So there was no option but to put the English estate into receivership and stand or fall by what he could make in Kenya. The loss of the dark red stone manor house which had been his childhood home was no great wrench to Delamere. He felt far more comfortable in the earthen-floor grass hut he shared with Lady Delamere, the occasional cow and a few sticks of antique furniture and china he had retrieved from England.

One day he would build his wife a proper stone house with doors and windows and a real roof. One day, but not yet. There was no time yet, and no money.

Delamere's day began at four in the morning, when he ate breakfast in the glare of a hurricane lamp. The meal was usually accompanied by his favourite tune *All aboard for Margate* played again and again on a terrible old gramophone.

By dawn he would be out in the fields, easily identifiable by the ginger hair growing over his shoulders as a protection against sunburn, discussing animal husbandry with his Masai herdsmen. He adored the Masai who worked for him. They in turn rather liked this autocratic oddball who had so captivated their imagination. They even named their favourite cows after him, a signal honour.

Sometimes Delamere's head would lift as he scented the far-off snort of an approaching train. Then, whooping, he would leap into his buggy, whip up his American trotter and race the train for ten miles or so, until both horse and rider had been thoroughly exercised. A good gallop through the bush always gave Delamere an appetite for lunch.

Lady Delamere, meanwhile, busied herself with running the house, feeding the poultry and attending to the various pigs which thrust inquisitive snouts into her hand. An acquaintance described her at this time as 'very lovely, graceful and charming, and quite out of place in this savage country'.

Whenever she had a spare moment, she was attempting to start a garden. Roses, carnations, irises and cannas grew like nobody's business in the fertile soil, though a plantation of oaks and chestnuts foundered for lack of a dormant season in Africa. More often than not, though, she was fully occupied coping with Delamere's crazy schemes, such as his plan for starting an ostrich farm.

Ostrich feathers were big business in Edwardian England, where society ladies could hardly be seen in public without half a dozen draped around their hats. Delamere therefore wrote off for five ostrich incubators he had read about in an advertisement.

Then he led his farm workers in an organised ostrich drive across the plain. They returned at the end of the day with a ragged collection of young chicks snatched from their angry parents to form the nucleus of his experiment.

The next step was to sneak up on a cock bird and lasso it to see if its feathers were valuable. Ambushing and lassoing proved comparatively easy, but clipping the cock's plumage was less simple. An ostrich is an irritable bird at the best of times. The one caught by Delamere did not take kindly to his attempts to strip its wings and tail of their finery.

Delamere tried to pacify it by pulling an old sock over its head in the hope that the sudden darkness would calm it down. Instead, the outraged bird battered a hole in the side of its pen and galloped off into the sunset, with absolutely no idea of where it was going. No one ever saw it again.

After that, Delamere handed over the ostrich business to his long-suffering wife. She took control of the young chicks and reared them in the imported incubators. Before they came to maturity, however, the ostrich market collapsed, killed by the new British fad for motoring, which was not conducive to large hats. Lady Delamere, for one, must have been extremely thankful.

One day, there appeared on the horizon a dot which swiftly transformed itself into a strange European. This was a transport rider, formerly a strong man in a circus, who had arrived in Kenya with no money but enough opium to buy a camel. By hiring out the camel, he had gradually built up a herd of cattle, until the railway had given him a transport contract.

With the profits from the contract he had bought up the empty land next to Delamere's and was proposing to set up in business as a cattle rancher. Even as Delamere stared in horror, the man could be seen driving his recently acquired herd along an old transport route that just happened to run across a corner of Equator Ranch.

Delamere was astride his mule in an instant and thundering down the trail to sort out this unwelcome intruder. Over his dead body would anyone settle the land next to his. He was all in favour of European settlement – had vigorously canvassed for it – but with the whole of Africa to choose from, he was not going to allow the view from his house to be spoiled by the sight of another human habitation on his doorstep.

The transport rider was trespassing on private property. Delamere told him so in no uncertain terms.

'I dare say,' replied the new neighbour tartly. 'But you can't stop me driving transport along the road I've used for eight years.'

'Right!' snarled Delamere through grated teeth. *'Right...!'* He gestured helplessly. 'Then you've better come in and have a cup of tea.'

Gradually, very gradually, the land around Equator Ranch began to tremble with the lumbering ox-carts of new settlers moving their goods and belongings from railhead to the distant patches of uncleared bush which the Government was pleased to call farming land.

Typically the carts would be piled high with all the settlers' worldly possessions: a disc plough, a grindstone, a few bags of seed, a couple of spades, a hurricane lamp, a chair or two, a bed and a few old family portraits, tended with loving care on a tedious journey across the sea and all the way up-country from Mombasa.

The Government's call for settlers had been answered from all parts of the globe. Men came from Australia and New Zealand, from South Africa and from Canada. They had been lured by amazing stories of Brussels sprouts which grew six foot tall and corn which shot up so fast that they had to stand back when they planted it.

Most had sold everything they owned to chance their luck in a fresh and untried country where the Government was practically giving away land to anyone with the nerve to take it.

The settlers came from the United States as well as all corners of the Empire. Northrop McMillan, a millionaire from St Louis, was said to be nearly seven feet tall. He was so fat that he had to go through doors sideways. He experimented with wildebeest farming on his Athi ranch and later received an honorary knighthood from the British.

Wherever the settlers came from, they were all men of courage and resourcefulness, prepared to break in wild land with a lick and a prayer and a loan from the bank. They were all independent-minded, all self-sufficient, all seeking the space and freedom to live their lives as they pleased in a way that they often wouldn't have been able to do in the countries that they had left behind.

There were as yet few rules in Kenya. It was still a frontier land. People sank or swam according to their own achievements. Money and social standing mattered less than the ability to make a success of their new lives in a harsh and unforgiving environment.

Enormous areas of bush had to be cleared before they could start farming. Trees had to be felled, boreholes sunk, streams dammed, fields ploughed and irrigated, roads built, quarries dug, boulders shifted, shade trees planted and seed beds tenderly nursed. There was little time at first for social nice-ties. Men of all backgrounds had to stand together in a constant struggle to remain afloat.

Many of the early settlers were fugitives in disgrace from Edwardian society. They had been exiled perhaps for losing too much at cards or for get-ting a debutante in foal. They brought with them the unmistakable stamp of the English upper classes and printed it firmly on the new earth.

Quite a few were titled. Delamere's brothers-in-law for instance, Berkeley and Galbraith Cole, younger sons of the Earl of Enniskillen, had followed him out to Africa to try their hand at farming. So had Lord Cranworth, who kept up his estate in Suffolk and ran the two holdings in tandem. So had Lord Hindlip.

Some, like Lord Cardross, came out as soldiers and stayed to settle. If they could not come themselves, they sent Tristram or Sandy, the idiot younger son who had been cluttering up the Blue drawing room since failing to get into the army.

It wasn't long before the country began to take on an undeniably patri-cian *élan*, a tiny pocket of high-altitude English madness in a bizarre world of croquet lawns and green box hedges some four thousand miles away from its proper setting of Ascot, Wimbledon and Henley.

'Having arrived up-country,' gushed Lady Cranworth, in a helpful article on hints for Kenya housewives derived from her own upbringing in London's Eaton Place, 'about the first operation will be to collect one's staff of servants. When one becomes accustomed to the sight of black faces, native servants will be found fairly good ...

'Unfortunately, as they learn the virtues of English domestics, they attain the drawbacks of the same with equal celerity. They have been known to sample the whiskey or to retire beneath the floor of the house with a full jam pot, there to lie *perdu* until it is empty; and a course of training will enable them to vie with any parlour-maid in crockery smashing.'

Always a problem, servants. If the ladies felt unable to cope, it was possible to fall back on a useful pamphlet put out by the Society for the Propagation of the Gospel, an all-purpose Swahili phrase book. 'The idle slaves are scratching themselves,' it counselled. 'Six drunken Europeans have killed the cook. Do not pour treacle into the engine.'

But Lord Cranworth had the final word on how to survive in Kenya when the odds were stacked against them. If in doubt, he sternly advised settlers at all times to bear in mind and act on the old maxim: 'Keep the spirits up, the bowels open, and wear flannel next the skin.'

One of the first settlers to arrive was Ewart Grogan, named Ewart because his father was a friend of William Ewart Gladstone. Grogan was to remain active in Kenya politics from the turn of the century right through to the 1960s. He had first heard about Africa while an undergraduate at Cambridge, just before being sent down for locking a goat in a don's rooms.

Later he had set out to walk the length of the continent, from the Cape to Cairo. By his own account, he had fallen in love with a girl and made the journey to prove his worth to her father. By other accounts, the girl was just a cover and he was on a mission for the British secret service, keeping an eye on French ambitions in Africa.

Whatever the truth, Grogan managed to complete his extraordinary journey, so achieving, as Cecil Rhodes pointed out, 'that which the ponderous explorers of the world have failed to accomplish'.

Thereafter he decided to settle in the Kenya highlands, where he was instrumental in stocking the Aberdare streams with trout imported from Scotland. He was also one of the settlers detailed to show a delegation of Zionist elders around the Uasin Gishu plateau in November 1904, with a view to deciding its suitability as a temporary home for Jewish refugees.

The idea was the brainchild of Joseph Chamberlain, then Colonial Secretary, who had made an official visit to Kenya in 1902. Like everyone else, Chamberlain had been struck by the emptiness and farming potential of the highlands. His visit had been followed by a savage pogrom in the Bessarabian capital of Kishinev. The event had triggered a renewed Jewish attempt to regain Palestine from the Turks and make it their permanent homeland.

The Turks refused to co-operate, so Chamberlain suggested to the Zionists that they might like to settle in Kenya instead, as a halfway house to the Holy Land. The highlands would be a safe haven for Russian and Polish Jews escaping persecution in Europe. Chamberlain offered them more than 3,000,000 acres of farming land, full autonomy under a Jewish governor, and the freedom to practise their religion under the protection of Great Britain.

The offer was received with incredulity by the would-be British settlers camped outside the Land Office in Nairobi until such time as their own requests to buy land should be processed.

Some of them had been waiting for more than a year, fretting impatiently while ill-equipped Government officials struggled to complete the survey and documentation without which no land could be handed over. Others had already given up hope and had gone home when their money ran out.

Yet here were their own people proposing to parcel out millions of acres to a diverse Jewish community with no interest in the country and nothing to contribute to it. The pogrom victims had no capital to sink into the land. They couldn't even speak English. Worse than that, they did not intend to become permanent settlers, merely guests in the country until Palestine was opened to them. The idea seemed outrageous to the British.

The Zionists were equally upset, interpreting the offer as an official admission that Palestine would never be theirs. It was with distinctly mixed feelings that a delegation of three Jewish representatives set out for Kenya. They were to be shown around by Grogan and a couple of others on a three day fact-finding visit.

The Zionists seemed unlikely colonists to Grogan when he met them: 'scholarly types, but not farmers or settler-pioneer types'. He couldn't see them thriving in up-country Africa. British officials too were having second thoughts by now.

'I am sure, gentlemen,' one of them is reported to have told Grogan, 'that you will be able to show members of the commission many things that they would not otherwise see.'

A wink was as good as a nod to Grogan. Gravely he and Edward Lingham, the other settler guide, set out with the three elders and an official from the Foreign Office to march from Londiani station up the blistering escarpment to a view of the promised land from the top.

The climb was stiff and the Zionist commissioners were not accustomed to violent exercise. They were glad to reach camp on the edge of the forest that night, delighted to kick off their boots and relax at last in the canvas-chair comfort of their tents. Delighted, that is, until a herd of elephants suddenly appeared from nowhere and thundered through the camp while bearers panicked in all directions.

Next day the fact-finding party continued its sleepless safari in search of a new Zion. It found not Zion but a column of Masai warriors fully got up for war – and a long way from Masai country at that. Ostrich-feather plumes, red ochre, fiendishly painted faces and sharp-looking spears jerked back and forth in what appeared suspiciously like the preliminaries to a massacre. Only at incredible personal risk did Grogan and Lingham go forward to calm the warriors down.

Even then the Europeans quadrupled the guard around the camp next night and ostentatiously took it in turns to stay awake with a loaded rifle until daylight. It was just as well that they did, because at some time during the small hours the pug marks of what could only have been a lion appeared mysteriously outside the door of the tent in which the Zionists had spent a miserable night.

The commission stayed just three days in the promised land. Later it reported to the British Government that the Zionists, though grateful for the offer, did not consider the Kenya highlands suitable for occupation by Jewish refugees.

They were quite right. Away from the railway line, the highlands were no place for a mass settlement of urban Europeans accustomed to tenement life in crowded city streets. The country was still no man's land. Murder and massacre were very much the order of the day, which was why the likes of Lord Delamere had not been allowed to settle out of sight of the Government's watch towers.

Even at Equator Ranch, there were times when Lady Delamere was forced to lay down her secateurs in favour of a rifle.

'I suppose you have heard of our scare,' she wrote serenely to her husband, who was away on a trip. 'The Sotik looted two Masai villages on the other side of the line from here. Wiped them out, I understand. Then the Government sent word to the *el moru* [Masai elders] on our land that another party of Sotik were coming.

'So I borrowed two hundred cartridges from Mr Clutterbuck to reinforce Casaro [the Masai headman]; but as nothing more happened, I conclude the Government were misinformed.'

British rule in those days was dispensed from a chain of forts usually built near waterholes along the caravan route from the coast to Uganda. The forts were attacked with monotonous regularity by squads of local braves looking for a bit of excitement. They were accordingly of solid construction, on the laager principle.

Fort Smith, for instance, parts of which still survive at Kabete, 'was a formidable affair, oblong in shape, and surrounded by a ditch which was in itself a difficult obstacle; and this was still farther strengthened by a barbed-wire fence on the glacis. Flank defence was afforded by a bastion and two caponnieres, and the work itself was entered by two drawbridges.'

The fort was named after its founder, Eric Smith, a young Life Guards officer who had somehow lost one hand during his tour in Kenya. He became the first of many Britons to administer large portions of the protectorate singlehanded.

In another part of the highlands stood Fort Hall, named after the area administrator, a nephew of Lord Goschen. The local Kikuyu chief resented Fort Hall so much that he always used to go and fire blunted arrows at it after he had had a few drinks.

Although the slave trade had been abolished with the coming of the British, the actual practice of slavery continued well into the twentieth century. It was officially upheld by the Government as part of the treaty by which it leased the ten-mile-wide coastal strip from the Sultan of Zanzibar.

Slavery was, of course, forbidden in the rest of the protectorate. But at the coast, anyone registered as a slave before 1890 who came in front of the courts as late as 1905 could expect the British legal system to find against him and in favour of his master. There were still plenty of retired traders around with nostalgic memories of the old days.

An evil old reprobate named Mbarak, who had spent a lifetime tramping the caravan route, remembered without embarrassment 'that the castrated boys were best looked after as they were the most valuable but that over fifty per cent died before reaching the coast; the girls were not shackled but went free and were raped both at night and all through the day whenever the caravan halted. About ten per cent of the men died from fatigue and undernourishment; if a man showed fatigue he was shot and left.'

Cannibalism, too, was still rife among some tribes. An English doctor who removed the organs of a dead native for a post-mortem found himself treated with a certain wariness by the rest of his patients, who were not entirely convinced of the purity of his motives. And a Manyema tribesman, a corporal in the King's African Rifles, was severely reprimanded by his European officer for returning from a fighting patrol with five severed black hands stuck in his belt, even though this was not an offence under the Army Act.

The corporal explained that eating his enemies would give him their strength. He added for the officer's information that fingers were the most succulent part of the body, but the nicest part of all was the buttocks of a young girl.

The officer was Lieutenant Richard Meinertzhagen, an Old Harrovian on secondment to the KAR from his regiment in India, and a nephew of the Fabian socialists Sidney and Beatrice Webb. Terrified of stagnating 'in the narrow groove of regimental soldiering', Meinertzhagen was a strong, if fractious, character – he was once challenged to a duel in Germany – who had applied for the Kenya posting after a series of rows with his Adjutant.

Instead of buying a polo pony, as most newcomers to the regiment were expected to on arrival in India, he had splashed out on a cow elephant named Archibald. He kept her outside his bungalow, some three quarters of a mile from the battalion parade ground.

One day, when late for parade, Meinertzhagen jumped aboard Archibald in full fig and whipped her up to an impressive seven miles per hour in order to reach the square in time. But Archibald, once roused, was not an easy beast to stop.

Instead of depositing her rider gently at the edge of the parade ground, she careered straight on into the massed ranks of the Royal Fusiliers, scattering them left, right and centre. It was the first time since Napoleon's day that an English square had been broken by cavalry. The Adjutant was not amused.

Other incidents followed. When Meinertzhagen put in for the Kenya transfer, neither Adjutant nor Sergeant Major stood in his way.

On arrival at the KAR officers' mess in Nairobi, he immediately proceeded to pick a quarrel with the bulk of his brothers in arms. Most of them were regimental outcasts, alcoholics heavily in debt. They thought nothing of sleeping with black whores from the shanty town and bringing them quite openly into the ante-room of the mess.

The offended Meinertzhagen had the bad habit of saying exactly what he thought – never popular in subaltern officers. Undeterred by his lack of seniority, he sat down and wrote out an official complaint about the presence of black women in the mess. He threatened to send it to higher authority if the practice did not cease at once. Understandably, the guilty officers were livid, but they had no choice except to comply.

No surprise, then, to find Meinertzhagen rapidly posted out of sight up-country where, with any luck, he would get his head cut off while trying to impose British rule on the natives. For his part, Meinertzhagen was delighted to go. He relished the prospect of military action. It was what he had come to Africa to see. He did not want to be disappointed.

Word soon reached him that a European settler attempting to buy sheep from the Kikuyu had been murdered in a particularly disgusting fashion. The Kikuyu had pegged him out on the ground, wedged open his mouth, and then invited the whole community – men, women and children – to urinate into it until the unfortunate man drowned.

They then proceeded to dance around his mutilated body by firelight, while the war drums beat a primitive tattoo of triumph through the darkness.

The orgy continued throughout the night. While it was going on, Meinertzhagen's soldiers quietly surrounded the village and settled down to wait for daybreak. When dawn came, they knew what they would have to do.

'I gave orders that every living thing except children should be killed without mercy,' reported Meinertzhagen. 'I hated the work and was anxious to get through with it. So soon as we could see to shoot we closed in. Several of the men tried to break out but were immediately shot. I then assaulted the place before any defence could be prepared.

'Every soul was either shot or bayoneted, and I am happy to say that no children were in the village ... We burned all the huts and razed the banana plantations to the ground. In the open space in the centre of the village was a sight which horrified me – a naked white man pegged out on his back, mutilated and disembowelled, his body used as a latrine by all and sundry who passed by.'

Other clashes followed. Sometimes Meinertzhagen fought alongside his KAR soldiers, sometimes at the head of specially recruited Masai spearmen, jubilant at this Government-sanctioned opportunity to carve up their old enemies. One ambush, in which a band of Kikuyu raiders from Tetu were trapped inside a camp fence by fifteen Masai, was especially successful:

'We all broke from our ambushes with a yell, I rushed to the entrance, and there we had entrapped forty-nine fully armed warriors of the Tetu people. The Masai were out like lightning and began to kill at once.

'The whole affair was quick and quiet, and as it all occurred in the open and within a few yards of me I had an excellent view when I was not myself kept busy. I held the entrance with my bayonet, being shielded on either side by two Masai with their massive shields of buffalo hide.

'A good number of the enemy bolted for the door, but none got past me. I was surprised at the ease with which a bayonet goes into a man's body. One scarcely feels it unless it goes in to the hilt. But one frequently has to make a desperate tug to get it out. In the end not a single one of the enemy escaped, all being killed.'

Such slaughter might seem horrifying today, but it should be seen in context. Meinertzhagen was not really a bloodthirsty man. He personally liked the Kikuyu, whom he thought the most intelligent of the tribes he had met, and made many black friends – but he was doing a soldier's job in a savage country where human life traditionally counted for very little.

His was a *Sanders of the River* existence, where poisoned arrows turned his hand black and gifts of young virgins from suspiciously friendly native chiefs had to be searched for the poison concealed in their tail feathers. He had to keep discipline any way he could. He was perfectly capable of shooting his own troops for killing women and children against his express orders.

Nor was killing his sole preoccupation. In between punitive expeditions, Meinertzhagen seriously contemplated buying land in Kenya and settling down to become a farmer, only to have his hopes dashed when his father refused to lend him the money.

He was regarded as something of a black sheep in his family. They thought that he had let them down by refusing to work in the family bank in the City. They remembered him only at Christmas, when they posted him his annual plum pudding.

One morning, while out on his own, Meinertzhagen came across a cool river running heaven-sent through the dusty plain. It was a sweltering hot day, and he badly needed a wash. Off came the bush shirt, off came the boots and puttees, down came the trousers and he was as naked as nature had made him.

Meinertzhagen was free to soap himself in the tingling water just below the ford. He dried out afterwards by lying in the sun a million miles from the nearest outpost of civilisation. He was at peace with himself and the world in the middle of uncharted Africa. Yet not for long:

'I was sitting quite naked on a mossy rock when to my utter dismay and astonishment a very beautiful woman dressed in white nun's clothes appeared at the ford riding a white donkey. The apparition was so lovely that I simply stared. She was riding straddle-legs and, looking straight at me, smiled and wished me good morning in French.'

Ever the gentleman, Meinertzhagen was torn between an Englishman's natural instinct to stand up in the presence of a lady, and mortal dread of frightening her to death. He compromised by shuffling around inanely on his backside, making polite conversation of the *plume de ma tante* variety, until she at length put him out of his misery by bidding him farewell and continuing on her way into the wide blue yonder.

Was she really lovely, or was Africa getting to Meinertzhagen at long last? As any old sweat knew, *cafard* does strange things to a man who spends too much time on his own. Perhaps the long lonely months in the bush were getting him down.

He was certainly becoming more introspective. He had noticed himself brooding more and more as time went on, about the disappointment and bitterness he felt that his family should regard him as a black sheep, about his own deterioration, both mentally and morally. And about the conviction taking shape in his mind that Kenya could never become the white man's country that people like Sir Charles Eliot and Lord Delamere intended it to be.

The more he thought about it, the more certain Meinertzhagen was that settling Europeans in the highlands did not make any kind of sense. He once said as much to Eliot, who had invited him to dinner on the strength of his relationship to the Webbs. Eliot was not convinced:

'He would not have it; he kept on using the word "paramount" with reference to the claims of Europeans. I said that some day the African would be educated and armed; that would lead to a clash ... in the end the Africans will win ... Eliot's policy can lead only to trouble and disappointment.'

Lord Delamere wasn't impressed by Meinertzhagen's reasoning either: 'Delamere is still enthusiastic about the future of Kenya. I take the view, with which Delamere has no patience, that in a hundred years' time there may be 50,000 white settlers with flourishing farms and 5,000,000 discontented and envious natives; can the white man hold out against numbers without terrific slaughter?'

As so often in British history, the subaltern with a worm's eye view of the ground saw things much more clearly than the great statesmen. Meinertzhagen was remarkably accurate. A clash between black and white over land was inevitable. He was only wrong about one thing. It did not take a hundred years, it took fifty. He was still alive to see it.

CHAPTER FOUR
BIRTH OF A CITY

Just over nine miles from the old IBEA post at Fort Smith, the Nairobi river ran down into a fringe of papyrus swamp separating a wide treeless plain from a low hill screened by foliage. The plain was the windy domain of the Masai. The hill marked the beginning of the Kikuyu forest.

By mutual consent the boundary between the two tribes was formed by the river. It could be crossed only at the base of the hill. A series of stepping stones provided the main route for war parties to raid deep into each other's territory in search of cattle and women.

Today the stepping stones form part of Museum Bridge at the head of the Uhuru Highway, Nairobi City's most prestigious tree-lined boulevard.

The spot first came to the attention of the British in 1892, when the advance survey party for the Uganda Railway spent a night there on its way back from Lake Victoria. An older camp site already existed two miles north east at Pangani on the Mathare river, where ivory and slave traders usually stayed before heading up-country. In spite of the damp and mosquitoes, Captain Macdonald preferred to set up his own camp along the projected route for the railway line.

The first white man to spend any length of time in the wilderness that was to become Kenya's capital was almost certainly James Martin. As a railway official recruiting labour for earthworks along the line, he camped for ten days of 1896 on a site now occupied by the steam loco workshops behind the station.

Martin was followed five months later by a Corporal Brodie. In February 1897, Brodie was placed in charge of a transport depot in the Kikuyu forest in what is now the Westlands area of the city, but he did not stay long. In May he handed over the depot to Corporal, later Sergeant, George Ellis of the Royal Engineers.

Ellis supervised the training of mules and draught oxen for most of the next eleven months, until he returned to England in April 1898. Although he did not realise it, this prolonged residence was to earn Ellis the title of Nairobi's first citizen.

At the end of May 1899, railhead arrived at Nairobi, some 327 miles from the coast. The plain at the edge of the forest was the last level place to turn an engine round before attempting the steep gradient of the Kikuyu escarpment.

The line would corkscrew up two thousand feet over the next twenty-seven miles before plunging over the lip of the Rift Valley. The attendant engineering problems could not be handled from Mombasa, so a forward base had to be set up somewhere. Nairobi seemed the obvious answer.

Soon the full paraphernalia of a railway camp was being shuttled up the line and off-loaded amid an ever-widening jumble of tents, bungalows, workshops, turntables, shunting yards, lean-tos and tin shacks. Most of the buildings were only temporary. They were designed to accommodate the labour force until such time as the line had progressed beyond the escarpment into the Rift Valley.

There was no thought of making Nairobi anything more than just a halt on the line. It was far too unhealthy, for one thing. The swamp extended from the present Boulevard Hotel to Racecourse Road and was a strong breeding ground for malaria.

Smallpox had already driven the Masai away. The moisture-retaining black cotton soil south of the river made sewage drainage difficult. The place was useful for railway purposes, certainly, but no one would ever want to live there. Or so the authorities reasoned.

But one thing swiftly led to another, almost without anyone noticing. Shops built of corrugated iron began to blossom on Nairobi's only street as Indian coolies, their railway contracts expired, decided to invest their earnings in business rather than go home. European railway officials organised themselves into a club the other side of camp.

An English settler built himself a house, his wife had a baby. Prostitutes and sightseers crowded in from the surrounding African villages. Somebody opened a hotel where it was possible to get a drink at night.

Roman Catholics built a wooden church. The first white men to die, mostly of lion wounds, were given a Christian burial in the new cemetery. With amazing speed the railhead camp began to look more and more like a proper town, especially after the British Government, in the shape of Ukamba sub-commissioner John Ainsworth, took up official residence there.

Ainsworth had started out as an employee of the IBEA company. Later he had been hired by the Foreign Office to administer the Ukamba area from the former IBEA post at Machakos. Since Machakos had been by-passed by the railway line, it soon became obvious that the seat of government would have to be moved to the new town.

The transfer of power proved unpopular with the railway authorities. They jealously guarded their own jurisdiction, which extended over the land a mile each side of the track and encompassed most of Nairobi.

The authorities already possessed a complete legal and administrative set-up of their own, with police, fire and health departments and all the trappings necessary to oversee a fair-sized and diverse community. Only with great reluctance were they prepared to share this power with the British Government.

Nevertheless, Ainsworth's request for office space in Nairobi could not reasonably be denied. With him came a Union Jack on a pole. Once both Government and railway headquarters were assembled in one place, Nairobi's future as capital of the new country was all but assured. The town was growing so fast that nothing could stop it now.

For his HQ, Ainsworth chose a site now occupied by the National Museum on the hill above the tribal stepping stones. With his American wife Ina he took up residence on the spot filled since the 1970s by a full-sized fibreglass model of Ahmed, Kenya's most famous elephant.

From there he could keep an eye on the warring factions of not only the Government and railway chiefs, but also the Masai and Kikuyu. The tribes' young men were still tempted from time to time to cross the ford below in pursuit of ancient pastimes. Behind him, the nearest Kikuyu outpost was only four hundred yards away.

Despite its expansion, however, Nairobi remained a hideously unattractive town. Everyone who saw it remarked on its ugliness. Because it was never intended to be a permanent settlement, it was allowed to develop any old how. There was little attempt beyond the railway quarters at sanitary regulations or town planning.

As new settlers arrived by train from Mombasa, they spilled out over the station platform and spread in all directions. They waited patiently with their belongings gathered around them until the Land Office made up its mind where it was going to send them.

A convoy of Afrikaners, fugitives from South Africa's post-Boer War depression, arrived knee-deep in mud at the end of the long rains. They immediately dubbed their camp Tentfontein. Others, arriving in the dry season, remembered nothing so much as the thick red dust clogging the streets.

Far the most unpleasant part of the new township was the Indian quarter. Without adequate sanitation, the ramshackle buildings and overcrowded shacks quickly became a breeding ground for all kinds of disease. Matters came to a head soon after the railway's arrival, when plague broke out in the bazaar.

The situation was rapidly dealt with by J. H. Patterson of Tsavo fame. He gave the inhabitants an hour's notice to move out before, on his own responsibility, burning the whole place to the ground. His swift action made him highly unpopular with both his victims and the authorities, but it solved the problem. After that, the bazaar was rebuilt on higher ground and things began to improve.

By 1906 Nairobi had a permanent European population of almost six hundred against maybe twenty or thirty a couple of years back. A vociferous lobby was demanding installation of an electricity plant to supply light for streets and houses, and power for the factories that were sure to be built one day.

Revisiting the town after two years' absence, Richard Meinertzhagen noticed that trees had sprung up everywhere. Hotels existed where zebras once roamed and private bungalows covered the landscape where he used to hunt waterbuck.

He also noticed that somebody was proposing to build on a ten-acre plot of land he had bought for himself long ago, when it was inhabited only by duiker and guinea fowl. On inquiry, he discovered that the administration intended to erect a house for the Governor on his land. He said nothing but rubbed his hands in glee, anticipating a good fight once construction got under way.

The town was also beginning to attract tourists. The brand-new Norfolk Hotel, jumping-off point for many safaris, billed itself as 'The True Home of the Big Game Shooter'. It proudly recorded that in the 1905–6 season it had played host to one marquis, three earls, five lords, three foreign counts, nine honourables 'and many others of the World's Finest Sportsmen'. An impressive bag for what was still a hick town.

Sometimes the big game hunters did not even have to leave the hotel to collect their trophies. Lions and hippos could be shot in the swamp. Lions could also be seen stalking wildebeest in front of the hotel or zebra outside the KAR officers' mess. George Grey, brother of Lord Grey of Falloden, was killed by one.

An elephant blundering through Ainsworth's garden tore up his wife's newly planted croton bushes, and a leopard was once found under a bed in the house of Mr Sandiford, the railway manager. People going out to dinner usually took a rifle or spear with them, just in case. One lady, riding her bicycle to a rehearsal of *Trial by Jury*, was nearly trampled to death in the street by a herd of frightened zebra.

1906 was also famous for an official visit to the protectorate by one of Queen Victoria's sons. The Duke of Connaught sailed out with wife and daughter to inspect the latest addition to the imperial collection. An Old Etonian named Jim Elkington invited the three of them to lunch at his farm outside Nairobi.

Mindful of social niceties, Elkington went to considerable trouble beforehand to ensure that his servants were fully clued up on the correct way to serve a meal to the King-Emperor's brother. The operation went like clockwork until after lunch, when the party moved into the garden to have a cup of home-grown coffee.

Over the rim of his cup, Elkington became dimly aware of a warrior advancing stark naked across the croquet lawn. The Duchess, with young Princess Patricia in tow, levelled her lorgnettes, anticipating the presentation of a gift from a loyal subject.

She saw instead a tremendous specimen of Masai manhood – tremendous because they tie a brick to it during childhood to make it longer – bearing a note for the embarrassed host. It was the Duke who retrieved the situation. 'Ah!' he said smoothly. 'The Elkington livery, I presume?'

In his spare time Elkington was joint master of the Masara hounds, the first of seven packs of fox hounds to be imported from England, together with pink coats, top hats, hunters and all the correct equipment for the chase. The quarry was usually jackal or duiker, although drag hunts were also introduced. Meets took place at around 6.30 in the morning while the scent still lay heavily on the dew.

The hills and valleys of Kikuyuland echoed regularly to the sound of a hunting horn, accompanied by bloodcurdling yells as the horsemen thundered through the banana trees. Later, a few Kikuyu joined in. They became whippers-in and hunt servants, taking great pride in their pink coats and smart riding boots.

It wasn't only in Kikuyuland that strange sights could be seen. The streets of Nairobi witnessed a continuous series of exotic processions as the frontier town expanded. A man named Tarpon Dick, for example, made a speciality of lassoing lions and rhinos with a thirty-foot lariat and then parading them through the township before branding them in front of an enthusiastic crowd at the Norfolk Hotel. He released them later outside the municipal boundary.

W. D. Boyce, a Chicago newspaper owner, arrived with son Ben to take aerial photographs of big game from a balloon suspended over the Rift Valley. The American Balloonograph Expedition, as it was grandly entitled, set off for the Rift from Nairobi station, accompanied by two hundred puzzled porters waving the American flags which had been thrust into their hands.

The train was bedecked in red, white and blue bunting – probably left over from the royal visit – which was quickly set alight by sparks from the engine stack. By the time the expedition reached the floor of the Rift Valley, there had been enough ballyhoo to stampede all the wildlife into German East Africa.

Undaunted by the sudden absence of game, Boyce supervised the inflation of the balloon, from which he intended to dangle a movie camera operated from the ground. The balloon would be attached to the earth by a mule whose weight, he calculated, would provide a firm anchor.

He was wrong. A heavy gust of wind seized both balloon and mule and whisked them skywards. The last anyone ever heard of the unfortunate animal, it was kicking its hooves and braying miserably before disappearing into the clouds, never to be seen again.

The balloon safari would have appealed to 'Uncle' Charles Bulpett, a wild Englishman who had been everywhere and done everything before washing up in middle age on the shores of Nairobi. As a young man in the 1880s he had once wagered £100 to £25 that he could swim the Thames at Greenwich in frock coat, top hat and cane.

He eventually reached the opposite bank, having been carried a mile and a quarter downstream by the tide, and immediately offered to repeat the trip in reverse for the same bet. There were no takers.

Later Bulpett swam the Hellespont to keep his hand in, climbed the Matterhorn and performed numerous mountaineering feats in Mexico. He also became entangled with a Spanish dancer named La Belle Otéro, a famous courtesan who took him for every penny he had before letting him out of her clutches. She commented afterwards that she had had £100,000 out of him in six months, but had given full value for money in return. He agreed.

Women like Otéro were all too familiar to the shady characters hanging around Nairobi in the lotus years leading up to the Great War. Most of the men had a lurid past or they would not have been sent out to the protectorate in the first place.

The veranda of the Norfolk hummed with talk every evening as cads and bounders far from home enlarged upon some aspects of their personal histories over a drink and were discreetly reticent about others, before touching their companions for a few bob to tide them over until their next remittance.

Wearing his old school tie at the bar, Jim Elkington sold five hundred acres of land he had never seen to Elspeth Huxley's father. Pocketing the money, he blithely expressed the hope that he would meet the family back in Nairobi for the races.

Elkington came from the same mould as Fritz Schindelar, a good-looking Austrian with a boundless appetite for women. Schindelar could often be found sitting at the Norfolk's gambling table with several hundred gold sovereigns in front of him.

Lording it over everyone else, however, were the white hunters, kings of the *shikar*, legendary names some of them. The hunters emerged only infrequently from the bush but were always ready for a drink and a long talk when they did appear. They were almost larger than life, festooned with slouch hats, bullet loops and gaiters of buffalo hide, invariably accompanied by a jungly looking native tracker as part of the props.

Every hunter possessed a fund of stories of the 'There I was, breathing down its nostrils, gun-bearer up a tree and right out of ammo' variety. They saw no reason to spare their audience, when they could get one.

Their achievements seem like butchery to modern ears, but men like W. D. M. 'Karamoja' Bell, Paul Rainey, Arthur Hoey and R. J. Cunninghame were famous all over the world in the days before television brought wildlife documentaries into every home.

Jim Sutherland and Andy Anderson were both acquainted with Colonel Cody – the legendary Buffalo Bill. Philip 'Jungle man' Pretorius, credited with shooting more than five hundred elephants, is said to have become the model for Peter Pienaar, sidekick of Richard Hannay, in John Buchan's *Greenmantle*.

Two men, F. C. Selous and Frederick Jackson, both enjoyed a certain notoriety at this time as the original of Rider Haggard's *Allan Quatermain*. Haggard himself had always suspected Haggard of being the original, but nobody took any notice of *him*.

If the hunters only rarely came out of the bush, the same could be said of the farmers. They trekked into Nairobi maybe two or three times a year to buy stores, sell their produce, get their machinery repaired and trade gossip with anyone else who happened to be in town.

Serious men normally, the settlers always advanced on the capital with a purposeful glint in their eye. They were determined to cram six months' riotous living into a stay of a week or so, knowing that the opportunity would not come again for some considerable time.

Nairobi offered the chance to hear the swish of a woman's skirt, read a newspaper, have a drink with friends, and then investigate that skirt. The laws of supply and demand being what they are, a white woman in Kenya had to be very ugly indeed not to wrest a halting proposal from some hat-holding settler who had been practising his speech for weeks on his best Hereford and had now forgotten every word of it.

For those not interested in marriage, a new Japanese whore house had been established where men could take their chance with a slant-eyed Oriental bint and hurl the furniture into the street if they weren't happy.

Of course, not all Europeans had a craving for feminine company. Some people came to Kenya specifically to get away from women. A man who thought himself secure at the far end of Nandi country was dismayed to receive an irate message from his superior at Nandi fort: '*A woman in men's clothes who says she is your wife has emerged from behind my office safe. Come here at once and identify her or deny the allegation by helio message.*'

The biggest social event in Nairobi's calendar was Race Week, the one week of the year when everybody was certain to be in town. The entire European community made a point of gathering together at the races for a gala occasion combining business, politics and pleasure in a whirl of activity that usually only came to an end when the participants could no longer stand up.

At the races settlers could look for a wife, discuss crops, sell a dud threshing machine to an unsuspecting newcomer and lobby the Governor about quarantine regulations or his iniquitous native labour policy. Africans were reluctant to work on white farms, so settlers had to entice them by playing a gramophone or persuading them that a hurricane lamp was really a piece of star which had fallen to earth.

The Africans' recalcitrance was a source of considerable annoyance to the settlers. They argued that compulsory labour would do wonders for black education.

Later in the evening, the settlers liked to drink themselves stupid before hitting the town. Taking the tone from Lord Delamere, they worked off half a year's farming heartbreak by brawling in the bar of the Norfolk or staging drunken rickshaw races down Government Road.

Staying at the Norfolk when the races were on was always a risky business. As Elspeth Huxley observed: 'It was nothing to have an Italian baron or an Austrian count thrown through the window on to your bed in the middle of the night.'

Jack Riddell, a soldier turned ivory poacher, liked to ride his horse into the hotel dining room and jump clean over a table without disturbing the crockery. A lady with a taste for strong waters often rode backwards on her horse into the Norfolk bar and emptied her revolver at the ceiling after she had had a few.

Delamere himself, in full evening dress, enjoyed shooting all the bottles off the counter – he always paid for them next morning – before lurching out into the night to take pot shots at the newly installed street lights in Government Road. He was invariably egged on by a bunch of cackling onlookers.

His temper had not improved with age. When the manager of the Norfolk unwisely informed him that it was closing time and no more drink would be served, Delamere seized him by the scruff of the neck and locked him up in the meat safe alongside several dead sheep. And when the Land Office vetoed a site selected by Delamere for a flour mill, he reacted in the only sensible way – by organising a squad of natives to light a fire under the Land Office.

Deaf to the entreaties of the officials squawking from the veranda, Delamere sat back with folded arms as a pile of firewood was heaped around the stilts of the building. At the last minute the bureaucrats capitulated. Delamere got his site.

In his attitude to officialdom he found a soulmate in Ewart Grogan, who shared the average settler's contempt for anyone remotely connected with the administration of the protectorate. It was well known among the settlers that administrators were born fools. The bureaucrats interfered needlessly with the development of the country by promulgating all sorts of mindless rules and regulations to the detriment of progress and good sense.

A mining ordinance, for example, listed clay as a valuable mineral. It forbade settlers to use the clay on their land as a building material without first obtaining a mining licence. Once they had a licence, they were entitled to prospect for minerals almost anywhere they liked.

To draw attention to this absurdity, Grogan went round Nairobi in the middle of the night pegging out a perfectly legal claim to the entire town. He was about to dig up Government Road with a pickaxe when the ordinance was hastily amended.

Lord Cranworth was only half-kidding when he commented that a general knowledge paper as the outside world understood it might sum up Kenya as follows:

'The British East African protectorate is a huge tract of healthy highlands extending from Mombasa to Lake Victoria Nyanza. It is kept as a game reserve for lions and such-like, which millionaires and Americans get shot for them, and write about afterwards. There are some settlers who stone their Governors and shoot natives.'

But all was forgotten during Race Week. Settlers and bureaucrats drowned their sorrows together and every unsuspecting carthorse, providing it could muster a leg at each corner, became for a brief and glorious moment a racehorse.

Every nag in the protectorate was pressed into service for the day, usually with owner up. Later, after Berkeley Cole imported the stallion Bobrinski, a onetime Derby favourite, and Delamere matched him with Camsiscan, son of the Derby winner Spearmint, the quality of racing began to pick up.

The programme was organised by the East African Turf Club, which generally appointed three stewards for the meeting. On one occasion two of the stewards fell out over some technical point and began to take a swipe at each other.

Delighted onlookers called for the third steward – Harry Penton, owner of the Blue Posts hotel at Thika – who had gone missing. He was sitting stark naked on the roof of the Norfolk, wearing a tin bath over his head and insisting: 'I am a mushroom. I *am* a mushroom!'

Now and again an incident took place at the racetrack to remind the crowd that although this was a part of old England, it was also indubitably Africa. Richard Meinertzhagen remembered one such:

'As the second race was finishing a silly rhinoceros was seen trotting towards the galloping horses. We all shouted to the riders to look out, and they returned at a pace which seemed to exceed that of the race; the rhino could not make head or tail of the flags, the horses, and the general noise of shouting and laughter, and with his tail in the air he kept making little charges here and there. Nobody had a gun to scare him away, and we just had to wait for at least half an hour before he took himself off.'

While a schoolboy at Harrow, Meinertzhagen had once bumped into 'an uncouth reserved lad' three years his senior, 'a lonely boy, usually walking by himself, but everyone in the school knew him because he was out of the ordinary'. Bumped is the right word for it, because it was a matter of some pride at Harrow as to who would walk on the pavement and who would be pushed into the road.

The loutish Meinertzhagen, choosing to argue the toss with his senior, 'cannoned into an object like a brick wall and found myself in the gutter, for he was as hard as nails and even in those days was a fierce opponent of wilful aggression'. Meinertzhagen had just bounced off Winston Churchill.

He remembered Churchill as a precocious, bumptious and talkative boy who, though respected, was little understood. In Meinertzhagen's opinion, Churchill would have had a much rougher time at school if he had not enjoyed the protection of his kinsman Dudley Marjoribanks, later Lord Tweedmouth.

But school is not adulthood. In his subsequent career Churchill was doing rather well for himself. By making full use of his connections and climbing ruthlessly over the backs of other people he had risen, at the age of thirty-one, to become Under-Secretary of State for the Colonies. In that capacity, he made an official visit to Kenya in 1907, an event recorded by him in the grandiloquently titled *My African Journey*.

'Every white man in Nairobi is a politician,' he wrote, 'and most of them are leaders of parties. One would scarcely believe it possible, that a centre so new should be able to develop so many divergent and conflicting interests, or that a community so small should be able to give to each such vigorous and even vehement expression.

'There are already in miniature all the elements of keen political and racial discord, all the materials for hot and acrimonious debate. The white man *versus* the black; the Indian *versus* both; the settler as against the planter; the town contrasted with the country; the official class against the unofficial; the coast and the highlands; the railway administration and the protectorate generally; the King's African Rifles and the East Africa Protectorate Police; all these different points of view, naturally arising, honestly adopted, tenaciously held, and not yet reconciled into any harmonious general conception, confront the visitor in perplexing disarray.'

What struck Churchill most about the young Englishmen he met in the Kenya highlands was that they were a tough breed – Spartan is the word he used – who wore few clothes to protect their bodies from the powerful sun. He recorded with surprise that most of the Europeans he saw were dressed in khaki shorts cut 'five inches – *at least* – above the knee'.

He may have been thinking in particular of Phil Percival, a white hunter who had gone with him on a lion-hunting safari at Thika. There was clearly something about Percival's knees that attracted the attention of great statesmen, for when Theodore Roosevelt, ex-President of the United States, visited Kenya in 1909, he too felt moved to write about them in a book.

Roosevelt had bowed out of the White House at the end of 1908. He set sail for Kenya three months later on an expedition financed by the Smithsonian Institution to collect specimens of big game and other mammals for the National Museum in Washington.

For the retired politician, the African trip was the realisation of a life-long ambition. 'I long also for the other wilderness which I have never seen, and never shall see, excepting through your books,' he had once despondently written to F. C. Selous.

With Roosevelt were his son Kermit – a nineteen-year-old Harvard undergraduate – and three naturalists. Between them, the party slaughtered more than a thousand creatures in the name of science, a score that left even hardened Kenya hunters shocked.

The former president himself despatched 296 animals. He might have killed more except that his 'bulk and conversational powers somewhat precluded him from tracking, since the utmost caution and lack of noise are essential'.

In honour of the Roosevelts, Lord Delamere and Berkeley Cole arranged a hunt for bongo, Kenya's rarest antelope, in the Aberdare forest. The results were laconically described by Lord Cranworth:

'Kermit Roosevelt was led up at once to two good bulls, which unfortunately, eluded his eyesight in the open jungle, where their colouring is most distinctly protective. Proceeding further, a herd numbering at least thirty or forty were encountered; the sight of so many of such a rare species grouped in his proximity not unnaturally so excited the young sportsman that his shooting became somewhat erratic. Luckily, the bongo shared his bewilderment, and remained until he eventually obtained a cow and calf, prizes which he richly deserved ...'

Hunting apart, Roosevelt senior made a good impression on Kenya's settlers. Charmed by his down-to-earth manner, they were happy to overlook the slaughter in view of the publicity his trip was bringing the protectorate. Roosevelt's former high office did not sit at all heavily on his shoulders.

He made friends with everyone he met, whether fellow Americans like Northrop McMillan — Roosevelt called him a trump — or Boer farmers on whom he tried out his few words of Dutch, the common language of their ancestors. He had a happy knack of telling people that Kenya's wooded hills were just like Middle Wisconsin, and that Africans were very similar to the Red Indians he knew back home.

At Meru he was introduced to the District Commissioner, a onetime Wyoming cow puncher, with whom he found much in common. Wherever he went he created a stir in the protectorate such as probably had never been seen before, not even for the Connaughts' visit three years earlier.

The only people not immediately impressed were the Masai. Accompanied by a string of porters and a dead lion, Roosevelt called at a *manyatta* late one evening to request shelter. A number of mud-plastered warriors' heads thereupon appeared over the eight-foot fence and looked dubiously from Roosevelt to the huge American flag which appears to have followed him everywhere, to the porters and back to Roosevelt.

The warriors were inclined to be suspicious. Only after it was explained to them that the fat one had been president of the United States of America did they agree to open their gates to him.

While on safari, Roosevelt received a telegram at Nyeri — brought to him by native runners — announcing that the American explorer Robert Peary had succeeded in his attempt to reach the North Pole. A year before, while still president, Roosevelt had seen Peary off on his Arctic voyage. The telegram said: '*Your farewell was a royal mascot. The Pole is ours — Peary.*'

In his book *African Game Trails*, Roosevelt diplomatically paid tribute to the British he had met on his journey, praising them for their steadfast qualities at a time when Imperialism was not yet a dirty word.

He saw the British in Kenya as 'quiet, modest men whose lives have been fuller of wild adventure than the life of a Viking leader of the ninth century'.

For a portrait of vintage 1909 Empire builders, he offered this impression of his fellow passengers on the sea voyage south from Suez towards Mombasa:

'The Englishmen included planters, magistrates, forest officials, army officers on leave from India, and other army officers going out to take command of black native levies in out-of-the-way regions where the English flag stands for all that makes life worth living. They were a fine set, these young Englishmen, whether dashing army officers or capable civilians … Moreover, I felt as if I knew most of them already, for they might have walked out of the pages of Kipling.'

Since Roosevelt was travelling on a German ship, he also met plenty of Germans on the voyage. About them, he was just as enthusiastic:

'I was not as well prepared for the corresponding and equally interesting types among the Germans, the planters, the civil officials, the officers who had commanded, or were about to command, white or native troops – men of evident power and energy, seeing whom made it easy to understand why German East Africa has thriven apace.

'They are first-class men, these English and Germans; both are doing in East Africa a work of worth to the whole world; there is ample room for both, and no possible cause for any but a thoroughly friendly rivalry; and it is earnestly to be wished, in the interest both of them and of outsiders too, that their relations will grow, as they ought to grow, steadily better – and not only in East Africa, but everywhere else.'

A nice sentiment, but unhappily it was not to be. Although people in Kenya were only dimly aware of it, political events in Europe were shaping up for the biggest military confrontation the world had ever seen. Before very long, the Germans and British in East Africa – having always forbidden anything of the sort among the natives under their control – were to discover a new and calamitous diversion.

War.

CHAPTER FIVE

LOTS OF FIGHTING

News of the outbreak of the Great War reached Uasin Gishu settlers in the middle of an agricultural meeting at Eldoret. They did not hesitate for a moment. Without bothering to return to their farms, they jumped onto their mules and rode through the night to the nearest railway station at Londiani. Next day they arrived in Nairobi, tired, hungry and slightly bemused, but raring to go into action against their German neighbours across the border.

They found Nairobi seething with excitement and rumour. The war had caught the capital unprepared. There was just one battalion of KAR troops to defend a frontier that stretched from Lake Victoria to the sea. For much of its length, the unprotected tracks of the Uganda Railway – Kenya's lifeline – ran within fifty miles of German territory, an easy target for sudden guerrilla raids.

There were German gunboats on Lake Victoria and a German battle cruiser roaming the sea lanes off Mombasa on the Indian Ocean. It was also rumoured that a large number of German aeroplanes was poised for a bombing attack on Nairobi.

The settlers lost no time organising themselves into armed units. Within a few days of war being declared, irregular groups of mounted commandos carrying all sorts of weapons had converged on the capital and were pawing at the ground, waiting for someone to tell them what to do.

The Uasin Gishu contingent, some of whom had settled in Kenya to get away from the British after the Boer War, christened themselves the Plateau South Africans and were itching to do battle for King and country.

Other units took their names from the most powerful personalities in the group: Wilson's Scouts, Ross's Scouts, Wessell's Scouts, Arnoldi's Scouts (Arnoldi was killed in 1915 when his foot caught in a stirrup and his skull smashed against a tree).

Russell Bowker, a South African built along the lines of Mount Kilimanjaro, recruited all his drinking companions into Bowker's Horse. Like the Afrikaner citizen-army of the Boer War, his men wore whatever clothes came to hand: bush jackets, khaki trousers, any kind of hat, boots, gaiters, hunting knives, neck cloths and home-made bandoleros.

Bowker was proud of them. They were the sort of men who would gallop into battle with a weapon in each hand and the reins between their teeth. He himself proposed to fight the Germans in a slouch hat on which he had mounted a leopard's head, complete with bared fangs.

(As it happened, Bowker's Horse came to an untimely end when a four-man German patrol crept up on them when they were not looking and rustled fifty-seven of their horses. After that, they became known as Bowker's Foot.)

Eventually these commandos were all amalgamated into one and restyled the East African Mounted Rifles. In the light of the Bowker experience, they took to camouflaging their horses by decking them out in black and white zebra stripes, indistinguishable at a distance from the real thing.

Styling themselves 'Monica's Own' after the Governor's daughter, the most pretentious of the EAMR's six squadrons imagined that they were Lancers because they carried red and yellow pennants at the tip of their bamboo spears. The EAMR fancied the idea of being soldiers, but not the discipline that went with it. When the real army tried to lick them into shape, one cowboy lasted only forty-eight hours before collecting a discharge paper which said: '*Length of service:* two days. *Reason for discharge:* hopeless and incorrigible.'

Altogether, over one thousand settlers joined the colours in the first fortnight of the war, serving either in the EAMR, or as infantry in the East Africa Regiment, or else going back to England to fight on the Western Front. There was also a contingent of eight hundred Somali volunteers mounted on mules and known as Cole's Scouts after their leader, Berkeley Cole.

His sister, Lady Delamere, had died of heart strain earlier in the year at the age of thirty-six. With nothing to tie him to the farm, Lord Delamere was busy recruiting Masai warriors for scouting parties along the German border. And the Game department, whose anti-poaching patrols knew the country as well as anyone, had been transformed into an intelligence-gathering unit on a full war footing.

But was there really going to be a war? Would the two administrations of Nairobi and Dar-es-Salaam allow the natives under their control to witness the unedifying spectacle of great white bwanas slaughtering each other, with all its grave implications for the future, or would they shelter behind Article Two of the Congo Act 1885? The Act allowed for neutrality in German and British East Africa in the event of a war between the two powers in Europe.

Neither Monica's father, Sir Henry Belfield, nor German East Africa's Governor Heinrich Schnee, whose wife was a New Zealander, wanted to see a war. Nor did the more reflective of Kenya's settlers. They realised that even a few months away would be enough to undo years of hard work on their farms.

If they went to war, the Africans left behind might rise in revolt. They might massacre the settlers' wives and children while they were away.[1] Both sides understood that they had far too much to lose in a war.

Unfortunately, as Tolstoy observed, events control people, rather than the other way about. Four days after war was declared, the British cruisers *Astraea* and *Pegasus* fired the opening shots of a campaign that was to last until after the Armistice – and end in tactical victory for the Germans – by bombarding the radio tower at Dar-es-Salaam as a hint to Governor Schnee not to defend the town.

Schnee promptly hauled up the white flag and disappeared inland, leaving behind a subordinate to agree a kind of truce with the Royal Navy. The British officer who signed it was at pains to point out that it was not binding on the British Government. Nor did it extend beyond the ports of Dar-es-Salaam and Tanga.

The Royal Navy was a powerful presence off the East African coast, but it did not have everything its own way. Germany possessed a trump card in the form of the *Königsberg*, a swift light cruiser armed with twin torpedo tubes and ten 4·1-inch guns. The guns roared so mightily that a peacetime salute in harbour shivered coconuts out of palm trees all along the shore.

In the few days preceding the outbreak of war, HMS *Astraea* and HMS *Pegasus* had formed part of a squadron shadowing the *Königsberg*. They were determined to keep her within range of their guns and so prevent her becoming a menace to British shipping. But the *Königsberg* had used her superior engine power to lose the squadron during a sudden squall which blew up just as night was falling. Where she was now was anyone's guess.

On land, too, Germany possessed a trump card of a different kind. The colony's Schutztruppe – white-led native troops – were commanded by a Prussian officer of outstanding ability, genius even. His charismatic personality and understanding of guerrilla warfare were to make him the only German commander in any theatre to come out of the war undefeated.

Colonel Paul von Lettow-Vorbeck had arrived in East Africa in January 1914 after a long career on active service. He had learned the ins and outs of his profession in places as far apart as China, during the Boxer rebellion, and South West Africa during the Herero uprising, where he had come to admire the skill and bushcraft of his Hottentot opponents.

If Governor Schnee was in two minds about opening hostilities against the British, von Lettow, though he liked and respected them, had no such doubts. He realised from the start that he could never hope to defeat the British outright.

Königsberg or no *Königsberg*, the Indian Ocean was dominated by the Royal Navy. There was no way that the Schutztruppe could hope to receive significant reinforcements of men or materials from the Fatherland. Whereas Kenya had unrestricted access to the vast resources of the world's largest empire, von Lettow would just have to make do with what he had got.

But if he could not defeat the British, it did not follow that they could defeat him. There was more than one way to skin a cat.

Von Lettow knew that the real war would be fought out in the mud and blood of Belgium and northern France. If he could divert stores and badly needed troops from the Western Front and bog them down in the malarial and disease-ridden bush of East Africa, he would be doing more than his bit for his country.

He acted swiftly. Immediately after the shelling of Dar-es-Salaam by the *Astraea* and *Pegasus*, a small force of commandos crossed into Kenya, the only part of the British Empire to be invaded by Germans during the entire war. They had orders to blow up railway bridges, cut telegraph wire and confuse the enemy.

The men were led by Tom von Prince, a Scotsman with a German mother, who had taken service with the Germans after being turned down for a commission by the British army. The 'von' was a personal present from the Kaiser, a reward for the considerable fighting qualities he had displayed during a long and colourful career.

Before the English knew what had hit them, von Prince had captured the railway station and telegraph office at Taveta. He triumphantly reported to his superiors that the German flag was flying on British soil.

Though von Prince's force was soon repulsed, and with it any German hopes of a quick victory, the British reacted precisely as von Lettow had intended them to. Pointing out that von Prince had got within twenty-five miles of Mombasa, they demanded reinforcements to counter the threat of invasion.

The India Office hastily re-routed two expeditionary forces of Indian troops. One was sent to back up the KAR in Kenya, the other to capture Dar-es-Salaam. Eight thousand troops set sail from India at the beginning of October 1914.

The men arrived off Mombasa at the end of the month, after a cramped and unpleasant voyage in which most of them had been unable to exercise properly and were heartily seasick. Even then, their miseries were not at an end.

Intending to send them into action straight away, East Africa Command left the troops to swelter beside the reef while their staff officers went ashore to be briefed. The officers learned that the invasion target had now been switched to Tanga, German East Africa's second most important port.

Soon after dawn on 2 November, the expeditionary force hove to on a greasy sea just out of sight of Tanga. Instead of going straight ahead with the invasion, it waited twenty-four hours while the cruiser *Fox* put in to Tanga to remind the German authorities that the truce agreed earlier with the Royal

Navy was no longer valid, and to demand the surrender of the port. This the Germans refused to do.

Instead, having had time and place of the invasion handed to him on a plate, von Lettow evacuated all civilians from the area and rushed more troops into the town. They arrived in time to gun down the advancing Indians from behind carefully prepared defensive positions. Right from the word go, the invasion was a fiasco.

Originally General Aitken, the expeditionary force's commander, had intended to land his troops on the jetties of the harbour. But the navy, fearing that the approaches might be mined, insisted that he land them instead in breast-high water leading to a mangrove swamp. The swamp lay at the foot of a fifty-foot cliff nearly two miles from the town.

In full moonlight, under continual sniper fire from Schutztruppe patrols, the Indians struggled raggedly ashore after nearly a month at sea. They were thoroughly demoralised by the time they reached dry land and had little interest in anything beyond saving their own skins. Small wonder that the ensuing battle was a fiasco.

'It was too piteous to see the state of the men,' wrote Richard Meinertzhagen, now a Colonel, who somehow contrived to do a great deal of his soldiering in East Africa. 'Many were gibbering idiots, muttering prayers to their heathen gods, hiding behind bushes and palm trees and laying down face to earth in folds in the ground with their rifles lying useless beside them. I would never have believed that grown-up men of any race could have been reduced to such shamelessness...

'I do not blame the men, still less their officers. I blame the Indian Government for enlisting such scum and placing them in the King's uniform.'

By next afternoon the British had lost officer after officer, shot down while trying to rally the troops. Meinertzhagen himself made free use of his boots and pistol. He killed several Indians who tried to run away, but to little avail.

The troops were poor quality, inadequately trained, and strangers to their officers. Many of the officers had only joined them just before the convoy left India. The sole British unit in the expeditionary force, the 2nd Loyal North Lancashire Regiment, did not carry enough respect to stiffen the Indians' resolve.

When the Indians did attempt to advance, they immediately ran into trip wires thoughtfully arranged by the Germans to trigger off a series of flags giving the precise range of the oncoming troops. At a critical moment a huge swarm of bees, probably knocked out of their hives by the defenders' gunfire, descended on the Indians with sudden fury and unleashed a battery of bee stings for which the suffering soldiers were totally unprepared.

The situation was not as comical as it sounds. An African bee sting is a very unpleasant experience. One man was stung three hundred times in the head. Another, laid out by a bullet wound, was jerked back into consciousness by the bees and probably owed his life to them.

The battle lasted two days, with the Germans outnumbered eight to one, before General Aitken admitted defeat. Pulling his men back to the beachhead for re-embarkation aboard the convoy, he left behind sixteen machine guns, 455 rifles and 600,000 rounds of ammunition. The weapons were picked up by the incredulous Schutztruppe and used against the British in the coming campaign.

Not surprisingly, the War Office relieved Aitken of his command at once and shipped him back to London, where Lord Kitchener refused point blank to see him. He spent the rest of his life explaining to anyone who would listen that the disaster had not been his fault.

In truth, the British operation at Tanga was unprofessional and amateurish in the extreme, the sort of performance that only an English general who has passed high out of Staff College can achieve. It had been based on two fundamentally faulty premises – that Indian troops were superior to the black tribesmen of the Schutztruppe fighting on their own terrain, and that an Englishman could lick a German any day of the week.

The only British officer to question the wisdom of this thinking appears to have been Meinertzhagen, himself of German descent.

Even with a battle raging in front of their eyes, the English still did not fully appreciate that they were at war. In the middle of the shooting, the crew of a ship's dinghy landed at Tanga harbour and got out to see if they could buy something to eat in the town.

At the height of the subsequent evacuation, with the Schutztruppe in full control of the port, a squad of North Lancs arrived ashore from a transport and began to bathe within fifty yards of the nearest German officer. Meinertzhagen, carrying a white flag through enemy lines to negotiate evacuation of the wounded, was severely embarrassed to see a British quartermaster wandering around making an inventory of the abandoned stores.

Later, while waiting in the hospital, Meinertzhagen had a drink with a German doctor and chatted freely about the war. Outside the window, he could see German snipers shooting at HMS *Fox* from among the trees. The whole business had a surreal and unsoldierlike quality about it which disturbed him deeply.

Indeed, for an exhibition of how not to carry out an invasion, the Tanga charade was almost impossible to beat. Nursing its humiliation as best it could, the expeditionary force stood off from land and limped slowly back to Mombasa.

There, four Customs officers very properly refused to allow anyone ashore until five per cent *ad valorem* duty had been paid on such stores and equipment as had been salvaged from the débâcle. Their minds were changed for them by Meinertzhagen and ten friends armed with bayonets.

First blood then to the Germans, and not just on land. Two days after the declaration of war, the *Königsberg* sighted the SS *City of Winchester* carrying two million dollars' worth of tea off the coast of Aden and blew the bottom out of her – and out of the London tea market as well. Then the cruiser disappeared back into the blue, leaving every Royal Navy captain for hundreds of miles in a fever of anxiety to know where she had gone.

HMS *Pegasus* found out on 20 September. Plagued by engine trouble, *Pegasus* was undergoing a much needed boiler cleaning in Zanzibar harbour when a huge grey ship loomed up out of the half-light of dawn and began to pulverise the helpless British cruiser into scrap metal.

Inside thirty minutes the *Pegasus* ceased to exist as a fighting force. At two o'clock in the afternoon she keeled over and sank in deep water. By that time the *Königsberg* was nowhere to be seen.

But the very efficiency of this operation sealed the German warship's destruction, for it brought down on her the full wrath of the Royal Navy. Three more British cruisers, the *Chatham, Dartmouth* and *Weymouth*, were ordered into East African waters to seek out and destroy the enemy raider as a matter of the utmost priority.

So long as he remained on the high seas, Captain Looff of the *Königsberg* still held the initiative and could afford to ignore this threat – but his ship was already overdue to go into port for a refit. There, if he was not careful, the British would have their revenge.

Looff weighed up the pros and cons in his mind. On a hostile ocean, it was out of the question to run for shelter in Dar-es-Salaam or Tanga. The Royal Navy controlled the offshore islands of Pemba and Zanzibar, and the memory of the helpless *Pegasus* was still vivid in his imagination. What he really needed to do was to take the *Königsberg* all the way back to Germany, but his engines would never last the distance without an overhaul.

That left just one alternative. Find a secret base somewhere along the two thousand miles of tangled, treacherous friezework that made up the coastline of German and Portuguese East Africa.

After some thought Looff selected the Rufiji delta in German East Africa. The Rufiji's maze of creeks and mangrove swamps contained ten large water courses in a sea of mud that stretched thirty miles along the coast. The delta was so overgrown that nothing was visible from the seaward side. The *Königsberg* had sheltered there before to make running repairs before the *Pegasus* sinking.

After the Zanzibar raid, Looff steamed back to his hiding place as fast as he could go. He made use of an exceptionally high tide to coax the vessel over shallow water far into the delta, where he calculated the deeper draught British cruisers would be unable to follow. Then he anchored and began to dismantle his engines.

The overhaul was a mammoth task. The nearest place capable of handling the operation was Dar-es-Salaam. It was too risky for the engines to travel there by sea, so they had to go by land.

With help from nearby German planters, Looff recruited upwards of one thousand Africans to transport the *Königsberg*'s dismembered boiler from the engine room onto a pair of specially constructed wooden sleds, enormous contraptions. They were then hauled through a hundred miles of uncleared bush to Dar.

Until the boiler returned, the *Königsberg* would have to lie helplessly at anchor, as the *Pegasus* had done. The crew could only pray that the avenging snouts of the other British cruisers would not poke too deep into the murky confines of the delta.

The British knew something was up, all right. They could tell by the presence on land of red and white flags, or fires at night, keeping pace with Royal Navy ships along the coast. They could tell by the presence of Schutztruppe patrols on the beach, clearly visible through field glasses.

Most of all, they could tell by the capture of the German merchantman *Präsident*. She claimed to be a hospital ship, yet had papers showing that she had recently unloaded a full cargo of stores at the mouth of the Rufiji. It did not take a genius to put two and two together.

For their part, the Germans did everything in their power to protect the *Königsberg*'s hiding place from the prying eyes of the Royal Navy's lookouts. The ship herself was heavily camouflaged, her sides streaked with green and her masts disguised as trees.

Along with the full complement of 47mm guns, her machine guns were dismounted and carried ashore. They were then concealed in well sited positions covering the seaward approaches to the delta.

To prevent the heavy armament firing blind, several miles of telephone cable linked the cruiser's big guns to forward observation posts hidden along the sea shore. Captain Looff did not believe in taking chances.

By 30 October he was nearly ready to leave the delta again. The *Königsberg*'s boiler had been dragged back from Dar-es-Salaam. A test run of the engines established that they were working almost perfectly.

After a few simple adjustments, the *Königsberg* would be ready to slip out into the Indian Ocean and begin the long journey home around the Cape to the Fatherland. She would pause only to sink any British merchant shipping she might encounter on the way.

There was just one snag. Five miles offshore, as close as she dared go at low tide, lurked the *Chatham*. She was newer and faster than the *Königsberg* and easily outgunned her. The *Chatham*'s captain was working on a hunch that his quarry was in the Rufiji somewhere not far away.

His suspicions were confirmed when Looff made an unavoidable mistake. While testing his engines, the German captain moved the *Königsberg* several hundred yards upstream. The sight of a pair of coconut trees behaving so oddly did not go unnoticed aboard the *Chatham*.

Closer inspection revealed that the trees were really the *Königsberg's* masts. She had been tracked down at last. But how to deal with her? She would not come out of the Rufiji, and the Royal Navy could not go in.

Since this was the week of the Tanga pantomime, the British army expressed a marked lack of enthusiasm for a land assault. A futile attempt at bombardment from the sea – for which the *Chatham* had to shift her ballast to gain maximum gun elevation – only prompted the *Königsberg* to raise anchor and disappear even further up the creek. There was nothing the navy could do to stop her.

Admiral King-Hall, commander of the British squadron, pondered his options. His first priority was to find the *Königsberg's* new hiding place. The most obvious way to do that was to send search parties up-river in small boats. Even if they weren't annihilated by the Germans, however, the job might take weeks or even months.

Fortunately, there was a quicker way. King-Hall knew of an aeroplane in South Africa. He would be able to sweep the whole of the delta in a single day if he could only get hold of it.

The aeroplane belonged to a civilian named Cutler. He was incautiously walking abroad in Durban one morning when a couple of sailors jumped out from nowhere and voted him a temporary commission in the Royal Navy before he had a chance to open his mouth. Of such beginnings was the Fleet Air Arm born.

Cutler's single-engine Curtis hydroplane was the only serviceable flying machine in British hands anywhere along the coast. Along with its pilot, it was promptly packed onto a ship and transported to the Rufiji. There, after only one flight over the river, the radiator fell off – whereupon Lieutenant Cutler thankfully assumed that his fighting days were over.

He could not have been more wrong. A helpful mechanic remembered seeing a Ford car in Mombasa with a similar radiator. The navy sent a ship steaming northwards to steal it. Once tacked on, it worked like a dream.

Inevitably perhaps, Cutler soon managed to crash his machine, though not before he had successfully located the *Königsberg's* latest hideout up-river. After a hurried search the navy got hold of other, more up-to-date aircraft. They did sterling recce work over the Rufiji in the first air-sea operations of their kind ever attempted.

This being the age of hop, skip and jump flying, the job was not without teething troubles. A message to the Air Department in London told much of the story: *'Glue not holding on any propellers. Wood for only one more propeller. Has india-rubber tubing been sent? As all ours perished.'*

But the *Königsberg* had been located. Now that he knew for sure where she was, Admiral King-Hall could draw up a blueprint for her destruction. The charts at his disposal were woefully inadequate, so he ordered a full-scale reconnaissance of the channels around the trapped warship to determine exactly which ones were navigable at low and high tide, and which were not.

It was rumoured that Captain Looff had set up his two 17·7-inch torpedo tubes in ambush positions along the river bank. This, and a hundred and one other things, had to be checked out before any attack could go in.

King-Hall was too good a commander to commit his forces until the area had been thoroughly explored. What he needed for the reconnaissance operation was a European with the right skills to infiltrate the mangrove swamps and spy out the land. He needed a European who could find his way blindfold around the delta if he had to. Happily, he knew just such a man.

Philip Pretorius was an Afrikaner – Pretoria is named after one of his *voortrekker* ancestors – with an extraordinary gift for bushcraft developed during a varied career as wanderer, white hunter and part-time fighter. He had first gone into action at sixteen against the Mashona. Later he had trekked so deep into the Zambesi bush that he never heard about the Boer War until it was over.

In the 1900s he drifted into German East Africa and settled down on a small farm by the Rufiji, only to see his land summarily confiscated after he had refused to sell it to a Schutztruppe officer who had taken a fancy to it.

Disenchanted with all things German, Pretorius then made a public vow to poach ivory on the Kaiser's territory to the value of his stolen farm. He did exactly that, despite intensive efforts to track him down. Come 1914, there was little or nothing Pretorius did not know about outwitting Germans.

Besides featuring in *Greenmantle*, his exploits more recently formed the basis of Wilbur Smith's fictionalised account of the *Königsberg* adventure, *Shout at the Devil*. Smith always insisted, however, that it would be most unfair to Pretorius to infer that the characterisation of Flynn Patrick

O'Flynn – played by Lee Marvin in the film – bore any resemblance to the original. Biggles would be closer to the mark.

Accompanied by six Africans in a dugout canoe, Pretorius made several trips up the Rufiji on spying missions for the Royal Navy. Having pinpointed the *Königsberg*'s exact location, his most important task was to find out whether her big guns were still in working order, and whether the two torpedo tubes had in fact been taken ashore.

This he achieved by disguising himself as an Arab – twenty-five years of malaria and blistering sun had already tanned his flesh the appropriate colour – and stepping boldly with a black companion into a native labourers' camp set up by the Germans not three hundred yards from the cruiser. By bribing a German sailor with a basket of chickens, Pretorius obtained permission for his 'servant' to meet his son, a temporary stoker aboard the *Königsberg*.

The meeting was a success. The son confirmed that 'the long bullets that swim in the water' had indeed been removed from the ship. They were probably mounted on small boats near the mouth of the estuary.

Pretorius reported back to Admiral King-Hall, who asked him to go back into the swamp and search for a navigable approach route to the *Königsberg*. He did so by taking soundings with a pole over the side of the canoe, often in broad daylight and under the noses of the enemy. They assumed he was a fisherman.

Pretorius established that there was no completely clear channel. The best route was effectively blocked by a solid reef running from bank to bank. By pacing out the distance from there to the *Königsberg*, he discovered that the cruiser would be well within range of 6-inch guns firing from the seaward side of the reef.

Encouraged by this news, King-Hall sent to England for two flat-bottomed monitor boats, the *Severn* and the *Mersey*. Each had a draught of only four feet, but was armed with two 6-inch guns fore and aft. The monitor boats would easily outgun the *Königsberg* if it came to a shootout.

While waiting for them to be towed out via the Mediterranean, Pretorius spent a solid month, the dreariest of his life, making an hour by hour record of the rise and fall of the tide close inshore by the reef. By the end he had become so bored that he was almost 'glad of the relieving sense of adventure brought by the possibility of a Teutonic face suddenly peering at me out of the bush'.

The final act of the *Königsberg* drama was not played out until the arrival of the *Severn* and *Mersey* at the end of the rainy season in July 1915. Using Pretorius's painstaking chart, the two monitors – little more than floating gun platforms – nosed cautiously up-river in the early light of dawn.

Their engines were turning over at a pathetic maximum speed of seven and a half knots. Their sides were reinforced with sandbags and steel plating against the steady stream of gunfire aimed at them from the bank.

Above them flew a spotter plane, waiting to direct their fire onto the *Königsberg* by radio. The target itself was invisible behind a solid belt of forest. Out at sea, their comrades aboard the British cruisers paced the deck furiously, powerless to do anything except watch and pray that the mission would be a success.

It was not. The first attempt to sink the *Königsberg* ended in total failure. The battle lasted eleven hours, during which the monitors fired 635 shells, but received aerial corrections for only seventy-eight. Though neither side could see the other, both achieved direct hits or straddled their targets so closely that the decks were piled with dead fish and dismembered crocodiles.

The *Mersey* was soon hit and began to leak below the waterline. German snipers added to the troubles of both monitors by upsetting the aim of their gunners with relentless fire from the swamp. At length, just before four in the afternoon, with the *Königsberg* still very much afloat and the ebb tide drawing to a close, the two British ships were forced to withdraw while they could still clear the shoals. Though not for long.

Five days later, having carried out extensive repairs, the *Mersey* and the *Severn* returned to the fight. This time they made no mistake. An early shot from the *Severn* destroyed the *Königsberg*'s telephone link with her main observation post on Pemba Hill. From then on, the cruiser's fire became more and more wild, while that of the monitors improved steadily.

Soon the *Königsberg* was blazing from stem to stern. Bodies lay in untidy piles by the forecastle. Her decks were awash with blood, sprinkled with sand to make the gangway passable.

In the space of twelve minutes, four of the *Königsberg*'s gun turrets were knocked out of action, the centre of the three funnels was blown overboard, and a tremendous explosion sent a funeral pyre of black smoke mushrooming upwards thousands of feet above the trees. The warship was doomed.

The Germans themselves administered the *coup de grâce* by setting off a torpedo to break the cruiser's back after all the dead and wounded had been ferried ashore. At two in the afternoon, bracketed by spumes of water from falling British shells, the *Königsberg* turned slightly onto one side and slowly sank to her upper deck into the muddy reaches of the Rufiji.

Her flag was still flying as she went down. In Looff's words, she had been 'destroyed but not conquered'.

He and his men had not been conquered either. Their ship might have sunk, but they still had her 4.1 inch guns. As soon as they were ashore, they mounted the guns on wheels and delivered them to the Schutztruppe for the defence of Dar-es-Salaam.

The loss of the *Königsberg* was a blow to Germany, but a battery of artillery proved a godsend for Colonel von Lettow in his protracted guerrilla war against the British. He knew exactly how to make use of it.

1. In Nyasaland, for instance, followers of a teacher trained by the American Baptist Mission decapitated the grandson of David Livingstone and stuck his head on a church pulpit while the teacher preached a sermon on Africa for the Africans.

'This peak and silvery line formed the central culminating point of Mount Kenia'

Fort Jesus, once commanded by a teenaged midshipman, which dominates the old harbour at Mombasa

The round house of Fort Smith at Kabete, the old-
est building still standing in the Nairobi area

The early settlers moved out from Nairobi in ox wagons such as
this one, which now stands in the grounds of the Norfolk Hotel

Richard Meinertzhagen (*Randle Meinertzhagen*)

A meet of the Molo Hunt in the white highlands

The Prince of Wales rides in front of the engine to
get a better view of the wild life, 1928

Lord and Lady Baden-Powell at Nyeri

Theodore Roosevelt's East African safari, 1909. Left to right:
Theodore Roosevelt, F. C. Selous (possibly the original of Rider
Haggard's Allan Quatermain), Edgar Mearns, Kermit Roosevelt

CHAPTER SIX

AND LOTS OF FUN!

Von Lettow's strategy had not altered since the Schutztruppe's victory at Tanga. His aim was still to draw as many enemy troops as possible to East Africa by a combination of surprise attack and steadfast refusal to commit his forces to a pitched battle. He would only commit to a battle when he judged that the outcome would justify the loss of irreplaceable men and equipment.

Live to fight another day was the Schutztruppe motto. Von Lettow's men obeyed the order with alacrity. Whenever the invading British moved forward in strength, the Germans would linger just long enough to inflict heavy casualties before slipping away into the bush, leaving their enemies to pick up the pieces and plod on with the advance as best they could.

By January 1916 the number of British Empire troops on active service in East Africa had swelled from a few thousand to two divisions, totalling more than thirty thousand men. A large percentage of these lost their lives during the campaign, not from enemy action, but from disease.

If malaria did not claim them, then bacillary or amoebic dysentery did. Chills, heatstroke, blackwater fever and rotting feet caused by jigger fleas were commonplace. Many soldiers were driven out of their minds by thirst.

Others died of exhaustion, brought on by endless weeks of half-rations augmented only by whatever food could be found along the line of march. For the British, stubbornly persisting in their belief that any troops had to be better than the relatively immune natives of the Schutztruppe, German East Africa was proving to be a death trap. Just as von Lettow had planned.

Yet for all the discomforts of the campaign, the war was fought with great good humour on both sides, as if it was just a great big boy-scout exercise that had somehow got out of hand. Von Lettow in particular captured the imagination not only of the German public at home but also of his opponents in the field. The British warmed to him for the efficiency with which he outwitted them at every turn.

In their estimation, and they yielded to no one on this, a man who could make fools of them so successfully and so often had to be pretty extraordinary. Von Lettow was indeed an energetic and capable front-line soldier. He led by example and believed in seeing everything for himself. Often the easiest way to do this was by bicycle. On one occasion, in the finest tradition of generalship, he had it shot from under him.

Since von Lettow was cut off from Germany and could get no news from home, the lines were continually parting to let through a British officer with a white flag bearing personal messages from the Kaiser by way of the British commander. Von Lettow had been promoted General, the British offered warm congratulations. He had been awarded the Blue Max, Germany's highest medal, the British were thrilled.

Every now and again they sent earnest solicitations after his health, which was not good. It comes as a surprise to learn that they did not shut down the entire war effort to send him a cake on his birthday.

He appears to have presided over his own army as a father over one big family, provided they all did their job: at least two officers committed suicide rather than face the General's wrath over a bungled mission. Indeed the Schutztruppe really was a family. It consisted almost entirely of native troops who insisted on bringing their women and children to war with them. More than one *askari* went into action with a baby clamouring for attention on his back.

In view of the harsh conditions, von Lettow permitted the troops as many home comforts as possible, although there were times when he was forced to draw the line. He gave orders that any cock crowing before 9 a.m. would be shot as a traitor, body forfeit to headquarters.

He was once badly let down by a company of Arab troops, upset that he had forbidden them to take along their boyfriends on a particularly tricky operation. They fired their rifles in the air, folded their arms and refused to take any further interest in the proceedings.

At every level, relations between the British and Germans were unusually friendly, showing few signs of the animosity that characterised the war in the trenches. When a British vet was captured by the Schutztruppe, his friends swapped him back for two bottles of whiskey.

A wounded British prisoner, nursed back to health by a German officer's wife, married her after her husband was killed. And after fully twelve months of war, the Mombasa Club held an extraordinary general meeting to debate a resolution that it was about time the German members handed in their resignations. The resolution was defeated on the grounds that the offended parties might sue for breach of contract.

Indeed, British admiration for von Lettow and his men was matched only by the disgust they felt for their own generals, who appear to have been as desperate a shower of no-hopers as has ever been wished on Empire troops in battle. General Aitken, of course, had been sent home under a cloud after Tanga – although officially he was absolved from any blame.

Aitken was replaced by General Wapshare, known to everyone as Wappy. Wapshare was a nervous old gentleman who developed a fit of the vapours at the mere mention of von Lettow's name. He had to be doped with champagne by Meinertzhagen before being packed off to bed.

On arrival at Mombasa to take up his post, Wapshare distinguished himself in an incident with a rickshaw boy that almost defies belief. The Swahili for 'Good morning, sir. How are you today? Would you like me to run you to the top of the hill?' is of course *'Wapi? Juu?'*

Hearing these words as he clambered into the rickshaw, Wappy interpreted them as an unwarranted assertion that his family came from Israel. He beat up the boy with his stick, not stopping until the unfortunate native had fled and the rickshaw lay abandoned in the road.

Sadly, this show of ferocity did not repeat itself in battle. In April 1915 Wapshare was quietly shovelled off to the Persian Gulf. As Meinertzhagen put it: 'His removal is for the public good, for he was a public danger.'

His replacement was General Tighe, a no-nonsense fighting man with plenty of thunder in his belly, but well on his way to death by alcoholic poisoning. Meinertzhagen described him as a bear with a sore head. This assessment was amply borne out by an incident aboard ship on Lake Victoria:

'Why is the propeller reversing?' demanded General Tighe after a good dinner.

'It isn't, we are going full steam ahead,' Colonel Meinertzhagen told him.

'If I say the ship is going back, it's going back. Send for the captain.'

The captain agreed with Meinertzhagen, but Tighe would not budge. 'If the bloody ship isn't going backwards, I'll eat my boots and what's more, if I say she's in reverse she jolly well is in reverse, so just get that.'

Tactics, as the old army saying goes, is the opinion of the senior officer present. On shore, Tighe's soldiers were dying in droves. His reputation with the enemy was such that when the Germans learned of a railway journey he was scheduled to make, von Lettow personally forbade any attempt to destroy the train in case his opposite number was then replaced with some-one competent.

Even worse than Tighe was the junior General Malleson. He was a thoroughly nasty piece of work who shared the universal concern of British generals in this campaign to preserve their own careers intact at no matter what cost in other men dead and wounded. There are recorded instances of vital information being withheld from one general by another on the grounds that it might be useful to a rival. Malleson was a leading exponent of this art.

It wasn't long before Tighe sent for his subordinate to give him the sack. Arriving in Nairobi twenty-four hours before the showdown, Malleson set off for a lion shoot at a farm about seven miles outside the town. He had ordered his driver to return for him at tea time, but he was missing when the driver arrived. A massive search revealed no sign of him anywhere.

By next afternoon Malleson's obituary was already being written when he turned up out of the bush, pale, haggard and unshaven, recounting a doleful story of having spent the night in a tree fighting off an angry pride of lions. General Tighe was so upset to hear this that he forgot all about sacking Malleson and insisted that he go straight to bed instead.

In fact, Malleson's ordeal was pure invention. Since no lions had been known in the area for at least twenty years, Meinertzhagen made discreet inquiries and discovered that Malleson had made a beeline for the nearest farmhouse on leaving his driver and had asked permission to stay the night. While troops under his command were fighting and dying, General Malleson was pretending to be up a tree.

In reality he was relaxing on a comfortable sofa, making himself agreeable to his host's fifteen-year-old daughter, prior to winning Tighe's sympathy with a story that was fiction from beginning to end. It was wholly in character that he was later relieved of his command after being taken ill very suddenly in the middle of a battle. The last his troops saw of him, a car was speeding him to the rear with a cigarette dangling from his lips.

Happily, not all the generals were like that. At the opposite extreme was General 'Ha ha splendid' Sheppard. A fire-eating lunatic of the old school, Sheppard liked nothing better than to take himself where the fighting was. According to Lord Cranworth, he had earned his nickname from his habit of plunging into the thick of the action with a cry of 'Ha ha splendid! Lots of fighting and lots of fun!'

In the end the War Office had to call in a civilian to do the generals' job for them. Jan Christiaan Smuts was a career politician from South Africa, already well on his way to becoming a leading world statesman.

Although not a soldier, Smuts had fifteen years earlier led a commando of 340 Transvaalers on a thousand-mile raid into the Cape Province that had come to be regarded as one of the most dazzling exploits of the Boer War. In Jan Smuts the War Office reasoned that it would at last be matching fire with fire.

Joining the British army with the rank of Lieutenant-General, Smuts arrived in Nairobi in February 1916 to take overall command of the Empire forces ranged against von Lettow. He immediately set about imposing his own stamp on the direction and attitudes of the campaign.

His first task was to get rid of the dead wood at the top. 'I am now beginning to understand how it was that we always outwitted your leaders in South Africa,' he confided to Meinertzhagen. 'Are they all like this?'

They were. One by one Smuts disposed of them, either arranging for them to be posted abroad or else resorting to less conventional methods as circumstances dictated.

He sent Ewart Grogan, then a captain, to Uganda with instructions to locate a British general who was making an ass of himself and lead him gently into the Belgian Congo, where he could do little harm for the rest of the war. Learning of this mission, a German patrol went racing around Lake

Victoria to intercept Grogan and the general. They got lost and were eaten by cannibals instead.

With the playing fields of Eton now discredited as a breeding ground for generals, Smuts turned to more suitable officers of his own choosing. One of the first he selected was General Jacobus van Deventer, an Afrikaner like himself. Van Deventer never spoke above a whisper because of a throat wound caused by a British bullet during the Boer War.

Like many of the South African Dutch, Smuts and van Deventer were now wholly committed to Britain's cause in the war. They believed that their support must inevitably win political concessions for South Africa in the peace that followed.

German South West Africa had already come under Pretoria's control. It did not seem impossible that German East Africa could also be annexed as a colony, particularly since a great many South African troops were now in action against the Schutztruppe.

Besides South Africans, Smuts later commanded soldiers from the West Indies, the Gold Coast and Nigeria. They had been imported for the campaign in belated recognition of the fact that Africans make the best fighting men in tropical conditions. The West African troops were preceded by a reputation for cannibalism which they had done nothing to deserve, but did their best to live up to.

Having captured a group of Schutztruppe officers, a company of Gold Coasters advanced upon their prisoners with eating irons at the ready, only to dissolve into helpless laughter at the discomfiture written on the faces of the unhappy Germans. A squad of local porters allotted to the Nigerians flatly refused to travel in the train with them. They sat on the roof instead, where they could be quite certain they would not end up as anybody's lunch.

This was unfair to the Nigerians, but it was true that their eating habits were not entirely normal. One company, ravenous with hunger, fell upon a road bridge tied together with strips of rawhide and ate the lot, whereupon the wooden spars collapsed into the river below and floated away.

This news would undoubtedly have interested General Dealy, the campaign's chief engineer officer. A lateral-thinking man, he liked nothing better than to turn a problem on its head and look at it from a fresh angle.

Having built himself a lovely trestle bridge, he lacked only a river to fit it. Some were too wide, others too narrow.

The bridge accompanied him all round East Africa, blocking roads, getting stuck in the mud, losing its way in the bush and visiting each river in turn, hoping to find a suitable home. After failing to find one in the British sector, Dealy was all for advancing against the Germans in the hope of striking lucky behind enemy lines.

As well as colonial troops, a fusilier battalion of Kitchener's new army, known semi-officially as the Legion of Frontiersmen (Driscoll's Tigers), was sent out from England to support Smuts. Among its officers were Northrop McMillan, the American millionaire so enormous that his sword belt measured sixty-four inches in circumference, and sixty-three-year-old Frederick Courtney Selous, easily the most famous big game hunter of his generation.

Selous may have been one of the models for *King Solomon's Mines*' Allan Quatermain, although he and Rider Haggard disagreed strongly on the Boer question. An Old Rugbeian, he seems to have spent a boyhood remarkably similar to Tom Brown's in evading gamekeepers and locking up schoolmasters in cow sheds. His idea of testing the accuracy of a new rifle was to stick it out of a window in Regent's Park and blow five chimney pots off a neighbour's roof.

Selous was killed in action on 4 January 1917 while leading an attack against the Schutztruppe. His death prompted his friend Teddy Roosevelt to comment: 'It is well for any country to produce men of such a type; and if there are enough of them the nation need fear no decadence.'

A memorial to Selous in the shape of a bronze buffalo can be found today in the Nairobi Club. This buffalo was later adopted as the cap badge of the Kenya Regiment, a body of European settlers who performed much the same role against Mau Mau as the Selous Scouts did against guerrilla fighters in Ian Smith's Rhodesia.

As for the rank and file of the Legion of Frontiersmen, they must have been the oddest ragbag of troops ever stitched together under one banner.

The Frontiersmen included 'a millionaire from Park Lane, a late subaltern from the Garrison Artillery, Colour Sergeants from the Brigade of Guards, men from nearly every line regiment in the Army, a flunkey from Buckingham Palace, several late members of the French Foreign Legion,

Sappers, Gunners, men from the 9th and 21st Lancers, a Naval wireless operator, circus clowns of ten years' standing, cowboys from Texas, publicans (and many sinners), an ex-colonel of the Honduras army (a real hard nut and I should think a wrong-'un!), musicians from the old Empire Band, members of the London Stock Exchange, sufficient officers of the Mercantile Marine for two large liners, Americans from the US Army, men who have poached seals in the Arctic and who have worked in the convict gold mines on the Lena and a light-house keeper from Scotland.'

Once he had sacked the incompetent generals and reorganised his command, Smuts addressed himself to the daunting task of bringing von Lettow to heel. He was not an outstanding tactician, but his strong personality and aura of self-confidence soon communicated itself to the men under him. They became convinced that at last there was someone at the top who knew what he was doing.

If Smuts had a fault, it was that he would direct a battle from somewhere slightly ahead of the front line, instead of getting an overall view from the rear. He once rode so far forward on a recce that he appeared in the gun sights of von Lettow. The Prussian was about to squeeze the trigger when he recognised his opposite number by his hat and red beard.

Von Lettow held his fire in the belief that it would be unsporting to kill an enemy commander in such circumstances. When he heard about it, Smuts commented: 'Von Lettow is a fool – but a gentleman. But of course, it was the only thing to do. There must be honour and chivalry, even in war.'

Gradually, inexorably, von Lettow was beginning to lose impetus. The problem was not so much Smuts – von Lettow had learned his soldiering in the same part of the world and was easily a match for the Afrikaner – as a question of logistics and resupply.

The Germans surpassed themselves with the limited resources at their disposal, but no amount of ingenuity could disguise the fact that the weapons of war were not available to them in the same quantities as to their enemies. That the Schutztruppe was able to survive as a fighting force as long as it did was a miracle in itself.

Once initial stocks had run out, everything in the blockaded colony had to be built or manufactured from scratch, not only for the army but also for the substantial civilian population. German farmers' wives soon taught themselves how to spin and weave on hand-made looms. The cloth they made was dyed khaki with a substance obtained by trial and error from the roots of the *ndaa* tree.

Tyres for motor cars and bicycles were initially manufactured by tapping rubber trees onto rope and kneading the rubber to the right thickness. Later, a supply of sulphur was discovered which enabled rubber to be vulcanised in the usual way.

Paraffin and gas were made from copra. Quinine – vital for the army – was made from cinchona bark. A factory was established at Dar-es-Salaam to produce ammunition. After British troops overran the mint at Tabora, brass and copper currency was knocked up out of old cartridge cases.

The Germans learned to make soap out of quillaia bark and to build a hospital without using a single nail. Because paper was scarce, they wrote messages on bamboo slips and kept their latrines supplied with top secret documents instead of lavatory paper – something they would not have done if they had known that Meinertzhagen, as head of British intelligence, was employing an army of spies to retrieve the bumf for his subsequent perusal.

Towards the end of the war, the Schutztruppe's plight became so desperate that some genius in Berlin conceived the idea of resupplying the troops with a Zeppelin airship from Bulgaria. The journey would cover more than three thousand miles, almost all of it over British-held territory. The plan was to deliver fifty tons of arms and ammunition to von Lettow, and then to dismember the Zeppelin for use among his men.

Tents, sleeping bags and bandages could be made out of the airship's skin. Its catwalks were treaded with leather that could be made into boots. Its skeleton would provide the framework for a radio tower. A good use could be found for almost every part of the airship.

In fact, although it started out in fine style, the Zeppelin never reached East Africa. After twice being turned back by bad weather, it got as far as Khartoum before receiving a wireless message from the Admiralty in Berlin. '*Abandon mission,*' said the message, '*von Lettow has surrendered.*' It had been sent by the British.

With the Zeppelin out of the picture, the British were now in effective control of most of German East Africa. Von Lettow was pushed back towards the Rovuma river and the border with Portuguese East Africa.

Accepting that he could no longer hold Germany's colony for the Kaiser, he abandoned the attempt and crossed the river on 25 November 1917. He knew full well that by invading Portuguese territory he would oblige the British – who counted the campaign almost over – to keep coming after him in support of their allies. So it proved.

November 11 1918 found von Lettow and the remnants of the Schutztruppe creating havoc in Northern Rhodesia (now Zambia). They had led their enemies a will o' the wisp dance all around Portuguese East Africa and then back into German East Africa before crossing the border to Northern Rhodesia.

On the day of the Armistice, the Germans were occupying a key town on an important British supply route, wondering where to strike next. They did not actually hear of Germany's defeat until two days later, when they captured a dispatch rider bearing instructions to organise an immediate ceasefire.

As a personal gesture from General van Deventer, all Europeans in the Schutztruppe were allowed to retain their side arms in tribute to the magnificent fight they had put up. It was surrender, nevertheless. With as much grace as he could muster, and with dignity too, General von Lettow-Vorbeck swallowed his pride and gave the order for his men to march themselves into captivity. The German flag had vanished from Africa for ever.

Von Lettow became a national hero when he returned to Germany. In a country torn apart by defeat and revolution, he was one of very few leaders whose reputation had emerged without blemish from the traumas and tumults of the past four years.

Led by their general on a black horse, the last European survivors of the Schutztruppe made a triumphant entry into Berlin through the Brandenburg Gate. They were mobbed by ecstatic crowds, celebrating what was for Germany the only victory parade of the war.

Later, after marrying the fiancée he had not seen for five years, von Lettow resigned his commission for a career in politics and spent ten years as a deputy in the Reichstag. He became great friends with Richard Meinertzhagen, and dined with him whenever he was in London. Indeed, when Meinertzhagen had a meeting with Hitler ('Heil Meinertzhagen' he introduced himself) he suggested that Hitler should make von Lettow Germany's ambassador in London.

Hitler was agreeable, but von Lettow was not a Nazi lover. He told the Führer in no uncertain terms what he could do with his offer. After that, his career went into decline. In the years following the Second World War he was able to survive only with the help of food parcels and cash handouts sent to him by Meinertzhagen and Jan Smuts. He died in 1964.

As a result of the 1919 peace conference, German East Africa passed into British hands under the new name Tanganyika. With the war over, and a new mood upon the world, the work of constructing a new order could begin. For the settlers of Kenya, eighty-five per cent of whom had seen service in the army, the first priority was to return to their land to count the cost of four years' neglect.

CHAPTER SEVEN

CONTINUAL FLOW CHAMPAGNE

Like so many countries in the aftermath of the Great War, Kenya went into the peace with a strong sense of hope for the future. Survivors were determined to forget the horrors of the past four years and put the war behind them.

Casualties had been relatively light in East Africa and there was little physical damage to repair, but the feeling was widespread that things could never be quite the same again. The country had reached maturity, or so everyone thought. Men of all colours expected to be rewarded for the part they had played in the struggle.

The war years had seen a world boom in agriculture, but Kenya had not been able to share in the bonanza. Although prices were high, markets were frustratingly out of reach. In any case, the boom quickly turned into a peacetime slump as the economies of the major trading nations adjusted to new and painful post-war circumstances.

This did not deter British people from trying their luck as farmers in Kenya. Once the Suez Canal had been reopened, every available ship from England was crammed with settlers either going back to their farms after war service in Flanders or else travelling out for the first time in search of an escape from the depression of post-war Britain.

The new settlers were overwhelmingly ex-servicemen lured by the Kenya Government's promise of free land (up to 160 acres) in the white highlands. The land was offered on a 999-year lease at an annual rent of just ten cents an acre.

By June 1919, more than two thousand applications had flooded into Nairobi to take their chance at a grand draw held on the stage of the Theatre Royal. It took two revolving drums all day to distribute the empty acres by lottery to an audience of would-be farmers seeking a place in the sun for themselves and their families. For the lucky ones, this was indeed land fit for heroes.

Behind the Kenya Government's apparent generosity in distributing free land lay a carefully conceived plan to ensure the future economic and political wellbeing of the protectorate. The land was free because it was idle, undeveloped and often a long way from the railway line.

Its only value lay in its potential. This could best be realised by new settlers as producers of wealth – and not without years of hard struggle first. Most important of all, the immigrant farmers were white and knew how to fight if they had to.

As far back as 1915, the Kenya Government had drawn up a scheme for establishing ex-servicemen on the land after the war. It wanted an influx of trained soldiers to reinforce the small number of returning settlers surrounded by what it imagined would be a restive majority of blacks.

Kenya's Africans had played a major part in the German East Africa campaign, either as soldiers in the KAR or as porters in the Carrier Corps (their camp in Nairobi is known today as Kariokor). Nearly fifty thousand had been killed, wounded or died on active service. It was not inconceivable that those who had survived would consider themselves entitled to a share of the spoils.

Once the war was over, the young Africans who had enlisted or been conscripted into the army made their way back to the native reserves as older and wiser men. They had seen the world the other side of the hill and were reluctant to return to the dismal existence for which the established order of things had destined them. As predicted, many had seen white bwanas shot down like dogs during the war. The memory lingered.

During the campaign, some Germans had so far forgotten themselves as to organise the deliberate humiliation of British prisoners by African guards. White men had been harnessed like oxen to a wagon and forced to drag it through a bazaar in front of jeering tribesmen.

Count Falkenstein ordered a white South African to be lashed to a gun wheel and beaten by a native before being shot. It was also rumoured – though only rumoured – that the Schutztruppe had been promised all the white women in the town on the day they took Nairobi.

This deliberate lowering of British prestige, probably carried out without General von Lettow's knowledge, had greatly disturbed the Kenya Government. It was the prospect of native unrest that lay behind the call for old soldiers to come and farm Kenya's empty highlands.

The ex-officers answered the call in hundreds at first and then in thousands, putting the horror of the Great War behind them and beginning afresh in a brave new world. Like the first wave of immigrants, an astonishing number of them came from the upper classes, scions of the landed gentry and the aristocracy.

They found the life hard at first, often living in mud huts with their families as they struggled to develop the land. Later, as things got better, some of them managed to build comfortable manor houses for themselves with panelled drawing rooms and stone-mullioned windows, passable imitations of their ancestral homes in Britain.

The new arrivals also brought their ancestral pastimes with them. Hunting, shooting, fishing, gymkhanas and polo, grooms and gun dogs, all the country pursuits of the English gentry. Often they were pursued across a rolling landscape that looked uncannily like Suffolk or Gloucestershire on a sunny day, even as far as a church steeple in the distance.

Inevitably perhaps, the settlers also pursued each other's wives with enthusiasm. Adultery was commonplace throughout the white highlands. Combined with casual promiscuity and occasional drug-taking, it became particularly notorious in the 1920s among a tight coterie of aristocrats based around Naivasha, Gilgil and the farmhouses of the Wanjohi valley.

The antics in the Wanjohi ultimately earned it the nickname Happy Valley, shorthand for a certain kind of behaviour all over Kenya. The valley's most disreputable residents were the Earl of Erroll and his then wife, Lady Idina Hay, but there were others too. They were widely disliked by the majority of Kenya's Europeans, most of whom behaved well and worked extraordinarily hard for a living.

When they weren't up-country, Happy Valley types liked to gather at the Muthaiga Club in Nairobi. A rambling, pink-walled structure built on the site of a Masai *manyatta*, the club was a meeting place for landowners of the right sort – bureaucrats and administrators belonged to the Nairobi Club instead. In its heyday, the Muthaiga Club probably saw more high jinks and illicit couplings than any other club of its kind in the world.

Elegant pillars and comfortable cane chairs provided an agreeable rendezvous and a forum for settlers and well-born wasters to order a drink from a uniformed servant before sliding over for a chat with lovely girls made lovelier by a healthy climate and Kenya sunshine. A cool stare, an invitation to tennis, and they knew they would be all right for the night.

Throughout the 1920s, the club was a mecca for the well-bred, slightly weak, male faces bounding off the Mombasa boat in the certain knowledge that all Kenya women do. 'Are you married, or do you live in Kenya?' was the one local phrase they had all learned off by heart.

The influx of younger sons and hooray henries sent out to Nairobi for the good of their souls was continuous. The black sheep were still coming too, the remittance men in Brigade of Guards ties, furtively scanning the letter rack before deciding what to do about the next race meeting.

So were the fugitives from Evelyn Waugh's and Somerset Maugham's fiction, P. G. Wodehouse's Freddie Widgeon of The Drones club, and the bad hats written off for a sticky end in the plays of John Galsworthy.

If they blotted their books, they were parcelled off to Kenya to juggle plates in the Muthaiga Club on Saturday nights at parties that lasted well into Sunday morning, interrupted only by a discreet opening and closing of bedroom doors as the guests rearranged their accommodation for the night.

In this self-indulgent and slap happy society, there was only one bounder too awful to be acceptable. His mother said despairingly of Evelyn Waugh's Basil Seal: 'It isn't even as though he were the kind of man who would do in Kenya.'

It was a crushing judgment, but it was based on personal observation. Passing through Kenya for a couple of weeks on his way to the Congo, Evelyn Waugh had carefully noted down in his diary everything he saw in the country against the day that *Black Mischief* and other novels would be written:

'Train hour and a half late at Nairobi owing to three derailments. Very cool morning. Changed into flannels. Great luxury not to sweat. Drove straight to Muthaiga, lot of toughs round the bar ... Slept in the afternoon and went later to a pantomime given by amateurs: *Babes in the Wood*, full of local jokes and local patriotism. People behind said "Dem good bay jove" and clapped their hands ...

'Out to Muthaiga where met Raymond de Trafford, the Prestons, Gerard de Crespigny and others. Lunched with them. Everyone drank about ten pink gins before lunch. Went to races ... Continual flow champagne ...

'Tea in Governor's box and watched races from there. Back to Muthaiga, drank champagne with Boy Long. Met Lady Delamere who asked me to stay. Brawl in bar at Torr's ...

'Arrived Elmenteita before luncheon. Three houses on top of hill, magnificent view over lake of flamingos forest and hills ...

'Lady D fished in lovely stream where I was stung by nettles. Caught nothing. Returned to find Raymond arrived. He got very drunk and brought a sluttish girl back to the house. He woke me up later in night to tell me he had just rogered her and her mama too.'

Guy Crouchback, hero of Waugh's *Sword of Honour* trilogy about the Second World War, had been a Kenya farmer until his wife Virginia left him for a Guards officer. He did not see Virginia again until 1940, when they came across each other in London. Then:

'They talked of old times together. First of Kenya. The group of bungalows that constituted their home, timber-built, round stone chimneys and open English hearths, furnished with wedding presents and good old pieces of furniture from the lumber-rooms at Broome; the estate, so huge by European standards, so modest in East Africa, the ruddy earth roads, the Ford van and the horses; the white-gowned servants and their naked children always tumbling in the dust and sunshine round the kitchen quarters; the families always on the march to and from the native reserves, stopping to beg for medicine; the old lion Guy shot among the mealies.

'Evening bathes in the lake, dinner parties in pyjamas with their neighbours. Race Week in Nairobi, all the flagrant, forgotten scandals of the Muthaiga Club, fights, adulteries, arson, bankruptcies, card-sharping, insanity, suicides, even duels – the whole Restoration scene re-enacted by farmers, eight thousand feet above the steaming seaboard.

"Goodness it was fun," said Virginia. "I don't think anything has been quite such fun since."'

Spoiled and badly behaved they undoubtedly were, but tough and resourceful too. Much of the eccentric behaviour of Kenya folk has been blamed on the high altitude at which they spent their lives. Living as most did between 5,500 and 7,500 feet above sea level, and often higher, the set-tlers argued in their own defence that it was the rarified air that frequently made them belligerent.

Their view was supported by the findings of Sir Joseph Barcroft. His medical researches in the Andes mountains revealed a definite ten-dency for people working at high altitudes to become temperamental and quarrelsome.

Kenya ceased to be a British protectorate in 1920 and became instead a fully-fledged Crown colony. At the same time the Legislative Council was reconstituted to represent settler and commercial interests. The European community was rewarded for its good conduct during the war by being granted the vote.

Henceforth Kenyan affairs could be debated in the local Parliament, though it was stressed that the colony was still to be ruled from Whitehall. The settlers were delighted at the development. They were in no doubt that self-government – such as the Rhodesians were granted in 1923 – would soon follow. It was only logical, after all.

The Europeans had been amply rewarded for their contribution to the war effort, but what about the other racial groups in Kenya? What about the Indians, for instance, now firmly established as the colony's middlemen and small traders? Didn't they deserve a slice of the cake? They thought so, as did the powerful allies they recruited to their cause.

Arguing that they outnumbered Europeans in Kenya by more than two to one – in 1921 there were 9,651 whites against 22,822 Indians – the Asian lobby claimed that they had played a full part in pioneering and developing the colony and were therefore entitled to an equal franchise on a common roll. They also wanted to buy land for themselves in what in effect were the exclusively white highlands.

The Indians won strong support from politicians in India. They knew full well that Great Britain had made heavy calls on Indian manpower during the war and could not afford to appear ungrateful in the peace. Kenya's India question was no longer a purely internal matter. In the hands of New Delhi agitators, it was a convenient stick with which to attack British imperialism.

Predictably, the European settlers were horrified at the prospect of sharing power, or anything else, with the Indians, regardless of the fact that they had been living in the colony longer than most whites. Feelings ran high. The Europeans pointed out that the Indians were a bar to native development because they held down all the trading, clerical and semiskilled jobs that might otherwise be given to Africans.

More than that, they had brought syphilis into the country – or so the Europeans angrily contended. And if contributions to the war effort were to be taken into account, Kenya Asians were undeniably skating on thin ice. As Elspeth Huxley tartly observed, against the massive casualties sustained by Africans in the struggle with von Lettow, local Indian casualty figures were as follows: Killed, nil; wounded, nil; died of wounds, nil; executed for treachery, five.

Nevertheless, the British Government professed itself ready and willing to listen to the Asian case. The principle of colonial expansion was now operating in a way the British had never envisaged when they first set the ball rolling.

Where Anglo-Saxons had once colonised Canada and Australia, India was now claiming Kenya as an outlet for its surplus population. It was demanding the right for Asians to settle there on equal terms with whites from Great Britain. The Colonial Secretary, Winston Churchill, was not disagreeable to the idea.

This was heresy to the settlers. All over the colony, excitable groups of highly strung and bloodyminded men gathered in bars and club houses to discuss what they saw as a gross betrayal of European solidarity by Whitehall. Old soldiers every one, they were unanimous that there would be civil war before they would surrender the principle of white supremacy. They began to plan accordingly.

In the early months of 1923, the colonists' self-styled Vigilance committee went to work in secret on a scheme for setting up an emergency military and political organisation to seize control of Kenya in the name of the European settlers. A list was compiled of arms, ammunition, motor vehicles, petrol dumps and horses in each district of the colony. To prevent incriminating documents being found, orders were issued only by word of mouth.

Military aspects of the proposed *putsch* were handled by a group of retired generals. They were willing to jeopardise their army pensions for a rebellion that used the slogan 'For King and Kenya' and was intensely loyal to the Crown. If the generals were arrested, others were already earmarked to take their place.

The Governor, Sir Robert Coryndon, was to be taken prisoner and held hostage at a farm sixty miles from Nairobi. The farm had been carefully chosen for the excellent trout fishing it would offer him during his captivity. Railway stations and telegraph offices were to be seized as soon as the order was given. If General von Lettow could turn the country upside down, the settlers reasoned, then so too could they.

In the event the Kenya administration, sensing that all was not well with the difficult children in its care, took some of the tension out of the situation by arranging for both Indians and Europeans to send delegations to London to lay their cases before the Colonial Secretary. Churchill had by then been replaced by the Duke of Devonshire.

In due course, the Duke found himself confronted by an irate group of frontiersmen crowding into his office and threatening to put the colony to the torch if they did not get their way. They were led by Lord Delamere, and they meant business.

For their London base, Delamere had wired ahead and rented a smart house in Grosvenor Place. The house was equipped with full staff and a good cook for the entertainment of the influential people the delegation intended to win to its cause. Here, on a rainy night in March 1923, a sodden party of unkempt colonials still in safari clothes and awful old *terai* hats put down their bags and rang the door bell.

The door was opened by the hired butler. He quickly shut it again when he caught sight of the tramps outside. But Delamere had his boot in the jamb. He had not come four thousand miles to be turned away now.

Once settled in, Delamere's men set about capturing the attention of Fleet Street with the 'Kenya question'. It began to make regular appearances in headlines and editorials as the press responded gratefully to the boozy lunches thrust upon them by these strange people from the other side of the earth.

Whatever the merits of the broader question, Delamere himself was allotted many column inches on the strength of his exotic reputation and bizarre appearance in the capital. He was accompanied everywhere by two Somali servants, on their first trip abroad. The Somalis' function in polite society was never made entirely clear until their master jerked a laconic thumb at them one day and untruthfully explained: 'My sons.'

In the end the Government reached a compromise solution to the Kenya question. A minority of Indians were to be elected to the Legislative Council, immigration from India was to be restricted in the interests of the African natives, and the highlands were to be kept white because the altitude was essential for their health in a tropical climate. Though Delamere's delegation recommended acceptance of this formula, it remained thoroughly unpopular with all parties concerned.

The Indians regarded it as a howling injustice and a barefaced denial of everything the Empire was supposed to stand for. The Europeans were appalled that the Asians had been granted anything at all. Since vigilante groups of settlers were known to be stalking the land with loaded shotguns in their hands, looking for the slightest excuse to make a unilateral declaration of independence, it was vital that Kenya's whites should agree to the proposals.

What seemed eminently reasonable in SW1 could take on a much more sinister meaning the other side of Hell's Gate or in the dark brooding forests of Molo, where injuries became magnified out of all proportion because men had little else to occupy their minds. Whether the settlers would buy it was something the politicians in London would just have to find out. Having made their pitch, they sat back and waited uneasily for the colonists' reply.

The answer was expected hourly. In this highly charged atmosphere, with armed rebellion just below the surface, a telegram plopped onto the Colonial Office mat from a top Kenya official whose function was to look after the colony's military forces. The telegram consisted of just one cryptic word: 'Assistance.'

A great wail of high-pitched twittering thereupon broke out in Whitehall and disturbed the pigeons on the Colonial Office roof. Clearly the settlers had removed their weapons from the thatch and taken the colony by storm. Visions arose in London of Government officials being murdered in their beds by gap-toothed colonials bent on rape, arson and a peek at the administration's secret files.

The Colonial Office reacted at once by sending a telegram to the acting Governor demanding to know exactly what was going on in that troublesome corner of the Empire that looked so peaceful and far away on the map. When no reply came, the Colonial Office assumed the worst. Quite obviously the Governor's throat had been cut.

In fact the military official who sent the original telegram had some months before arranged with a friend in the Colonial Office that if ever anyone questioned the financial estimates for his department, he would cable the single codeword 'Assistance' back to London.

Somehow, with bigger things on his mind, the friend had forgotten this in the general excitement. Immediately after the telegram went out, a freak storm had dislocated the cable line, which was why nothing more had been heard from the colony.

It came as a terrible anti-climax when the settlers grudgingly signalled their assent to the proposals.

For the Indians then, second-class citizenship was the most they could hope for in a Kenya dominated by white bwanas and their memsahibs. Which left just the unfortunate Africans, millions of them, serfs in their own land.

In the settlers' view, the Africans were useful only as cheap labour on their farms. They had not been impressed by a recent and very important declaration by the British Government about the colony's future:

'Primarily, Kenya is an African territory, and HM Government think it necessary definitely to record their considered opinion that the interests of the African natives must be paramount, and that if and when those interests and the interests of the immigrant races should conflict, the former should prevail.'

Quite so. The African natives were no longer the simple souls who had peered wonderingly up Joseph Thomson's trouser legs to see where his ankles went. With the benefit of European education and medicine, they were beginning to thrive and develop at an amazing rate.

One tribe in particular, the Kikuyu, possessed an intelligence and willingness to learn that set them head and shoulders above other tribes in the race for self-advancement. Already many Kikuyu were perfectly capable of handling jobs monopolised by Indians. With increasing self-confidence came increasing aspirations. With non-fulfilment of those aspirations came bitterness and anger.

Focal point of the tribe's unrest was a mission-bred trade unionist named Harry Thuku, founder of the Young Kikuyu Association. He pointed out that his people's reward for taking part in the Great War had been a reduction in farm wages, a doubling of Hut and Poll tax and the introduction of a compulsory identity card.

Thuku was an articulate and ambitious politician, a militant man who made no secret of his distaste for Government and Europeans. His downfall came after a meeting attended by thousands of fellow Kikuyu at which he publicly urged everyone to hire lorries, fill them with the new identity cards and dump the lot outside Government House. On 14 March 1922 the authorities used the speech as a long-awaited excuse to arrest him.

He was detained in the Nairobi Police Lines alongside the Norfolk Hotel. Two days later, a crowd of six or seven thousand Kikuyu gathered there to demand his release. Some eyewitnesses assert that the crowd was angry and intent on violence. Others that it was peaceful and law abiding.

Whatever the truth, a jittery African policeman discharged his rifle into the crowd, whereupon 150 of his comrades followed suit. When the shooting stopped, some twenty-five Kikuyu, including a few women and a teenage boy, lay dead or dying on the ground.

No matter how genuine the regret of the authorities at this incident, no matter how accidental the circumstances leading up to that first shot, the affair was a great embarrassment to the British administration. Thuku was exiled to the NFD, Kenya's inhospitable northern frontier district, but the Kikuyu tribe's new-found political awareness continued to flourish without him.

Beside the relatively minor grievances of taxes, wages and pass laws, the main issue troubling the Kikuyu was land. Land was the fountainhead of all wealth, the measure of a community's pride and the barometer of its political stability. Without land, a tribe was nothing. As they understood it, the Kikuyu were without land.

'When the Whitemen first came, we did not understand that we were to be deprived of any of our land, nor that they had come to stay,' they told a Parliamentary Commission in 1924. 'A small piece of land here and there was sold voluntarily by its owners to a few of the first pioneers in the time of the Imperial British East Africa Company.

'When the British Government took over the administration of the country we were still unaware that our possession of our land would be questioned or challenged. Then from 1902 increasing numbers of Whitemen arrived and portions of our land began to be given out in farms ... these lands were not bought from the Kikuyu owners, and any compensation they received was quite inadequate.'

The settlers' reaction to this was that it was pure hogwash. The Kikuyu had known perfectly well what they were doing in releasing idle land of no value to them. They had only begun to want it back when they saw what could be made of it under white ownership. Anyway, they had plenty of land of their own in the native reserves which they were not using efficiently.

The settlers argued that the Kikuyu would not even have known they had a land grievance if the idea had not been put into their heads by unscrupulous rabble rousers like Harry Thuku. Moreover, the Europeans observed cynically, it had taken the Kikuyu twenty years of careful husbandry by the settlers to notice this injustice and put their complaints into writing.

On the other hand, it could not be denied that some land had indeed been taken unintentionally from the Kikuyu in the early years of the century. This had happened mainly as a result of pressure on the Land Office from prospective European settlers clamouring for early completion of the paperwork without which no farm could be bought. Faced with this pressure, Government surveyors had accidentally cut corners – Kikuyu corners – in an attempt to distribute the land with maximum speed.

The land thus filched from the Kikuyu had been temporarily unoccupied because of famine or disease in the local community. It could by no means be described as a large amount, but it had multiplied a hundredfold in the mouths of the *sabuni* box orators stirring up the passions of the mob. Whatever the truth of the matter, the only thing that counted in the final analysis is what the Kikuyu themselves believed – and they believed they had been robbed.

They found a curious ally in a Danish baroness named Karen Blixen, sometimes known also as Tania or Isak Dinesen. She had immigrated to Kenya at the end of 1913 to become the owner of a six thousand-acre coffee farm just outside Nairobi.

That Karen was the owner of the farm came as news to her Kikuyu labourers, many of whom had been born on the land and had imagined it to be theirs. They warmed to her anyway for the enthusiasm with which she invariably espoused the black man's cause against the white.

'I am so angry with the English, because they've raised the taxes on natives,' she wrote to her brother. 'They talk of a poll tax of twenty shillings. When you think that the most a man can earn is about 150 shillings a year, it's outrageous. If only people knew at home, but this country is so strangely beyond law and justice.

'The upper classes haven't improved in the slightest since the Revolution. When they're not afraid of the lower classes, they're quite without shame; natives are starving here, and will die of starvation, while the Governor is building a new Government House for £80,000 and champagne flows in rivers at their races etc.

'Lord Delamere has just had a dinner in Nakuru for 250 people, where they consumed 600 bottles, and they have *no* idea; the women here are quite capable, when they hear that natives cannot get posho, of asking why they don't eat wheat or rice, just like Marie Antoinette ... One would like to let fly at them sometimes, when that truly English stupidity brays too loudly!'

Despite her irritation, Karen Blixen was a keen Anglophile, albeit with no illusions about the upper classes. A strong-minded woman, she became a pillar of Nairobi society in the years following the Great War. Few people of any consequence, including the Prince of Wales on his visit to the colony in 1928, failed to have dinner at her farmhouse at the foot of the Ngong Hills.

She was great friends in particular with Berkeley Cole and with Denys Finch-Hatton, brother of the Earl of Winchilsea, who was her occasional lover for much of her time in Kenya.

Finch-Hatton too was an interesting character, although not perhaps as remarkable as Karen Blixen liked to make out. A tall, bald aristocrat, very gifted at sport, he had been president of Pop at Eton. He was played, not entirely convincingly, by Robert Redford in the film *Out of Africa*.

He is said to have been deep on safari once, hundreds of miles from anywhere, when a telegram reached him all the way from London. It had been carried in a cleft stick from Nairobi by relays of sweating natives who had strained every nerve to get the message to him.

The telegram consisted of just one sentence: 'Do you know Gervase Pippin-Linpole's address?' Finch-Hatton thought hard, then apparently scribbled a reply for the runner to carry through the bush back to civilisation. 'Yes,' he wrote.

When not on safari, he spent long evenings with Karen at her house, teaching her Latin and an appreciation Greek poetry. He struck a chord in Karen that was to inspire her in later years to write what is still one of the great classics of African literature, *Out of Africa*.

The book is the story of her farm at Ngong, of her servants and animals, of the waifs and strays both black and white who came knocking at her door for help, of attempts to juxtapose civilisation with a culture still locked firmly into the Dark Ages.

The story is hardly original – all Kenya settlers could have told similar tales if they had found the time and talent to set them down – but it is written with a perception and insight that make it several cuts above other books of the period. Most rely on long lists of animals killed and places visited to keep the covers apart.

The book is all the more remarkable because Karen was writing in English, having failed to achieve success in her native language. Along with her other writings, it made her Kenya's one and only near-Nobel prizewinner for literature. She won the first ballot of the Swedish academy in 1957, but was eventually beaten into second place by Albert Camus.

Karen first travelled to East Africa on the same boat as Colonel von Lettow-Vorbeck, heading south to take command of the Schutztruppe. They soon became shipboard friends. A year later, when the two colonies were at war, this friendship brought her into bad odour with the British military authorities. She was suspected of being a spy until she cleared herself by leading an ammunition convoy down to the troops on the border.

Further proof of good faith came when her brother, a Prussian-hating Dane, won the Victoria Cross near Amiens while serving as a private in Canada's Quebec Regiment.

Accompanying Karen on her first trip to Africa was her fiancé, Baron Bror von Blixen-Finecke. He was a shadowy figure of no great intellect but good with a gun on safari. They were married in Mombasa on 14 January 1914, with Prince Wilhelm of Sweden as a witness.

Unfortunately, the marriage was not a success. In 1915 Karen returned to Denmark via France, Switzerland and Germany to be treated for the venereal disease she had caught from her husband. The illness left her sterile and probably contributed to the bad health that dogged her for the rest of her life.

Once back in Kenya, she spent more and more time alone on the farm while her husband absented himself on hunting expeditions. They separated in 1921 and were divorced four years later. Karen kept the title though, even after Bror found himself another baroness.

She was one of those women who always have to dominate the proceedings, who become petulant and irritable if they are not at once the centre of attention. She had a way with bank managers that mesmerised them into lending her money on the farm when the rule book absolutely prohibited it.

Men flocked to her house to sit at her feet and revel in her company, white and black alike. She adopted a paternalist approach to the Africans on her farm and was for ever giving them free handouts of food and medicine, as well as slaughtering five cattle for them every Friday.

Karen must have attracted the men through a combination of charm and personality, because she was no great shakes to look at. The Duke of Portland, then a young settler named Ferdinand Cavendish-Bentinck, remembered her as 'plain, fat and very tiresome'. He liked her husband better.

Karen was always coming into conflict with the Government over the *ngomas*, native dances, staged at regular intervals on her land. Since these usually consisted of naked men and women waggling their private parts at each other before dashing off into the darkness, it was Government policy that they should not be encouraged.

Karen thought otherwise. She would sometimes invite as many as two thousand Kikuyu to dance on her lawn, extracting permission from the

District Commissioner for them to brew *tembu* beforehand. *Tembu* is a deadly hooch derived from sugar cane that always spells trouble. It certainly did on the memorable occasion when twelve young bucks from the Masai tribe crashed one of Karen's parties.

There were a number of excellent reasons why it was against the law for Masai and Kikuyu warriors to attend the same *ngoma*. Like so many settlers, however, Karen took little notice of Government regulations. The Masai were honoured guests in her view, most welcome on the farm.

Her thinking was not shared by the Kikuyu braves. They fell back sullenly as the Masai pushed into the dancing ring. The newcomers were naked except for their weapons and head-dresses.

To the excitement of the Kikuyu maidens gathered around them, the Masai stood as God had made them as the dance began again. The atmosphere was no longer light-hearted as it had been before. It was filled now with resentment and foreboding.

Karen Blixen takes up the story. 'All of a sudden the ring swayed, and was broken, someone shrieked aloud, in some seconds the whole place before me was a mass of running, thronging people, there was the sound of blows and of bodies falling to the ground, and over our heads the night air was undulating with spears.'

Once the excitement was over, the crowd fell back to allow their hostess to take a body count of one Masai and three Kikuyu gravely wounded. Alert to her every need, Karen's cook ran to the house and re-emerged with a long threaded darning needle and her thimble. Another servant who had learned tailoring during a seven-year stint in prison volunteered for the task of sewing up the casualties.

They all survived, although the wounded Masai had to be concealed in a hut for a long time in case the Government discovered that he had flouted the law by attending the *ngoma*. The party itself broke up in disorder. Many guests stayed on until daylight to organise a spell guaranteeing the Masai no success in bed with Kikuyu women.

At the beginning of 1919, Karen's farm saw a ceremony of a different kind, the distribution of campaign medals to the Masai in recognition of their service as scouts during the war. Back in 1914, before they became disillusioned and uncooperative, squads of war-painted *morans* had eagerly made themselves available to the Government, rattling their shields, waving their spears and just itching to have a crack at the Germans. Or anybody.

The Government however had considered it unwise to encourage the Masai to make war on white men. Since they were far too proud to serve as porters in the Carrier Corps, their contribution to the war effort had been mainly as scouts under Lord Delamere.

His kinsman Berkeley Cole, who spoke Masai fluently, was delegated to distribute the medals from a grateful King-Emperor. An impressive ceremony was carried out from the veranda of Karen's farm. There being nothing he could pin the medals to, Cole pressed them into the palm of each naked warrior's hand. It had been, as the medals proclaimed: *'The Great War for Civilisation.'*

Whenever he stayed on Karen's farm, Berkeley Cole would treat himself to a bottle of champagne in the Ngong forest at eleven o'clock in the morning, always insisting that his hostess should dig out her best glasses for the occasion. He shared this fastidiousness with his brother Galbraith Cole, who farmed in the Rift Valley along the flamingo-pink shores of Lake Elmenteita. In the early days, Galbraith hardly ever travelled anywhere but by a landau harnessed to a team of oxen.

Berkeley owned Solio ranch at Naro Moru, the other side of the Aberdare mountains. One day he decided to ride over the mountains, no mean feat in itself, to deliver a herd of cattle to Galbraith. He took with him a house guest, Eleanor Balfour – niece of A. J. Balfour – who was visiting Kenya to keep a pregnant cousin company.

After she had been a few days at Lake Elmenteita, Galbraith Cole gave Eleanor a rifle and led her towards an impala to see if she could shoot it. She dropped it at once with a bullet through the heart. Galbraith was delighted. He had staked his future happiness on that shot. If she killed the impala, and only if, he would marry her. And did.

Both Cole brothers died prematurely during the 1920s, Berkeley of a bad heart in 1925, Galbraith of crippling arthritis in 1929, though not without first producing an heir. In due course Lady Eleanor Cole's eldest son succeeded an uncle to become Earl of Enniskillen and, much more important in a country of inverted snob values, a second-generation Kenya settler.

Lord Delamere followed his in-laws in 1931, dying of angina at the age of sixty-one. He was buried on a knoll overlooking Lake Elmenteita. A statue of him was later erected outside Nairobi's New Stanley Hotel looking down Sixth Avenue – the sixth road parallel to the railway station – which was renamed Delamere Avenue in his honour.

Today the statue is no longer there. When Kenya became independent it was moved to Lake Elmenteita, where Lord Delamere's descendants still lived. The road in which it stood acquired another change of name and became Kenyatta Avenue.

For Karen Blixen, the early 1930s were perhaps the most unhappy time of her life. She was deeply grieved by Berkeley Cole's death, but that of Denys Finch-Hatton was a blow from which she never fully recovered.

Denys was killed in a flying accident in May 1931. Taking off from Voi for a trip to Karen's farm, his Gypsy Moth suddenly went into a spin at two hundred feet and crashed to earth, killing Finch-Hatton and his passenger instantly. The news was broken to Karen by Lady McMillan, widow of Sir Northrop.

'That a person like Denys exists,' Karen had once written, 'which I have suspected before, I suppose, but never dared believe, and that I have been so happy to meet him during my life and live so close to him, even if there have been long periods of missing him in between, that compensates for everything else on earth, and other things mean nothing in themselves.' And now he was dead.

She had other troubles too. Despite regular infusions of cash from her family in Denmark, the Karen Coffee Company was losing money on a large scale. Year after year, the coffee bushes came into a rich bloom that promised a harvest of at least 150 tons. Year after year, a cold frost stole down from the highlands and bit deep into the crop, leaving just fifty tons to go to market, and sometimes as little as fifteen, not nearly enough for the farm to pay its way.

Drought and locusts played a part, but the main problem was one of altitude. The farm was just too high and too cold for coffee to flourish. No one had known that in the early experimental days when the Blixens first sank their precious capital into the land.

Not counting interest charges, it cost between £71 and £75 for a Kenya farmer to get each ton of coffee from railhead to the London salerooms, where it could expect to fetch around £120 in a normal year. At that price, an efficient farmer could just reckon to keep his head above water.

But in 1930 came disaster. As a direct spinoff from the Wall Street crash, the price of coffee slumped to a derisory £70. The fall wiped out the mainstay of Kenya's economy at one cruel stroke.

For Karen Blixen, and for many other Kenya farmers, the party was over.

CHAPTER EIGHT
LOCUST YEARS

It was not only coffee that fell disastrously in price. It was also maize, wheat, sisal, butter and other dairy products. All were slashed by more than half in the space of twelve months, then by half again, as the biggest slump the world had ever known got under way. For a developing country with no industry to fall back on, the collapse in farm prices was catastrophic.

Because the world's economists could not get their sums right, efficient, tightly run, hard-worked farms faced ruin. To cap it all, the turn of the decade saw an invasion of locusts on an unprecedented scale. The swarms were several miles long and so thick that they blotted out the sun wherever they struck.

The locusts left behind a trail of devastation that made suicides of some farmers and drunks of many. Through no fault of its own, the colony was being brought to its knees before it had even learned to walk.

When they began to burn coffee beans as fuel for railway engines, Karen Blixen recognised the writing on the wall. After eighteen years in Kenya, the time had come to quit. Unhappily, choked with emotion, she began to pack up her possessions for the long journey back to Denmark.

She was watched dumbly by her house servants – most of whom had been with her since the start – and by the herd boys and old men and women of the farm who came to stare in silent disbelief. Karen had been a memsahib in the grand manner. They could not imagine a world without her.

Nor could the European community. Half of Nairobi was at the railway station to see her off. She had been one of the great characters of the town. Her passing left many people nervous and uncertain of their own futures.

Once the floodgates of retreat had been opened, there was no telling where the process would end.

Before Karen left, her farm was snapped up by a Nairobi company with no interest in coffee but plenty in land speculation. The way the company saw things, Nairobi was a growing town which would one day begin expanding towards the Ngong Hills in the west. Strip out those coffee bushes, lay down roads and drainage systems, and before they knew it they would have six thousand acres of prime building land to take the overflow from Nairobi's European quarter at a very nice profit for themselves. So it proved.

Today the suburb is called Karen, although suburb is a misnomer for what in England would be considered fairly deep countryside. It is an elegant leafy place mustering one English Duke and plenty of lesser nobles among its inhabitants. Its only rival as a residential area of Nairobi is Muthaiga, which also boasts one English Duke – a paramount chief in his own country and not unimportant in Kenya either.

For the Baroness Blixen, however, there was only a tearful railway journey to Mombasa and third class deck space on the SS *Mantola* to Marseilles. There she was met by her brother, who hardly recognised her after such a long time away. Karen had given Kenya the bloom years of her life. In return she had nothing to show for it but a shrunken face, a bad case of malarial jaundice... and a treasure house of memories.

Once back at the family home in Denmark, it was several years before she could bring herself to unpack the crates of mementoes that had come with her from Nairobi. The mementoes included Denys Finch-Hatton's Bible, his letters, photographs of Kenya, pictures of the farm and her servants. One day she would set the whole story down on paper. For the moment, though, the greatest work of her life lay undisturbed in a rough wooden box.

In a sense the Depression helped to sort out the wheat from the chaff among Kenya farmers, enforcing as it did the Darwinian principle of survival of the fittest. Only those who really knew their jobs were able to weather the storm. The good-time charlies and freeloaders mostly sank without trace, and were not much missed.

Those who survived were usually mixed farmers whose investment in a variety of crops helped spread the risk of violent price fluctuations. They had one big advantage over their rival agricultural countries: low production costs based on an abundance of cheap native labour.

Two other factors worked to Kenya's advantage during the Depression. The gold fields at Kakamega came into production, providing jobs for a thousand Europeans and ten thousand Africans. The fields also provided an income for the railway and a very welcome source of tax revenue for the administration.

It was discovered too that good-quality pyrethrum, from which insecticides are made, flourished at an altitude of eight thousand feet or more. The yield was so high that Kenya was able to break the world monopoly of pyrethrum shared previously between Yugoslavia and Japan.

After Lord Delamere's death, leadership of the settler community in those difficult days fell on a son of the Duke of Buccleuch. Lord Francis Scott farmed at Deloraine near Rongai. He had been chosen in preference to Ewart Grogan. Grogan was the stronger personality, but a little too astringent for the Government pen-pushers with whom the settlers' spokesman would have to deal.

Age had not yet mellowed Grogan. When Nairobi Council persistently refused to tarmac Delamere Avenue, newly named after his dead friend, Grogan's riposte was to plant a row of banana trees all down the middle of the street.

'East Africa is the home of the leopard, the tick, the baboon and the amateur official,' he once remarked, rather forgetting that it was his home too. Governors of the colony were mere 'telephone girls' in his view unless they could prove to the contrary.

An opposition member of the Legislative Council for a quarter of a century, Grogan sometimes became so bored with debates that he sneaked out into the sunlight to play ball with the Clerk of the Council's small daughter. While they admired him greatly, and were fond of him too, the settlers felt that he was not the ideal man to represent them at the top.

Yet for all his asperity and wild colonial ways, for all that he had once killed a Portuguese with a single punch, Grogan was also an intelligent, well-read man. He was an occasional contributor to *The Times* and *Financial Times* in London and had attended the Versailles peace conference at the end of 1918 as an adviser to Lord Milner, the Colonial Secretary.

Lord Francis Scott was a completely different character, a more moderate and flexible man who believed in cooperating with the machinery of government wherever possible. A comparative newcomer to the colony, he had been severely wounded in the Grenadier Guards during the First World War and still walked with a pronounced limp. His leg was eventually amputated in 1933.

Perhaps his greatest success during the 1930s was his stint as one of two settler representatives on the Governor's Executive Council. This was a sort of cabinet which aimed at 'government by agreement' rather than by imperial decree. The settlers' dreams of self-government had vanished with the onslaught of the Depression. The fight had been drained out of them.

Instead, recognising that the administration was there to stay, they were content to go along with most of what the bureaucrats told them. It was better to do that than waste valuable time that could be more usefully spent salvaging something from their farms.

Differences remained, of course, leading at one stage to the resignation of both settler representatives from the council. The situation improved in 1936 with the departure of Sir Joseph Byrne, a tough and uncompromising Governor who had not been popular with the farming community.

From 1938 the other settler representative on the Executive Council was the future Duke of Portland, also badly wounded during the war, who had settled in Kenya because the climate was good for his lungs. With moderation and good sense, he and Lord Francis exerted considerable influence on an administration more accustomed to abuse from the local population than compromise and conciliation.

Among the most important concessions wrung from the administration at this time was a reaffirmation of Britain's commitment to keeping the scheduled areas of Kenya's highlands exclusively for Europeans. This victory was vital to the settlers, affecting as it did almost every white family. Without the highlands, their chances of making Kenya into another England were non-existent.

Wishing to enjoy the fruits of their investment, the settlers had developed the land on the understanding that it would remain theirs for life, and their children's to enjoy thereafter. But the vacillation and continually changing policies of successive British governments had planted in the settlers' minds the suspicion that politicians at Home might easily go back on their word and throw open the highlands to all comers.

In particular, they might open the scheduled areas to the Kikuyu, whose grievance about the alleged theft of their land had never ceased to smoulder.

The issue had flared up again in 1932, when the British Government set up the Kenya Land Commission under Sir Morris Carter to examine the boundary disputes between black and white farmers and decide once and for all the question of who owned which land. Though other African tribes also lived around the highlands, the commission's main task was to find a way of keeping the Kikuyu quiet without provoking open rebellion from the settlers.

To this end it patiently examined hundreds of different land claims. Some were genuine, some debatable, some openly fraudulent. All were extremely tortuous and complex.

The commission concluded that an injustice had indeed been done to the Kikuyu during the early years of European immigration. Because of drought, famine, rinderpest and smallpox, roughly a hundred square miles in the vicinity of Nairobi, normally used by the tribe, had been lying vacant at the time the British marched through it.

To put matters right, therefore, the commission now risked the wrath of the settlers by awarding the Kikuyu rather more than a hundred miles elsewhere, close to the forest. Justice, it hoped, had been done at last.

Needless to say, neither side was happy with the verdict. To the Kikuyu, the land award was not nearly enough. To the settlers, it was far too much. But there, for the time being, the matter rested.

Two new people added their voices to the land debate during the 1930s. Both of them were Kikuyu elders, one black, the other white. The white Kikuyu was L. S. B. Leakey, son of missionary parents. He had been brought up as a child of the tribe and spoke the language so well that he often caught himself thinking in Kikuyu.

No European could claim to know more about the Kikuyu than Leakey. He was a member of the Mukanda age group, to which many future Mau Mau leaders also belonged. In 1935 he set down his knowledge in a book on Kenya which summed up perfectly the passion felt by both sides in the land dispute:

'To the white man bushland, as distinct from cultivated land and grass-land, appeared to be unutilised land and many a settler who took up areas in the Kikuyu country in the early days holds firmly to the view that the land which he took over was unoccupied and unused, because it was virgin bush. But to the African virgin bush is the ideal pasturage for goats and sheep, and Kikuyu bushland was as much in use and occupation as are the great grassland farms of the European stock owners today.'

The other Kikuyu to take part in the dispute was an ex-mission boy born Kamau wa Ngengi at an uncertain date in what the Church of Scotland later told him were the 1890s. He had joined the mission after listening to a speech by a white man who introduced himself as the special messenger of God – a role the British often liked to allocate to themselves.

The mission baptised him Johnstone Kamau because his oriental-look-ing eyes reminded them of John Chinaman. They taught him to read and write, thereby giving him a head start in the white man's world over those of his fellow tribesmen who had failed to grasp the importance of self-improve-ment by education.

Drifting into Nairobi, Johnstone Kamau took a variety of jobs before building himself a mud and wattle shop which he called Kinyata Stores, *kinyata* being the Kikuyu word for brightly coloured beads, usually stitched into a belt. Since the name had a nice ring to it, he later decided to adopt it for himself. He became known to his friends as Johnstone Kenyatta.

It was under this name that he first got involved in Kikuyu politics, initially as a lieutenant of Harry Thuku, and subsequently his successor as political leader of the tribe. Thuku's trade union organisation had collapsed when he went into exile, to be replaced by a more vigorous body, the Kikuyu Central Association.

By 1928 Kenyatta was general secretary of the KCA. A year later he startled Kenya's Europeans by paying his first visit to England, over the heads of the Kenya Government. He went to lay the grievances of the tribe directly before the Colonial Office – just as the white settlers and Indians had done a few years earlier.

The trip was not a success. 'Here the sun is not often seen,' he wrote to his wife, and nor was Kenyatta. Pointing out that he ought to have gone through proper channels, the mandarins of the Colonial Office left him to hang around their outer offices while they got on with the sports pages. But if he achieved none of his stated aims, he at least saw something of how people lived in Europe.

He learned, for instance, that African representatives of the French empire held seats in the mother country's national assembly. Not only did nothing of the sort happen at Westminster, but 1929 saw only the first general election in Britain with all the adult population, both male and female, being allowed to vote. It was obviously out of the question, therefore, to put forward the idea that Kenya's blacks might be ready for some sort of representation in the Legislative Council.

After a brief return trip to Kenya, Kenyatta found himself back in England once more in 1931. This time he tried to get the ear of the Parliamentary select committee set up to examine the problems confronting East Africa. He did not yet realise it, but he was not going to see his native land again for a good fifteen years, not until the end of the Second World War, in fact.

Instead, he spent the rest of the 1930s completing his education in England, travelling around Europe – including Moscow – and living the life of an impoverished student in London. He became the darling of Hampstead thinkers and was seen to read the *Manchester Guardian*.

Black men were tremendously fashionable in Europe at this time. Millionaires' daughters and society women like Nancy Cunard and Margot Beste-Chetwynde – before she became Lady Metroland – openly took negro lovers, something that would have horrified the loose-living memsahibs of Nairobi, to whom preservation of caste was all-important.

For Kenyatta, accustomed to a social pecking order that placed Africans at the bottom of the heap, the open doors of London and Paris came as a very welcome change. He became friends with Paul Robeson, the American singer, who was in England to star in the film version of Edgar Wallace's unabashed tale of colonial supremacy *Sanders of the River*.

Robeson was Bosambo, the white man's friend. Kenyatta played one of a group of minor chiefs in loincloths who bow to Sanders and say 'Yes, Lord Sandy' on being ordered to keep the King's peace while the District Commissioner goes Home on leave.

The job was fun, and it put a guinea a day expenses in his pocket. He appreciated the cash, because he was not well off and work was hard to find in England. Yet he was belittling himself, in the opinion of his Hampstead friends, debasing both himself and his people for mere money.

Over tea and cucumber sandwiches in their comfortably furnished drawing rooms, they chided him vigorously for taking such a demeaning part. Then they rang for the maid to show him out.

During the mid-1980s, Kenyatta studied intermittently at the University of London, and in particular at the London School of Economics, where he enrolled for a course of anthropology under the famous Professor Malinowski. The outcome of this was a thesis on the Kikuyu tribe, later expanded into a book and published in 1938 as *Facing Mount Kenya*. By now the author had changed his name again. The book, when it appeared, was written by Jomo Kenyatta.

As might be expected, it gave a glowing appraisal of the tribe, of their customs, beliefs, clan structure and the way their affairs were conducted. It dealt expertly with tribal education, religion, division of land, ancestor worship, economic and social organisation – an entire community structure which, though different from that of European societies, was no less ordered and well arranged.

Facing Mount Kenya was a work of passion. It sought to defend the old Kikuyu ways from the unwelcome imposition of new western values, while being willing to learn in moderation from the west at the same time.

The idea was best expressed, perhaps, in a letter Kenyatta had written to *The Times* in March 1930, in which he had pleaded 'to be permitted to retain our many good tribal customs, and by means of education to elevate the minds of our people to the willing rejection of the bad customs'.

The letter had been written in response to an outcry then taking place in Kenya over the Kikuyu practice of circumcising their girls at puberty. This highly controversial custom had led to the murder two months previously of a missionary who had preached against it.

The issue was important to Kenya's Africans. On its outcome hung their right to a degree of self-determination in the conduct of their private affairs. Female circumcision was a test case of how far Europeans could, or should, be allowed to go in imposing their ideas on human beings of different beliefs who had lived on the same planet for just as long as the whites, indeed – as L. S. B. Leakey later discovered during his excavations at Olduvai – longer.

Its exact origins are unknown, but the practice of circumcising teenage females is probably as old as the Kikuyu tribe itself. What happens is that an old woman performs an extremely messy and painful operation, without anaesthetic, to amputate the clitoris and sometimes the outer lips of the young girl's vagina, thus depriving her of any sensual feeling during the act of sex. That way she will make a good wife unlikely to run off with the first man who catches her eye.

The side effects of the operation can be appalling. Without its natural elasticity, the vagina contracts into a ring of hard fibrous tissue which often sterilises the girl by making sexual intercourse impossible. Infections of the bladder and kidneys are commonplace. The unyielding breech can make childbirth not just difficult but downright dangerous.

To the European doctors called upon to deal with such cases, female circumcision was a repellent and barbaric practice that should have been outlawed long ago. White missionaries in Kenya were unanimous in their agreement. They insisted that the idea was unclean and an affront to Jesus Christ.

But the Kikuyu saw it as an ancient and sacred tribal custom, a much revered article of faith. It was no business of the doctors', the missionaries' or anyone else's. The complex ritual accompanying the operation heralded the girl's entry into the adult world. Without undergoing circumcision she could never hope to take her rightful place with her own age group as a wife and mother of the tribe.

This argument carried little weight with the many Churches represented in Kikuyuland. They had long ago won themselves a reputation for poking their noses into private native affairs, upsetting the traditional order of things and overturning long-established conventions. The Churches poured ridicule on cherished tribal superstitions and set up in place of old shibboleths their own variously denominated brands of mumbo-jumbo.

Too much religion all at once was more than the Kikuyu could bear. When the missionaries, fired more by zeal than good sense, made a serious attempt to stamp out the practice of female circumcision, the Kikuyu struck back the only way they knew how.

Hulda Stumpf was an elderly American lady, an implacable foe of female circumcision and for twenty years a hard-working member of the Africa

Inland Mission at Kijabe. In January 1930 someone entered her room as she lay in bed and forcibly circumcised her, for motives that may perhaps have been well intended. Unfortunately she protested so vigorously that a pillow was held over her face to drown the noise. She suffocated to death.

Brutal and obscene the murder may have been, an isolated incident certainly, but it drove home the point that tribal sensitivities were too important to be trampled on by outsiders, well meaning or otherwise, who did not know what they were doing. The Kikuyu were entitled to their own beliefs. If circumcision was one of them, then so be it.

Jomo Kenyatta said as much in his book. He also said so in the Department of Anthropology at the University of London where, in November 1935, he read a paper on female circumcision to Professor Malinowski's students.

Among those present on that occasion were Prince Peter of Greece, a friend of Kenyatta's, and L. S. B. Leakey, himself the author of a paper on the subject. He considered Kenyatta a potentially bad influence on the tribe of which he was an honorary member.

Leakey had attended the lecture especially to hear what the other man had to say about female circumcision. He did not like what he heard. In fact he disagreed so strongly that he and Kenyatta stood up in class and had a blazing row with each other in Kikuyu, to the mystification of everyone else in the room.

Yet there were far more important things to argue about in 1935 than anthropology or female circumcision. October, for example, saw the invasion of Ethiopia by an army of Italians equipped with the most up-to-date weapons available, bent on carving out a new colonial empire for Mussolini in the Horn of Africa. The Ethiopians put up a fierce fight with spears and arrows, but they could never hope to compete with bombs and mustard gas.

It was all over within a few months. Emperor Haile Selassie was forced to abandon his country in May 1936. He went into exile, leaving the victorious Italians to occupy Ethiopia alongside neighbouring Somaliland. Somaliland had been ceded by Britain to Italy in 1925 in return for the latter joining the wartime alliance against the Germans.

What that meant for Kenya was that more than eight hundred miles of her northern and eastern frontiers were now bordered by a sophisticated western power in the grip of rising fascism, and openly keen to expand. Even more alarming to the south, Germany was pressing for the British-mandated territory of Tanganyika – where many Germans still lived – to be restored to its rightful owner, Adolf Hitler.

Nineteen thirty five also saw publication of the book *Green Hills of Africa* by Ernest Hemingway, an almost word-for-word account of his safari to East Africa the previous year. Already established as one of the United States' most famous writers, the king of *machismo* had journeyed to Africa to shoot a lot of game and add to his carefully nurtured reputation for wide-shouldered, all-American masculinity.

Unfortunately, Hemingway was so *macho* that of the three male friends originally scheduled to accompany him on the safari, two dropped out, unable to face the thought of big Ernest competing with them every minute of every day to see who could kill the biggest and best of every kind of animal.

Only his wife Pauline and friend Charles Thompson were with Hemingway when he arrived in Nairobi to spend a few days pooped by the altitude while waiting for the epic ego trip to commence.

The party's white hunter was Phil Percival – he of the famous knees admired by Teddy Roosevelt – who took them down to Serengeti to begin blasting their way through the wild life. As expected, the safari swiftly developed into a contest between Hemingway and everybody else to see who could bring in the finest skins and the longest corpses measured nose to tail.

Hemingway, whose eyesight was so poor that he had to wear spectacles when shooting, lost. If he shot a buffalo, Charles Thompson shot a bigger one. The day Hemingway dropped a rhino at three hundred yards, Thompson killed a rhino whose lesser horn was longer than Hemingway's greater.

It was the same with waterbuck, lion and leopard. Also with kudu. One day Hemingway brought down two beautiful bulls, with curly horns so long and perfect that no one could possibly equal them. Except Thompson, who returned to camp with 'the biggest, widest, darkest, longest-curling, heaviest, most unbelievable pair of kudu horns' the enraged novelist had ever seen.

It was all too much. A photo of the trip shows Hemingway, Thompson, Percival and Percival's assistant posing in a smiling group with their trophies. The other three are holding kudu horns. Hemingway is holding oryx.

He loved the country, though. It was exactly his sort of place, a wide-open, sky-high world where a man could search long and hard and eventually find himself, something novelists are fond of doing. Besides one full-length book, it gave him the material for *The Snows of Kilimanjaro* and *The Short Happy Life of Francis Macomber*, two of his most successful short stories.

Phil Percival appears as 'Pop' in *Green Hills of Africa* and as Robert Wilson in the Macomber story. Also in Macomber is Baron Bror von Blixen, apparently not soured by writers after the failure of his marriage to one, who made good friends with Hemingway on the trip.

Although the safari game in the 1930s was still the private preserve of the very rich, the foundations of a hotel industry outside Nairobi were already being laid for those travellers who could not afford the enormous expense of tented camps, safari lorries, chop boxes and all the other luxurious extras. A pioneer in this field was:

> H. H. Aitken, licensed to sell what he
> likes, to whom he likes and when he likes.

Two supercilious young women once annoyed Aitken by braying out 'Steward!' in upper class tones, as if they expected him to collect their luggage from the car in which they had just arrived. He refused to let them stay at his hotel. They had to drive 140 miles to find another one.

Another early hotel keeper was a retired bootlegger who later won a unique position in Kenya folklore by playing host to Princess Elizabeth on the night she became Queen. Son of a parson, Eric Sherbrooke Walker had read Theology at Oxford before the Great War with a view to following his father and grandfather into the Church. He had abandoned the idea after deciding that he was too much of a sinner to make a go of it.

Instead he joined the Scout movement and became private secretary to Lord Baden-Powell. He held the post for six years before joining the Royal Flying Corps in 1914. His engine failed over enemy lines in 1915 and Walker spent the rest of the war making at least eleven attempts to escape from prison camp. Baden-Powell corresponded with him in code and sent him a pair of wire cutters hidden inside a ham bone.

Repatriated in 1918, Walker joined the British military mission fighting with the White Russian army against the Reds. He won the Military Cross in the Crimea for coolness under fire. Back in London in 1922, with only £400 of army back pay in his pocket and no qualifications of any sort, he was wondering what to do next when he met the sixth daughter of the Earl of Denbigh and fell deeply in love with her.

The way it is with Earls' daughters is that they ought to be kept in some sort of style, and Sherbrooke Walker was a man who was very broke indeed. In order to marry Lady Bettie, he looked for a job in the City, only to find that nobody wanted to employ someone so obviously unsuited to office life.

Increasingly depressed as the rejections kept coming, Walker was about to abandon the idea altogether when he bumped into an old friend in Fenchurch Street. His friend knew of an excellent job for a man prepared to take a risk or two.

In those days the United States of America had introduced a weird law prohibiting its citizens from having a drink, except for religious or medicinal purposes. As a result, doctors and priests were becoming very rich and bootlegging had the third-largest turnover of any American industry. Naturally the City wanted a piece of that turnover. A syndicate of London businessmen had put together a scheme – with A and B preference shares and all – of beautiful simplicity.

All it needed was a boat flying the Union Jack and stocked with alcohol to heave to off Long Island just outside territorial waters. In no time at all the boat would be swamped by American smugglers eager to buy the cargo at a profit of three hundred per cent to the financiers back in Fenchurch Street. Would Walker like to go along and keep an eye on things, in return for all the money he could reasonably spend? He certainly would.

It was not as easy as it sounded, of course. US coastguard cutters could not touch a British ship in international waters so long as it had no contact with the shore, but there was nothing to stop pirates from storming the vessel and hijacking its contents. The pirates off Long Island were not the kind of pirates to draw the line at taking a life or two, in international waters.

A kind American tried to dissuade Walker from having anything to do with the enterprise: 'You look the sort of Englishman whose ancestors for several hundred years have shot partridges and ruled natives, but never done any work or earned any money. How can you hope to compete with the cleverest brains in the American underworld?'

'Tush,' was Walker's response. 'An Englishman who has cut his way out of prison camp with a ham bone and holds the Order of St Stanislaus (2nd class) can deal with anything.'

Nevertheless he always kept a revolver loaded and well oiled in his coat pocket. There were times during a successful smuggling career – he drew a distinction between that and bootlegging - when he was called upon to point it at people. In his memoir of that time, a Runyonesque account of gangsters called Izzy or Sam and pretty girls who tucked flasks of liquor into their garters, Walker recounted a friendly tip-off of trouble ahead:

'An hour ago I saw that dark Dago, Jalleno,' sang a canary into his ear. 'He was loading his gun, and said that he was going to pump your guts full of lead for interfering in his business.'

This was disturbing news, for Jalleno was 'immensely powerful, with a body like a gorilla and a face like a large black pansy'. In the event, though, he proved no match for Walker, whose years at an English public school had left him more than equal to the challenge.

Rather more dangerous were a gang of hijackers who surprised Walker on dry land at a time when he happened to have dropped his revolver into a doll's pram lying at his feet. Two of the gang covered Walker and his men while the rest began to steal his liquor. In the darkness, with his hands above his head, Walker contemplated his next move:

'Very gradually lowering my right arm, I picked up the revolver from the perambulator and covered the dark man to hit him about the middle waistcoat button. With luck there would be just time to get him and then drop the other with a quick snapshot before he had time to swing his revolver round.'

It never came to gunfire. Instead Walker bolted into the night, sneaking around in a full circle to counter-attack from the rear. He rapidly obtained what Sir John French often referred to as a 'moral ascendancy' over the enemy – who gave him his liquor back.

In between smuggling trips, Walker would go home to England, where his clergyman father had no idea what his son did for a living but proudly informed his parish that the boy was doing awfully well. All went swimmingly until his last trip, when Walker shot and badly wounded a corrupt state trooper and was forced to flee the United States in a hurry. After that, he married Lady Bettie and sailed for Kenya before the Americans could catch up with him.

Their plan was to buy a coffee farm with their earnings from Prohibition. While looking for somewhere to buy, they found themselves in Nyeri, a pleasant township on the plains between Mount Kenya and the Aberdares. Nyeri had been founded by Richard Meinertzhagen in 1902 by dint of pitching a tent and building a thorn fence all round it.

He described it thus: 'It has an ideal field of fire for six hundred yards in all directions, a complete barbed wire entanglement, and a ditch and parapet which would defy the most ardent savage. It could be easily defended by fifty rifles.'

Twenty-four years later, Nyeri had blossomed into a busy Kikuyu market town boasting one small inn, The White Rhino (that charges at sight) but nowhere to have a bath. Spotting a gap in the market, the Walkers decided to open a hotel instead of buying a farm. They bought seventy acres of land, built The Outspan and opened for business on New Year's Day 1928. One of their first guests was Neville Chamberlain, a family friend.

Once prices had improved the Walkers diversified into agriculture, taking up land at Naro Moru and living in an elegant farmhouse, famous for trout and strawberries, that later served as headquarters for the film crew of the movie *Born Free*. But far and away Walker's most inspired achievement, after he had been at Nyeri a little while, was his decision to build his wife a house in a tree.

The idea owed something to Peter Pan and something to the Swiss Family Robinson. It also owed quite a lot to Lady Bettie, who had passed much of her childhood in a treehouse looking at naughty postcards out of reach of the Earl of Denbigh. Where an Earl could not go, could a rhino or an elephant?

Just inside the Aberdare forest, a few miles from The Outspan, lay a waterhole frequented every night by elephants on their way to trample the local settlers' coffee bushes. At one side of the clearing was a large *mugumu*, a wild fig tree. It proved ideal for the construction of a branch hotel enabling guests and animals to study each other at minimum inconvenience to themselves. The place was dubbed Treetops. The first tourists from The Outspan visited it in November 1932.

Among the most famous of Treetops' early guests was Walker's former boss, Lord Baden-Powell, who dropped in to Nyeri on his way to South Africa for a scouting jamboree. Baden-Powell had paid his first visit to Kenya in 1906, as part of the Duke of Connaught's entourage. By 1937 he was an old man whose strength was fast failing, despite the loyal support of his wife.

Instead of pressing on to South Africa, he decided to spend the winter months at The Outspan. He had discovered that Kenya's climate suited him very well, as did the countryside.

'*Never* could we have imagined a more perfect place,' wrote Lady Baden-Powell. 'Exquisite view over forty miles of wild Africa and the snow-covered peak of Mount Kenya beyond – just indescribably lovely. And this Hotel is unique as we each have our own sort of little house with verandah, looking on to a garden *ablaze* with cannas, roses, salvias, madonna lilies, geraniums, arum lilies, stocks and snapdragons, and besides that all the lovely tropical things like jacaranda, flamboyant tree etc ... It is absolutely perfect.'

The Baden-Powells liked it so much that they bought shares in The Outspan company. In return Walker built a cottage in the grounds for the old man to live out the rest of his days sketching, pruning roses and taking his pet hyrax for walks on a leash.

There was little problem over what to call their new house. The Chief Scout had named his English home *Pax* because he bought it on Armistice Day 1918. He wanted to call the new one *Pax* too. *Paxtu* it has remained ever since.

At the time, however, Peace was hardly the most appropriate name for it, as the Baden-Powells found out all too soon. It had been their intention to go back to England in the early months of 1940 to enjoy the summer living quietly at Pax Hill, their country house in Hampshire. Instead they were forced to remain at Nyeri. The lights had gone out again and Kenya was at war for the second time in a generation.

Karen Blixen (*Popperfoto*)

The 4·1-inch gun taken from the German cruiser *Königsberg*,
used by General von Lettow-Vorbeck in his campaign
against the British during the First World War

A Mau Narok settler talks to his Ndorobo shepherd

A settler's house in the white highlands

After months of preparation, a Masai youth waits tensely for
the moment of circumcision that will make him a man

Using the contents of a sheep's stomach, one of Her Majesty's Witch
Doctors cleanses a Kikuyu tribesman of his Mau Mau oath (*Popperfoto*)

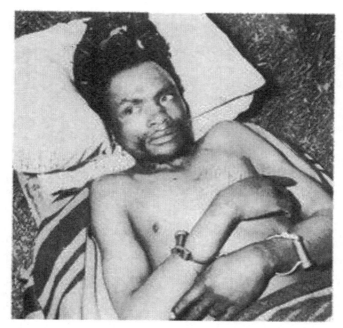

Dedan Kimathi, the Mau Mau leader, on the day of his capture (*Popperfoto*)

President Kenyatta, 1975 (*Popperfoto*)

CHAPTER NINE

WAR AGAIN – AND MURDER TOO

This time Kenya was ready for a war, perhaps even expecting it. In 1936, a few months after Italy's victory in Ethiopia had redrawn the face of East African politics, a man with a strong service background had been appointed Governor of Kenya in the shape of Air Chief Marshal Sir Robert Brooke-Popham. The new Governor had been a light infantryman before joining the RAF. He lost no time in drawing up a contingency plan for Italian entry into the war.

Calculating that any Italian invasion of Kenya would come along the coast road towards the key port of Mombasa, Brooke-Popham and his military advisers intended to defend the harbour with the small force at their immediate disposal, while leaving Nairobi and the highlands almost bare of troops.

They reasoned that the natural barrier of Kenya's unwelcoming northern frontier district would be protection enough for the highlands in the short term. To reach the settled areas of Kenya by that route, the Italian army would have to cross a pitiless expanse of desert. It was rough, arid country, best summed up by the ship-shaped Royal Wajir Yacht Club – a wry British comment on the lack of water for hundreds of miles. An advance through the desert was feasible but unlikely.

Nevertheless, the Italians were close enough for Eric Sherbrooke Walker to keep a car loaded with petrol, oil, blankets and food hidden behind Lord Baden-Powell's cottage, ready to whisk the old man to safety at a moment's notice. The precaution proved unnecessary, because Baden-Powell died on 8 January 1941. He was buried in Nyeri churchyard, where his gravestone carries the Scout symbol for 'gone home'.

As it turned out, Mussolini delayed Italy's entry into the war until June 1940, when the British defeat at Dunkirk made it quite certain that Germany's was the best side to join. The delay was used by the Kenya Government to consolidate its position in the north of the colony.

To the south, the Tanganyika administration had already secured its territory by rounding up and interning Tanganyika's few thousand German residents. Many of them had been under surveillance for years as known members of the Nazi party.

Although the Italian forces in Ethiopia and Somaliland overwhelmingly outnumbered the British in the south, the expected invasion of Kenya never took place. Rather it was the other way about. Kenya suddenly found itself the centre of attention and an object of strategic interest as the base from which allied forces rolled up Mussolini's East African empire in a matter of months.

The campaign began on 23 January 1941 when black and white troops of the East African Brigade, supported by other Empire forces, pushed towards the border with Italian Somaliland. On 6 April they entered Addis Ababa, having averaged 76·6 miles for each day they advanced. One unit had managed to cover no less than 2,800 miles in six weeks.

'Take petrol for 900 miles and go until you can go no more' was a typical order of the day. By February 1942 the Italians had surrendered almost a million square miles of territory and had lost an army of 200,000 men, together with all their equipment.

Their morale was so poor that one heavily laden lorry and its crew in the middle of Ethiopia was captured singlehanded by the *Königsberg* adventurer Philip Pretorius. Now an old man, he had little trouble persuading the driver to take him back to the British lines.

Yet for all the excitement of a war on their doorstep, it was not the invasion of Somaliland that occupied the attention of Kenya's European community in the days and weeks immediately following 23 January 1941. From that same day a much more absorbing drama was being enacted under their own noses. It was playing daily to packed houses in Nairobi and via radio and newspapers to an audience across the free world.

The drama involved the murder by shooting of an English aristocrat, allegedly by another aristocrat in a fight to the death over a beautiful woman.

The victim was Josslyn Victor Hay, 22nd Earl of Erroll, 30th chief of the Hays since 1160, baron of Slains, 26th Hereditary High Constable of Scotland and widely reputed to be very exciting in bed. A Kenya settler since the early 1920s, Erroll had been one of the original residents of Happy Valley. He represented Kiambu in the Legislative Council and held a temporary commission in the Kenya Regiment.

Erroll was thirty-nine at the time of his murder, impoverished, good looking and notorious even in a promiscuous society for sleeping around. He was a compulsive womaniser, of whom the judge in a very messy divorce case had once observed: 'It is obvious that the co-respondent is a blackguard.'

The man accused of his murder was Sir Henry Delves Broughton, 11th baronet of that name, deaf, arthritic and fifty-seven years old. Rich by anybody's standards, Broughton owned a coffee plantation in Kenya, an estate in Cheshire and a string of eighteen race horses. He had abandoned his previous marriage to wed a young girl thirty years his junior, a girl whom he loved to distraction and who was described in open court as his 'most cherished possession'.

Sir Delves had married Diana Caldwell in South Africa on 5 November 1940. A week later the happy couple arrived in Kenya and went to stay at the Muthaiga Club, prior to taking a house the other side of Nairobi in the newly fashionable suburb of Karen. They bumped into Lord Erroll, whom Sir Delves already knew and liked, on their first evening in Kenya.

By mid-January 1941, having been married to her second husband for as long as two and a half months, Lady Broughton informed Sir Delves that she had fallen in love with another man.

Under the circumstances, the old boy took the blow as well as could be expected. He was not happy about it, but he accepted it. He had fully realised the risk of marrying a flighty woman less than half his age. They had made it a condition of their marriage that if either fell in love with anyone else they would not stand in each other's way. It appeared that the time had come already.

A racing man of many years' experience, Sir Delves resigned himself to cutting his losses with as much dignity as he could muster. Win a few, lose a few was his watchword. To show that there were no hard feelings he invited his wife and her new lover to a champagne dinner at the Muthaiga Club.

The party, if it can be called that, took place on the evening of 23 January. Besides Sir Delves, his wife and Lord Erroll, there was a fourth person for dinner, the Broughtons' house guest Mrs June Carberry. She was married to the tenth Lord Carbery, who had given up his title and added an 'r' to his name on becoming an American citizen in 1919.

The four of them began with champagne cocktails before dinner, then went on to split a couple of bottles with their meal. Since Sir Delves was not normally a drinking man, the alcohol must have gone to his head. Towards the end of dinner he raised his glass and cheerfully proposed a toast to the prospective happiness of his wife, Lord Erroll and their future heir. Then the party broke up.

Lord Erroll took Lady Broughton off to dance at the Claremont Road House. He promised to return her to her husband's house in Karen by three o'clock next morning. Sir Delves and Mrs Carberry lingered on at the Muthaiga Club until the small hours. Then the chauffeur drove them home.

They arrived back at Sir Delves's house in Marula Road just after 2 a.m. Sir Delves was so drunk that he had to be helped upstairs by Mrs Carberry, herself suffering from a slight touch of malaria.

A quarter of an hour or perhaps twenty minutes later, Lord Erroll drove up to the house in a Buick saloon, accompanied by Lady Broughton. He stayed for ten minutes, talking and laughing in the hall, then slammed the car door and drove away. The time must have been about 2.35 or 2.40.

Somebody shot him immediately afterwards, because his body had been discovered and reported to the police by 3 a.m.

The body was found on the floor of the Buick, hanging over the edge of a murram pit alongside the Ngong Road exactly 2.4 miles – as the police later calculated – from the Broughtons' house. Two bullets had been fired from a .32-calibre revolver. The first had missed. The second had hit Erroll in the head, killing him instantly.

Uproar followed. This was news with a capital N. *Passionate Peer Gets His* is how the American press saw it, and the English papers agreed. For months afterwards, nobody around the Muthaiga Club bar could talk of anything else.

The war, crops, local politics, even women all paled into insignificance against the fascinating question of who gave Lord Erroll what he had long been asking for. More than one cuckolded husband with a perfect alibi for that night raised his glass and silently drank to the eternal damnation of Erroll and the good health of his murderer, whoever it might be.

With the attention of the entire European population focused on them, the Kenya Police strained every nerve to bring the case to a satisfactory conclusion. Casting around, the way policemen do, they searched for a man with a motive for murdering Lord Erroll – and found one straight away.

Nobody fitted the bill more perfectly than Sir Delves Broughton. He had retired to his separate bedroom after returning home that night and had no one to vouch for his presence around the time of the killing.

Assuming that Sir Delves's calm and reasonable attitude to the proposed divorce was a sham. Assuming that he had feigned drunkenness after the Muthaiga Club dinner – or perhaps was taking Dutch courage – was it not possible that the 3 a.m. deadline he had imposed on Lord Erroll's return to Karen was simply to provide Sir Delves with the opportunity to eliminate a hated rival?

Despite the toast earlier in the evening, surely any red-blooded male in Sir Delves's predicament would want to make sure that the 30th chief of the Hays never lived to father a son? The police thought so. With that in mind, they asked Sir Delves to show them his revolver, so that they could compare the murder bullet with one fired from his gun. And there they discovered something very curious.

According to their information, Sir Delves possessed two revolvers, a Colt ·45 and a Colt ·32. Just two days before the murder, he had reported both stolen. Now that they came to think about it, the police recalled that they had found no signs of a break-in when they inspected his house after the alleged burglary.

Karen was an area with an almost non-existent crime rate. Anybody might think Sir Delves was planning a murder and was taking steps beforehand to remove the incriminating evidence.

At this point the police had a brainwave. They might not have Sir Delves's revolver, but they did at least know where he had fired it in the past. With luck, and a fair amount of diligence, they might yet be able to procure a bullet fired from his gun.

Jack Soames, an old friend of Sir Delves's from Eton days, owned a farm at Nanyuki, some 120 miles north of Nairobi. While staying there for a week soon after his arrival in Kenya, Sir Delves had done some revolver shooting at a hunting camp on the property. It was just conceivable that the bullets from that target practice could still be retrieved.

Soames took the police to the same firing point as he and Sir Delves had used and set up similar boxes as targets. At the police request he fired his ·38 revolver at the boxes. The bullet was seen striking a thick clump of grass.

After a careful search of the grass, the police were rewarded with the discovery of four spent ·32-calibre bullets almost concealed under a light covering of earth. Adding these to three live ·32 cartridges and some empty cases they had found by the firing point, they sent the whole lot off to be examined by two Government ballistics experts.

The experts' report virtually wrapped up the police case against Sir Delves Broughton. In their view there was no room for doubt. The two bullets fired at Lord Erroll and the four found at Soames's farm had come from the same gun.

More than that, one of the live cartridges discovered at the farm contained black powder, such as had been found on the murdered man's ear. Black powder cartridges were very rare. They had gone out of production before 1914 and were no longer obtainable in Kenya colony. The conclusion was obvious. Whoever killed Lord Erroll had fired the same weapon at Soames's farm.

The trial of Sir Delves Broughton for the murder of Lord Erroll opened in the Supreme Court on 26 May 1941. It lasted twenty-three days in front of a jury of twelve Europeans and such of Nairobi high society as was not away at the war. The prosecution case was quite straightforward. Sir Delves was a wronged husband with a very strong motive for killing Erroll.

As *The Times* reported at the hearing of the murder charge: 'Lord Erroll's native valet gave evidence of occasions on which Lord Erroll and Lady Broughton had stayed alone at night in Lord Erroll's house.'

Sir Delves had motive, he had opportunity (in the Crown's contention) and he had a ·32-calibre revolver which had most conveniently been stolen just before the crime. Though there was very little evidence linking the accused man directly to the murder, none at all in fact, the Crown rested its case on the coincidence of Soames's farm being more than enough to hang Sir Delves.

It reckoned without his lawyer, a South African KC named Henry Morris. He was a firearms specialist who had built up an impressive career at the bar by always paying strict attention to detail.

Flying up to Kenya to take on the case, Morris immediately spotted a flaw in the prosecution's argument. The flaw seemed so obvious to him that he instinctively mistrusted his own judgment. Surely the prosecution could not have made such an elementary mistake? Surely it was not going to be that simple?

Now was the time to find out. From the Government witnesses who testified that the murder bullets and the Soames's bullets had been fired from the same weapon, Morris extracted the technical information that the weapon had a five-grooved barrel with a right-hand twist. Just as he had hoped.

'It is true, is it not,' he pointed out, 'that all ·32 revolvers manufactured by Colt have a six-grooved barrel with a left-hand twist? And since Sir Delves's stolen revolver was a Colt, by no stretch of the imagination could it possibly have been the weapon used to kill Lord Erroll.'

The Crown coughed. The Crown had not thought of that.

It rallied swiftly, still pinning its case on the remarkable coincidence connecting the murder weapon with Soames's farm. Obviously the accused must have possessed another gun, a *secret* gun unknown to the authorities. This, the Crown now announced, was the weapon he had used to destroy his enemy.

So why fake a robbery of the two revolvers and declare it to the police?

The Crown was coming unstuck and there was no avoiding it. It suffered a further blow when Morris produced a ballistics expert of his own who argued that the two sets of bullets had been fired by different weapons. He defied anybody to prove him wrong in the absence of any of the guns in question.

The prosecution case stood or fell by the evidence of the ballistics experts, and the accused was entitled to the benefit of any disagreement between them. Strong motive alone was not enough to convict Sir Delves. With insufficient evidence to connect him to the crime, the jury had little hesitation in bringing in a verdict of Not Guilty. The verdict was greeted with a spontaneous outburst of applause from the spectators in the court.

Sir Delves stepped from the dock a free man. As he did so his friends, who had been punctiliously avoiding him since the murder, crowded around to declare that they had never for a moment doubted his innocence. But although his reputation was vindicated, the saga did not have a happy outcome for him.

A few months later he injured his back in a fall, damaging his spine and losing all sensation in his right side. Combined with the strain of the trial, the pain was more than he could bear. At the end of 1941 he killed himself in a Liverpool hotel with an overdose of Medinal.

Lady Diana Broughton had left him by then and was already recovering from her ordeal. In due course she married Kenya settlers as her third and fourth husbands. She ended her days as Lady Delamere.

As for the murdered Lord Erroll, Happy Valley died with him and is buried in the same grave. Though the police worked for some time on the theory that an angry husband or a jealous woman may have killed him, his murder has not been solved to this day.

The affair still excites great interest. Everyone in Kenya knows exactly who did it. The only trouble is, everyone's suspect is different. Despite what was said at the trial by the defence, one of the Government ballistics experts was never shaken from his view that the chances of the murder weapon not being identical to that fired at Soames's farm were three and a half million to one against.

Lord Carbery's daughter Juanita, a teenager in 1941, claimed that Broughton confessed his guilt to her four days after the murder. He told her that he had thrown the murder weapon into the Chania Falls at Thika. She kept the information to herself at the time, knowing that he might be hanged if she told anyone.

With the Broughton trial out of the way and the Ethiopian campaign over by the beginning of 1942, attention in Kenya was now drawn towards the Far East, where the sudden entry of Japan into the war had created a new threat. The speed of the Japanese advance through South-East Asia was so rapid that it looked for a while as if nothing could stop their forces spreading across the Indian Ocean towards the eastern seaboard of Africa.

Fresh from the desert war in Ethiopia, thousands of African troops were hurriedly retrained for jungle fighting. Towards the end of 1943, men who until recently had never set foot outside their tribal reserves found themselves on board ship and crossing a sea they had never seen before towards India, Ceylon and Burma. There they played a full part in dislodging the Japanese from the British Empire's Asian possessions.

In Madagascar too, black Kenyans fought in the successful campaign to wrest control of the island from the Vichy French. They learned in the process that a white man is just as scared as anyone else when a gun is aimed in his direction. It was a thoughtful lesson for the future.

The Madagascar operation had been mounted from Mombasa. The port basked in hitherto undreamed-of glory during the war as a naval base for policing the Indian Ocean and as the main port of call for convoys steaming up the coast to resupply the British armies in the Middle East. Such was the importance of Mombasa to the war effort that the Macupa railway bridge connecting the island to the mainland was dismantled and replaced with a causeway, less vulnerable to enemy bombing.

If Mombasa was popular with the Royal Navy, the rest of Kenya was no less so with other branches of the armed services. To the RAF, the colony's remote airfields were ideal for training pilots, of whom there were never enough. To the army, Kenya provided a staging post between Britain and the Far East at a time when North Africa was constantly changing hands.

The colony was also a dumping ground for the myriads of Italian prisoners, seventy thousand from the North African campaign alone, who had cheerfully surrendered to the British at the first opportunity. The Italians all had to be fed, as did the many thousands of Allied servicemen passing through Kenya.

The Depression became a distant memory and the local economy enjoyed a boom of unprecedented proportions as Kenya's farmers buckled down to the task. For the first time in their lives, the market for their produce was no longer tantalisingly out of reach elsewhere in the world. It was camped in their back garden, quite prepared to eat anything they could grow and more besides.

Since shipping space was at a premium, local production of foodstuffs was actively encouraged and farming became a reserved occupation of high priority. Many Kenya settlers obtained early release from active service to go home and do whatever was necessary to meet the ever-rising demand.

They did not always succeed. Meat products were in such short supply that the Government resorted to shooting out herds of game to keep bellies filled. The Laikipia plains around Rumuruti and over towards Nanyuki were virtually denuded of wild life during the war.

Zebra, kongoni, Grant's gazelle and topi were all slaughtered wholesale, leaving the grazing land free at some future date for cattle and sheep and tight wire fences. If it achieved nothing else, the Second World War did at least set the agricultural economy of Kenya firmly on its feet, in a good position to face the future. At a price.

The war years also saw construction of one of the country's most important tarmac links, the road from Nairobi to Naivasha, a much acclaimed showpiece that was the work of Italian prisoners of war. It followed the route over the Escarpment and down onto the floor of the Rift Valley taken half a century earlier by Captain Macdonald's survey party for the Uganda Railway.

Macdonald himself was probably pursuing an elephant trail, since elephants can always be relied upon to take the line of least resistance along a slope. Towards the bottom of the Escarpment, the Italians built a Chapel of Thanksgiving beside the road, overlooking the site of the 1895 Kedong massacre just beyond. They dedicated it to St Mary of the Angels. The first service was held there on Christmas Day 1943.

When not engaged on outside work, most of the Italians were concentrated in large prison camps close to townships such as Gilgil, Nanyuki or Eldoret. Not all were soldiers. The entire male population of Italian civilians in Ethiopia had also been interned by the British at the end of the campaign. Some came with useful trades and skills which they put at the disposal of their captors in a variety of projects beneficial to the colony.

For the bulk of the captives, however, there was only the endless monotony of life behind bars, a tedious round of daily routine and nightly boredom, not leavened by any possibility of escape. If anybody did succeed in getting outside the wire, there was nowhere to run to. The nearest neutral territory was Portuguese East Africa, the other side of Tanganyika. It might as well have been the moon.

The Italian PoWs whiled away the long hours of captivity in much the same way as other wartime prisoners were doing all over the world. At

Nanyuki camp, for instance, nestling at the base of Mount Kenya, there were keep-fit classes and games of football or tennis.

The camp orchestra performed wonders on musical instruments made out of old packing cases. Some men built wireless sets in secret, some played cards, some took up carpentry. Others got themselves involved in boxing or chess.

Many went in for amateur dramatics – always a popular pastime with Italians. One man specialised in mesmerising chickens until they fell asleep, whereupon he bought them from their worried African owners at a knock-down price on the grounds that they did not look too healthy. Anything to keep boredom at bay.

Among the inmates of Nanyuki camp was Felice Benuzzi, a thirty-two-year-old official of the Italian colonial service. He had been posted to Addis Ababa shortly before the war, only to be declared a PoW with the rest of his colleagues. Born in Vienna of an Italian father and an Austrian mother, Benuzzi had been brought up in Trieste, where the family moved when he was a child.

Both his parents were keen mountaineers. Since Trieste lies within easy reach of the Julian Alps and the Dolomites, it was only natural that Benuzzi should have picked up the rudiments of the sport at an early age. By the time he arrived at Nanyuki, though, it was almost eight years since he had done any serious climbing.

Since his arrival coincided with the long rains, some time elapsed before he came to appreciate what is surely one of the most attractive aspects of Nanyuki: the view it provides of Mount Kenya.

Benuzzi had heard about the mountain certainly, but though its summit was not more than twenty miles away, it remained hidden behind a bank of grey cloud as thick and immovable as an Afrikaner *vrou*'s petticoat. Until one day, the clouds briefly drew back in an unguarded moment to permit Benuzzi a tantalising glimpse of the first 17,000-foot peak he had ever seen.

There it stood, looking – as all agreed – almost exactly like Monviso viewed from Turin. Benuzzi was enchanted. Hours after the vision had disappeared again behind its protective screen he remained, in his own words, spellbound. Like so many before him, he had lost his heart to the compelling magic of one of the world's most glorious mountains.

It came as no surprise to him to learn that African tribes living around Mount Kenya addressed their prayers to the mountain top in the belief that the distant snow line provided a home above the world for their God. No surprise at all.

Even today, climbing parties on Mount Kenya sometimes come across elderly, dazed Africans wandering hopelessly towards the snow, as if in search of something. Occasionally they are too far gone to speak, and die within a few hours.

Other times they recover sufficiently to explain that they heard the call of God from on high, and that He commanded them to leave the plains and seek Him among the cathedral-like pillars and glaciers of that sepulchral white place. The mountaineers nod. They understand what the old man means. They have felt it too.

So it was with Benuzzi. Face towards the barbed wire, footballs flying all around him, he looked at the mountain and knew that he would have to climb it or die. The snow-clad summit was calling him, just as surely as it called the Africans. There was no resisting the command.

Well why not? He would escape from prison camp, he would plant an Italian flag on Mount Kenya's highest peak, and he would return in triumph to Nanyuki to face twenty-eight days' confinement in the punishment cells. *Ecco*, because it was there.

It was mountain madness, and Kenya madness too, but it was a wonderful way to prove to himself that he was still alive – something he was beginning to doubt as the months of captivity began to blur indistinguishably into one another.

Now that the vision had been revealed to him, life inside the wire took on a new purpose as Benuzzi began to make preparations for the trip. It was obvious that he could not go alone. He would need at least two companions, one an experienced mountaineer to accompany him on the final assault and one other man, not necessarily a mountaineer, to help keep watch on their way up through the forest.

A larger party would be better, but it would make the task of assembling mountaineering stores and equipment from the scant resources of a prison camp just that much more difficult. Benuzzi had enough problems as it was.

The first candidate for the expedition presented himself almost immediately. Dr Giovanni Balletto was an old hand at rock climbing. He was also
a medical man who knew enough about high altitudes and the debilitating
effect of prison camp food to realise that Benuzzi was off his head to be con-
templating anything so ridiculous. Balletto counted himself in.

Using their weekly ration of thirty-five cigarettes each as currency, the
two men set about collecting equipment for the climb. Bartering unwanted
possessions for tins of meat and vegetables or heavy woollen clothing from
other prisoners, they stored the accumulated supplies under their bunks
until the great day should arrive.

Two stolen hammers were filed down into ice-axes. Crampons and spikes
were laboriously constructed out of metal removed from the mudguards of
an abandoned car. Climbing ropes could be made out of sisal bed strings. The
whole business took months of preparation, but it served admirably to pass
the time. The climbing season did not reach its zenith until the clear weather
of January, some eight months ahead.

A more serious problem was selection of the third man for the enterprise.
There was no shortage of candidates expressing extravagant enthusiasm for
the project, but they either cooled off the idea on reflection or were judged
unsuitable by Benuzzi. It was not until seven days before the off that the final
member of the team was chosen.

Enzo Barsotti was not fit, nor had he ever climbed a mountain in his life,
but he was an old friend of Balletto and widely regarded as a lunatic. This
was recommendation enough.

The three of them broke out of Nanyuki camp on 24 January 1943
by the simple expedient of unlocking a gate with a dummy key they had
made. Escape was comparatively easy, because the African guards were
lax and it was universally acknowledged that prisoners were much safer
inside camp than out alone in the bush. Intending to be long gone by
morning roll call, the three Italians set off for Mount Kenya under cover
of darkness.

A few hours later they slipped into the belt of mixed forest surrounding the mountain's lower slopes. The forest was so thick that often the only
way to move through it was to follow the narrow game trails, where buffalo,
rhino and elephant commanded right of way.

Now and again during the early stages they were forced to cross a man-made track, such as the path leading to a sawmill, where the chances of recapture were greatest. African trackers received a ten-shilling reward for every escaped PoW brought in. To confuse any pursuers, the three Italians crossed backwards, leaving behind footprints going in the opposite direction. Wherever possible, they avoided the paths altogether.

By this time Barsotti had been revealed as a sick man with a temperature of 101 degrees. He had been suffering from malaria for two days before the escape, but had kept his illness quiet, choosing to go ahead with the break-out rather than miss any of the excitement. He could not be left behind now.

Guessing correctly that the river Nanyuki must have its origin in the glaciers of the mountain, Benuzzi had decided that the quickest way to the top would be to follow the river back to its source. This was easier said than done, because its banks were often completely overgrown. The slippery stream twisted and turned and doubled back on itself with more energy than a lizard avoiding a hawk.

At one point it split in two, leaving the party with no idea which fork to follow. All they had to guide them was a map taken from a book about the Kikuyu, covering fifty miles to the centimetre. Otherwise they relied on sketches made in camp and a printed trademark of the summit borrowed from the label of a meat tin.

Using these unconventional aids, the party toiled upwards through the mixed forest until, at about 8,000 feet, they reached solid bamboo. The bamboo was of two kinds. Giant bamboo grew in diameter to the thickness of a man's upper arm and lay haphazardly across the way like the poles of an equestrian show jumping event.

Dwarf bamboo, though no more than an inch across, grew in tight clumps which had to be circumnavigated. This became increasingly tiresome as the dwindling oxygen in the atmosphere began to take effect.

The going was further complicated by herds of elephant, which migrated to higher ground during the dry season. The elephants saw no reason to move over just for a group of human beings.

At length, towards 11,000 feet, the bamboo came to an end as abruptly as it had begun. From now on there would be no more forest. Instead, the PoWs had come upon a strange, weird-looking moorland, devoid of trees, as windswept as a blasted heath in Scotland and as uncharitable. Heather on the moorland grew fifteen feet tall. Lobelias stood at six feet and groundsel twice as high.

In the early mornings above the treeline it was possible to see elephant feeding on grass completely white with frost. The world had suddenly become an eerie, unreal place that reminded Benuzzi strongly of *Alice in Wonderland*. It was all so very different from the landscape he had left behind him.

Far below stretched out the great plains of Laikipia. With binoculars he could even make out his own barrack block in the prison camp, where men would still be queuing for the showers, shuffling forward to answer their names at roll call, quarrelling over a piece of soap or fighting for a drop of cooking oil.

That night, immediately it grew dark, he planned to carry out his promise to light a fire for the watching prisoners to see. The tiny stab of flame would signal to the prisoners that three of their number at least had won back their freedom for a few precious days.

Ahead of him lay Batian, tallest of Mount Kenya's twin peaks, solid and imposing against the deep violet blue of the summer sky. 'I had not expected it to be so near, so beautiful, so tantalising,' he remembered.

'There it was at last, our ultimate goal, its appalling north face armoured with ice, its jagged pinnacles not yet touched by the rising sun, dreamlike, overwhelming as it had appeared to me on that well-remembered May morning in the camp, when first I fell in love with it.'

Near, and yet far away. As the PoWs approached 14,000 feet, they noticed that the Nanyuki river was still fringed with icicles at midday. Their hearts and lungs worked overtime in the thin air, leaving them light-headed and weak from mountain sickness. They were even convinced that they could hear the tinkling of Alpine cow bells coming from somewhere not far off.

For the feverish Barsotti, it was all too much. Ill prepared for physical exertion, his heart suddenly failed. He collapsed unconscious to the ground.

The other two moved fast. Hurriedly brewing coffee on an alcohol burner, Benuzzi stood aside as Balletto forced a few drops of the hot liquid between the sick man's lips, enough at least to force him back into consciousness. For a long time nothing happened. Then, after another interval, he recovered sufficiently to sit up and take notice of his surroundings.

Later he managed to walk a little way with help to the shelter of a nearby boulder. Any further progress was out of the question.

His companions decided to make the best of a bad job. Since Barsotti could not move, they would have to establish the base camp where they were. It was too low to give them a good start for the assault on Batian, but they were not prepared to put the sick man's life in further jeopardy by taking him any higher.

After all they had been through, the two mountaineers deserved a fairy tale ending to their story, but the sad truth is that the attempt on Batian was earmarked for failure even before it had begun. It is not an easy climb.

The peak was first conquered by Sir Halford Mackinder in 1899. It was not reached again for another thirty years until Eric Shipton and Percy Wyn Harris – both of whom later made attempts on Everest – ascended Batian after becoming the first men to scale Nelion, the lower of Mount Kenya's twin summits.

What the Italians did not know is that Shipton had long ago classed as hopeless the route selected by Benuzzi for the climb. There was no time for the Italians to make a proper reconnaissance of the alternatives, because the party had brought food for only ten days and they were already on their tenth.

It had to be now or never. Empty stomachs, inadequate equipment, unyielding rock and a sudden icy storm which blew up as they clung to the rock face conspired to make it never.

As a consolation prize, they planted their flag on Mount Kenya's third highest peak, Point Lenana, a highly respectable 16,355 feet above sea level. After such a long time, it was a grand sight to see the Italian flag flying free once again. As Benuzzi readily confessed, the only flags he had seen in recent years had been white – and in large quantities.

The return journey down the mountainside was nothing short of a race to break back into prison camp before they died of starvation. When the three exhausted PoWs produced their key at the end of their frolic and secretly let themselves with shaky fingers into Nanyuki camp, they had been continually on the move for eighteen days. They had survived on a supply of food intended to be eaten sparingly over half that time.

The final days of the ordeal had been an agony of hunger, sustained by little more than crumbs of barley sugar and a few overlooked grains of rice. Indeed, when searching for a tiny brown smear they might have missed, they had proved it almost possible for a grown man to get his entire fist inside an empty bottle of Bovril.

When they did re-enter camp and reveal themselves to the inmates, no one believed they had climbed Mount Kenya.

Fortunately, their flag was discovered only a week later by a party of climbers from Nairobi, who duly reported the news to the *East African Standard*. As they had expected, the escapees were sentenced to twenty-eight days in the cells, a guaranteed solid month of a bed each to sleep on and food issued to them at regular intervals.

They could not have asked for anything better. They were a bit put out when the Camp Commandant released them after only a week in recognition of their sporting effort.

What made them do it? According to Benuzzi, it was purely for the romance of the thing: 'As knights of old crossed perilous seas, fought fiery dragons and even each other, for the love of their princesses, so nowadays mountaineers armed with ice-axes and ropes, crampons and pitons, make dangerous and wearisome journeys and endure every hardship for the sake of their mountains.'

Afterwards, the rest of the war came as something of an anti-climax for the three PoWs, dragging on interminably as it did. The end came at last and they were free to be repatriated to Italy for a reunion with their families, picking up the threads of life in a new and very different post-war world.

Like the European settlers and African troops flooding back to Kenya towards the end of 1945, they were to discover that much had changed during the past six years of strife. Not all of it was for the better.

CHAPTER TEN
LOSING THE PEACE

Every war is followed by a difficult period of readjustment as young men who have known no adult life except soldiering find themselves in civilian clothes for the first time. Rootless and disorientated, not knowing what to do with themselves, they often get up to no good if there's nothing else to do, as there always was in the services. The rate of petty crime in London and New York rocketed with the return of demobbed troops at the end of the Second World War.

The same happened in Kenya, where the black tribesmen of the King's African Rifles came back from overseas to find that life in the tribal reserves could not compare with all that they had seen and done during the war, not only in the big city of Nairobi but also in other lands across the wide water. Those who had stayed at home could have no idea of how much more there was to the world than hymn-singing at the mission church and a monthly bus ride to the nearest market town.

Words could not describe the ocean at Mombasa, or the enormous ships which had ferried the troops abroad. They couldn't describe the brown-skinned women who had welcomed the troops at the other end, or the sense of *being* somebody that the fighting men had experienced in Burma at Jambo Hill, Leik Ridge, Sadwin and Myittha Gorge.

Not all the Africans had fought. Many had served only as non-combatants in the labour battalions. This distinction tended to become a little blurred in the back rooms of Kenya's beer halls when the returning warriors recounted their experiences to an admiring audience of family and friends, old men, young brothers and available girls.

The war had given African soldiers much to think about. As fighting men they had shared the same misery and discomfort as their European officers. They had often laughed together in the same rain-filled foxhole as the Japanese lobbed down mortar bombs and heavy explosive onto their position.

Black and white together had participated in a joint war effort, comrades in arms, fighting and dying side by side in a battle which did not distinguish between the colour of their skins. The Africans had also met soldiers from England, other ranks like themselves, who were not afraid to accept and even welcome black men on terms of equality.

In the mud and stench of Burma, the blacks had found Europeans who regarded them first and foremost as fellow human beings. They rather liked the feeling. Conversely, although men of the KAR usually formed a close bond of affection with their Kenyan officers, they could not fail to notice that the great white bwana of the farm was just as likely as anyone else to become an undignified, whimpering wreck when he got a Japanese bullet in the stomach.

Time and again during the war they had seen their untouchable bwanas reduced from on high to the level of common mortality. The memory lingered.

Now that the war was over, there was still the peace to be won. The dismal prospect of two harvests a year, sowing and reaping, sowing and reaping year in year out, was rarely enough to entice the ex-soldiers back to their tribal reserves. Nor was the idea of working as a squatter on a European farm any more attractive.

Rather they would prefer the bright lights of Nairobi, where there was always something to see and do. There were cars, bicycles, bazaars, beer halls and brothels in Nairobi. Life could be lived there among their own kind, men who had seen the world across the sea as they had, men who knew what they were talking about when they exchanged their memories of the war.

Accordingly, thousands of old soldiers drifted into Nairobi after demobilisation, tramping the streets in an often fruitless search for work. Within a few months, finding good jobs hard to come by because so many trades were still monopolised by Asians, they had become angry and disillusioned.

The influx of ex-servicemen into the capital city was not confined only to Africans in the years after 1945. As at the end of the First World War, the Government put in hand a soldier-settlement scheme to distribute land in the white highlands to Europeans who had fought for King and country. Many took advantage of this opportunity to escape the austerities of post-war Britain.

Typical of those who immigrated to Kenya at this time were an Oxford rowing blue who had had most of his lungs shot away while serving with the Brigade of Guards, a former inmate of Colditz Castle, and a Scottish-born adventurer who claimed to have had dealings with Al Capone in his youth. His favourite trick at agricultural shows was to hold a revolver in each hand and shoot two bulls in opposite directions at the same time.

These men were not pioneers, in the strictest sense, because the pioneering days were over now that the land had been settled. Apart from the northern frontier district – always a law unto itself – there were no frontiers to push back and few warring tribes to contend with. Nevertheless, the pioneering spirit was still present in the sort of men who came out to Kenya in the late 1940s.

They were usually ex-servicemen, people like Digby Tatham-Warter, formerly of the Parachute Regiment. He had distinguished himself at Arnhem by leading a bayonet charge in a captured bowler hat, with an umbrella to protect him against mortar bombs. His feat was portrayed fictitiously by the character Major Carlyle in the film *A Bridge too far*.

After 1947 and the end of British rule in India, the new settlers were joined by a steady trickle of Indian Army officers and civil servants from the Raj who had chosen to retire to Kenya rather than return to the British Isles.

They were followed in turn by a number of Asian traders and craftsmen who had depended on the Raj for their livelihood. The Indians preferred to make a new life in Nairobi rather than suffer the horrors of Partition as India and Pakistan divided messily into two different countries.

Another immigrant was the Duke of Manchester, who arrived on safari in 1947 and immediately fell in love with the country. He had more reason than most to be disillusioned with post-war Britain. Both of his ancestral homes had been occupied by the army during the war. The buildings had suffered only slightly less damage than if the Germans had attacked them.

Attempts to obtain compensation had been rejected out of hand by a Labour government intent on creating a new order of things. Preoccupied with more pressing matters, the socialists were in no mood to help the aristocracy. Like many ex-servicemen, therefore, the Duke upped sticks and emigrated.

Intending to become a rancher, he first considered buying a property at Nanyuki, but turned it down because there was not enough land to make ranching a viable proposition. The house later became a hotel before being sold to William Holden and a consortium of Hollywood film stars. They transformed it into a major tourist attraction, the Mount Kenya Safari Club.

The Duke eventually settled at Hoey's Bridge, where he bought the farm of Cecil Hoey, the first European to reach the area. Hoey had succumbed to an altitude of 7,000 feet and was looking for somewhere to retire more amenable to his blood pressure.

The Duke had no such health problems. Adapting readily to the altitude, he set up home in the bush with the Duchess and seven ancestral portraits by Van Dyck. He was soon on good terms with his fellow chiefs of the neighbouring Nandi, Cherangani and Marakwet tribes.

Nineteen forty six saw the return to Kenya of Jomo Kenyatta at the end of his fifteen-year sojourn in Europe. He had spent the war doing his bit for Britain as a farm labourer at Storrington. They had known him at the *White Horse* as Jumbo, a popular village character who liked his pint, and the second more than the first.

In 1942 Kenyatta had married as his second wife an English governess named Edna Clarke. A condition of the marriage had been that if he ever had to choose between her and Kenya, she would be the loser. When he set sail for Mombasa four years later, he sailed alone, leaving wife and son behind.

Nominally Kenyatta was still general secretary of the Kikuyu Central Association. In this capacity he had worked with Kwame Nkrumah of the Gold Coast to organise the 1945 Pan-African Congress in Manchester. The situation was awkward, however, because the KCA had been outlawed at the beginning of the war as a subversive organisation 'in contact with the King's enemies or potential enemies', by which was meant Italian fascists.

Although the Kenya Government had found little evidence to support this charge, it arrested twenty of the KCA's leaders and did not release them until 1943. Kenyatta himself only escaped imprisonment because he was out of the country at the time.

On his return to Kikuyuland, he was quick to notice the mood of restlessness which had gripped his people while he was away. In general the Kikuyu had done well out of the war, sharing in the widespread prosperity it had brought to agriculture. They had even clubbed together to buy Spitfires for the war effort (the planes flew with the word 'Kikuyu' painted on the side).

Nevertheless, the old grievances still remained, in particular the feeling that the European community was waxing rich on land stolen from the tribe. Carter commission or no Carter commission, the Kikuyu were convinced they had been robbed.

Moreover, a new factor now had to be taken into account: the dramatic increase in the Kikuyu population. In the four decades or so since the introduction of proper health care and vaccination programmes, the number of Kikuyu mouths to be fed had more than quadrupled, while the acreage of land to sustain them had not.

What Malthus once called 'the perpetual struggle for room and food' had created a problem of real hardship in the native reserves, especially among the young. The settlers took the view that this problem could easily be solved, for a while anyway, by employing the surplus population as cheap labour on white farms. Their opinion was not shared by the Kikuyu.

The African sense of grievance was compounded by the experience of demobbed soldiers, desperately seeking work in Nairobi. All too often, they found themselves pressing back off the pavement out of the way of immigrant strangers from England en route for the empty acres of the white highlands. As the Kikuyu understood it, they had fought in the war too. If land in Kenya was going spare, as evidently it was, surely they were entitled to a small slice of it?

Just a few acres each, that was all they wanted. Enough to grow some maize and raise a few goats to support their families in the traditional Kikuyu way. It did not seem too much to ask.

To the European settlers, however, goats and maize were precisely why African farmers should not be allowed into the white highlands at any price. Goats were anathema in European eyes because they ring-barked the trees and pulled out grass by the roots instead of simply cropping it. To plant maize in soil heaven-sent for better things seemed a major crime in a country where optimum allocation of resources was essential for the economy. Nothing was calculated to arouse the settlers' ire more violently than bad farming practice.

Certainly, maize grew like a weed and yielded two or maybe even three crops a year without any effort. It was an easy way to feed the Africans' burgeoning families. Yet the land was often better suited to valuable crops like coffee, which did not yield anything at all for the first four or five years after planting, and required back-breaking supervision and care throughout all of that time if it was ultimately to be a success.

When the coffee harvest was gathered, however, the financial rewards of good planning and forethought could be enormous. A massive surplus could be ploughed back into the land for the benefit of everyone, white squire and black squatter alike.

The Europeans were just what their name implied, settlers. They did not remit their profits back to England. They kept the money in Kenya, where it formed the backbone of the economy and provided the Government with its main source of revenue.

The Europeans argued that Africans were not temperamentally suited to a farming ethos that involved waiting five years before seeing a profit. If Africans took over the highlands, claimed the settlers, they would squander it on maize and goats and uneconomical smallholdings.

With some justification, the whites drew attention to the innate conservatism of the Kikuyu. The tribe had resisted the benefits of European agricultural improvements for many years in favour of its own more wasteful methods.

What the country needed was large-scale, efficient farming to create a profitable surplus, asserted the whites. Surrender the highlands to a legion of smallholders concerned with growing only enough to feed themselves as far ahead as they could see, which was not very far, and the treasury would very soon be bare.

The Kikuyu countered by pointing out that advances *had* been made in their traditional methods of agriculture as the benefits of European experience became clearer to them. This was particularly so in the terracing of hills to conserve water and soil.

Younger farmers were more than willing to put right the mistakes of their parents. It was undeniable that the few Africans who had attempted to grow coffee had been prevented from doing so by pressure from Europeans afraid of the competition.

As for the charge that Africans were incapable of planning ahead, concerned only with feeding themselves this week, what else could they do when arable land in the country of their birth was so difficult to obtain?

The problem was not simply a case of black against white. It was also a question of capitalism versus subsistence farming, further complicated by the unprecedented upsurge of population in the Kikuyu reserves. The problem was not solved when the whites did eventually vacate the highlands, nor has it been solved to this day.

Neither side in the dispute could claim a monopoly of justice or virtue. From their respective viewpoints both sides were right. Tragically, both were also wrong.

The land issue surfaced again soon after Jomo Kenyatta had returned to take his place as unofficial spokesman for the Kikuyu tribe. Right from the start the problem was dominated by the Kikuyu, just under one fifth of the colony's black population, because they were the tribe geographically closest and mentally most in tune with the Europeans.

Kenya has around forty-two different tribes, depending on how they are classified, but only the Kikuyu – and to a lesser extent their cousins the Embu and Meru – were to take any part in the coming clash over land.

As an example of how the Kikuyu dominated African thinking, eight out of nine central committee members of the Kenya African Union – a non-tribal party set up at the end of the war to represent the political interests of all Kenya Africans – were Kikuyu by 1951. President of KAU from 1947 was Jomo Kenyatta. He used the party as a respectable front for the still-proscribed Kikuyu Central Association.

Kenyatta's aims were the same as they had always been: to obtain freedom from colonial rule, and to get hold of the white highlands. The difference now was that people were beginning to listen to him.

Among his earliest recruits were the old soldiers, tough dissatisfied men who felt that the world owed them a living and did not shrink from talk of bloodshed to achieve their aims. Many of these Kikuyu were comrades of the same age group, having been circumcised together in the initiation rites of 1940.

They called themselves the Forty Group, a close-knit body of young men pledged in allegiance to Jomo Kenyatta and bound by their circumcision oath to ask no questions and help each other at all times. They provided the muscle to back up their leader's political organisation.

By the end of the 1940s there was no longer any doubt in the minds of a million or more Kikuyu that the white highlands must be given back to Africa. The only argument now was over how the goal should be achieved. Older men, most of whom had a small patch of land to call their own, favoured negotiation and compromise. They believed that the issue simply was not worth fighting for.

Younger men demanded blood. For one thing, the new generation of warriors recognised a need to assert their masculinity in front of the girls of the tribe. Most important of all, however, they argued that violence was the only way to make the Europeans part with the land.

They were quite right. The Europeans would fight, sure enough, before they would be pushed off their land. The idea seemed as ludicrous to them as giving New York back to the American Indians.

Most of the settlers had come out to Kenya with a dream, a dream that one day the virgin bush they had cleared and planted – with African labour – would be bludgeoned and pummelled into a broad green paradise. They intended to live out the rest of their days there in well-deserved contentment, watching their children grow up healthy and strong in the sunny uplands of God's own country.

Many settlers had devoted a lifetime to making the dream come true. Many had died in the attempt. Theirs was the planning and forethought, theirs the initiative and enterprise, theirs the trial and error and costly experiment, the lying awake at night and the worry and the strain.

The settlers believed they were carrying the country on their backs. Most had staked everything they possessed – and a good deal of the bank's money as well – on the green baize of the highlands, leased to them for 999 years in good faith by their own government.

They felt entitled to the prize money. They were good farmers and clear-eyed hard-working men, nobody could deny that, the kind of stubborn opinionated visionaries who could make water run uphill and turn barren scrub into a flowering garden of a thousand delights.

The settlers loved the land and they meant to stay on it. They had not struggled through half a century of disaster and Depression simply to hand over their life's work to the first African who demanded it. They would die first. And some did.

With God on both their sides, a holy war between Kikuyu and European had become inevitable. The Kikuyu began to organise themselves for the struggle. It would not be an armed insurrection at first, merely a campaign of intimidation to persuade the British that the time had come to go in peace.

Arson and the bush knife called panga would be the weapons. Burnt crops and hamstrung cattle the means. Just as the Irish had once mutilated the livestock of English landlords in the cause of Home Rule, so now the Kikuyu would employ the same methods to the same end.

How it started and where it started nobody ever knew for sure. Nor even who was responsible. The British later tried to put the blame on Kenyatta, but failed to prove their case to everyone's satisfaction in court – which did not prevent them finding him guilty anyway.

At first it took the form of an oath of unity and brotherhood among the Kikuyu. The oath was a solemn pledge intended to draw the tribe together against the common enemy, even if individually that enemy might be a good friend.

The Kikuyu are a deeply religious people with a mystical faith in ceremonial rites. They were originally forest dwellers. Forest dwellers all over the world believe strongly in magic sprites which live among the branches and whispering treetops of dark leafy places, where no one can ever see them.

Oathing ceremonies based on such a belief might seem naive to sophisticated westerners, but they are no sillier than the initiation rites of a European freemasons' lodge and no less binding.

A Kikuyu oathing ceremony has been described by Josiah Mwangi Kariuki. Then a young man, he later went on to become one of Kenya's most prominent politicians:

'I took off my trousers and squatted facing Biniathi. He told me to take the thorax of the goat which had been skinned, to put my penis through a hole that had been made in it, and to hold the rest of it in my left hand in front of me. Before me on the ground there were two small wooden stakes between which the thorax (*ngata*) of the goat was suspended and fastened.

'By my right hand on the floor of the hut were seven small sticks each about four inches long. Biniathi told me to take the sticks one at a time, to put them into the *ngata*, and slowly rub them in it while repeating after him these seven vows, one for each stick. (After each promise I was to bite the meat and throw the stick on to the ground on my left side.)'

The seven oaths which followed are too lengthy to repeat in full. Two should suffice to indicate the enormity of the pledges which Kikuyu people were undertaking as the land freedom movement gathered pace in the late 1940s and early 1950s:

I speak the truth and vow before our God
That if I am called to go to fight the enemy
Or to kill the enemy – I shall go
Even if the enemy be my father or mother, my brother
 or sister
And if I refuse
May this oath kill me,
May this he-goat kill me,
May this seven kill me,
May this meat kill me.

I speak the truth and vow before our God
That if I am called during the night or the day
To go to burn the store of a European who is our enemy
I shall go forth without fear and I shall never surrender
And if I fail to do this
May this oath kill me, etc.

Altogether, perhaps ninety per cent of the Kikuyu tribe went through some form of oathing ceremony during these years. Many were very unwilling and did so only under duress. The reluctant ones – 'loyalists' as they were contemptuously called by the rest – were often dragged from their huts late at night and forced to undergo the ceremony on pain of death if they refused to comply.

Particularly unhappy were the Christian Kikuyu. They frequently found themselves torn between the old ways and the new, condemned to hell and damnation whichever path they chose.

For those who took the oath, however, the result was always the same. Once oathed, no matter how mixed their feelings, they became the creatures of the movement. They were transformed overnight from smiling pro-European to deadly enemy by the overriding power of an irresistible superstition.

Almost half a century after he first claimed to have forecast just such a conflict over land, Richard Meinertzhagen paid a return visit to Kenya to renew a few friendships from the pioneer days. One of the first places he visited was Nyeri, his old camp. There he met up with a Kikuyu chief he had known when both were young warriors.

What the chief told Meinertzhagen worried him so much that he immediately repeated it in a private letter delivered by hand to Government House:

'He fears an outbreak of violence against Europeans involving murders on a large scale under the direction of a secret society now in existence called "Maw Maw" whose influence in the tribe is rapidly growing and whose oaths, taken in utmost secrecy, are binding on those who are compelled to take them.'

Mau Mau is the name it came to be known by, a meaningless word whose origin is lost in the Kikuyu passion for secret signs and portents of mysterious significance. A meaningless word, but one that would dominate Kenya politics for more than a decade and find its way almost every day into newspaper headlines across the world before people began to understand exactly what it stood for.

By the end of the 1940s, the process of oath administration was rapidly gathering momentum among the Kikuyu. It was often carried out by strong-arm members of the Forty Group. The men charged a fee for their services. They were supposed to give the cash to a political campaign fund, but all too frequently kept it for themselves.

There were no formal links between Mau Mau and KAU or the KCA, because nothing was ever written down on paper. Police raids never yielded a membership list or anything that could be used as evidence in court. The authorities were convinced nevertheless that such a link did exist. In August

1950 they declared Mau Mau an illegal society and began to prosecute its members.

From then on the situation started to get out of hand. Oathing ceremonies were stepped up and for the first time included a pledge to kill a European if called upon to do so. Loyalist Kikuyu who refused to take such an oath were badly beaten up, yet remained strangely silent when the police asked them to make a statement.

Kikuyu chiefs and headmen who spoke out against Mau Mau found their huts burned in the night. District Commissioners in Kikuyuland reported an alarming increase in unexplained grass fires on property belonging to loyalists, and a peculiar mood of sullenness hanging over a normally cheerful people.

Richard Meinertzhagen was not the only one to hear rumours of a night of the long knives, when European farmers and their families would be massacred wholesale in the highlands as the prelude to a general uprising. Word right across Kikuyuland had it that the day was fast approaching when the white man would be driven out and his farm sold to any black man who could raise £50 to pay for it.

This, and hundreds of rumours like it, was scrupulously noted down by British district officers and despatched in confidential reports to the central administration in Nairobi. The officers in the field called for decisive action to be taken against Mau Mau while there was still time.

Nairobi did nothing. For a long time the official view of Government House remained that the Mau Mau scare was being greatly exaggerated, that the district officers in the heart of Kikuyuland were over-reacting to what was nothing more than a minor political irritation. A brush fire, as it were.

Report after report mounted up in Nairobi begging for stronger security measures, calling for a show of force, urging the administration to do something while it still had the chance. The reports were all discounted until it was too late.

Much of the blame must fall on the Governor, Major-General Sir Philip Mitchell. He was coming to the end of a career that had included forty years in and around East Africa. His tour of duty had been specially extended for two years to enable him to complete the political changes he had set in hand after the war.

These changes included a measure of black representation in the Legislative Council and a redistribution of seats to give a combined African, Indian and Arab bloc the same voting power as the elected Europeans.

Mitchell was eager to retire on a happy note. He did not wish to hand over to his successor a colony on the brink of civil war. To this end, while he acknowledged that there was certainly a problem of sorts, he chose to play down the intelligence reports emanating from Kikuyuland. He refused to admit even to himself that the situation might justify the adoption of emergency measures.

The Duke of Portland, who knew him well and admired him, believed that part of the problem was that Mitchell had been too long in the same job: 'He had very great qualities, but he got swollen headed, the way Governors do. They get fixed ideas if they stay too long.'

The crowning glory of Mitchell's career was to be a long-planned visit to the colony by King George VI and Queen Elizabeth on the outward leg of a royal tour of Ceylon, Australia and New Zealand. Unfortunately, the King was too ill with cancer to undertake the journey, so his daughter Princess Elizabeth and the Duke of Edinburgh were coming instead.

In view of the disturbed state of the colony at the beginning of 1952, opinion was divided as to whether the Kenyan part of their tour should take place. Many Provincial Commissioners and officers responsible for the safety of the royal couple were adamant that it should not.

The Commissioners repeatedly made their feelings plain to the Governor. They argued that it was impossible to guarantee the twenty-five-year-old princess's safety in the midst of the campaign of arson and lawlessness that was threatening to engulf the highlands.

In Mitchell's view, however, the danger was still much exaggerated. It was not easy to cancel a royal tour at short notice without a convincing explanation. Against the better judgment of many of his subordinates, he decreed that it should go ahead.

The royal pair left England on 31 January 1952. The King was well enough to see them off from London airport. Knowing that he was sick, the watching crowd gave him a particularly loud cheer as he stood bareheaded in bitterly cold weather to wave goodbye to his eldest daughter.

Next day the princess arrived in Nairobi to an enthusiastic reception at the airport and a varied programme of events which included a tour of Nairobi game park and a visit to the Ngong Road to open the new headquarters of the Kenya Regiment.

Those who had doubts about the trip need not have worried. Africans turned out in swarms along the route to greet her. They did not cheer, because that is not the African way, but they were happy to see her and they made no secret of the fact. It was plain right from the beginning that the visit would be a success.

On 3 February Princess Elizabeth and the Duke of Edinburgh drove up-country to Sagana, the colony's official wedding present to them, a fishing lodge built overlooking a trout stream in the Mount Kenya forest.

Sagana was a beautiful, isolated spot, with horses to ride before breakfast in the chill morning air. It had been carefully chosen as a place for the royal couple to relax far from the din and bustle of Nairobi – an ideal base for their engagements in the highlands.

Two days later, they left Sagana after an early lunch to drive to Treetops, the game-viewing platform in the Aberdare forest. They were to be guests that night of Eric Sherbrooke Walker, the retired rum smuggler, and his wife Lady Bettie.

As with every royal journey, the behind-the-scenes preparations for the Treetops excursion had begun weeks earlier. The planning had occupied hundreds of man-hours as every possible contingency was provided for in advance.

For several miles along the forest edge of the Treetops salient, a cordon of Africans waited with spears at the ready to keep out unwelcome sightseers. At The Outspan hotel, Sherbrooke Walker assembled the battalion of journalists and photographers covering the trip and explained to them that the scent of even one stranger in the forest might be enough to frighten off the wild life and turn the visit into a disaster.

With admirable restraint the press agreed not to follow the princess to Treetops. They opted instead to remain seated en masse at The Outspan bar. To give her a few hours' peace in the midst of a non-stop schedule, Sherbrooke Walker forbade anybody accompanying the royal party to take a camera with them. They would have made a fortune if they had.

So far as game viewing was concerned, Princess Elizabeth was in luck that day, because a herd of forty-seven elephants was awaiting her arrival. The nearest was not more than eight paces away as she climbed the ladder into the *mugumu* tree. Baboons, warthog and bushbuck were also much in evidence.

Sherbrooke Walker's ban on photography naturally did not extend to the princess's cine camera. She used it repeatedly from the viewing platform during the course of the afternoon. So engrossed did she become that when tea was announced in the dining room, she replied: 'Oh, please may I have it here? I don't want to miss one moment of this.'

The two royals spent most of the night sitting on the balcony watching game by the light of the artificial moon. After only a few hours' sleep, Princess Elizabeth was up again at dawn to film a pair of rhino squabbling over the salt lick.

Jim Corbett, the well-known naturalist and author of *Man-eaters of Kumaon*, had passed the night on the top step of the ladder to the ground, guarding against any stray leopard that might take it into its head to climb this particular tree this particular night. He noticed that despite her weariness the princess 'started that second day with eyes sparkling and a face as fresh as a flower'.

After breakfast, the party descended to the ground for the return journey through the forest to the transport that would take them back to Sagana. There were smug faces all round as the organisers congratulated each other on an unmitigated triumph.

The game had obligingly turned up in strength, which did not always happen, and like anyone else the princess could not wait to see her home movies developed. As she drove away, she waved to Sherbrooke Walker and said: 'I will come again!'

Later that morning a telephone call reached Martin Charteris, the Princess's secretary, who was lunching at The Outspan. The editor of the *East African Standard* had rung from Nairobi to ask if the reports of the King's death coming over the teleprinter were true.

Shocked, Charteris immediately got in touch with Prince Philip at Sagana. The Prince reacted 'as if hit by a thunderbolt' when he heard the news.

They waited for the story to be officially confirmed by radio-telephone before Prince Philip gave orders for the rest of the tour to be cancelled and preparations made for a return flight to England. Then, at 2.45 pm on 6 February 1952, he broke the news to Princess Elizabeth on the lawn beside the Sagana river that her father had died in his sleep the previous night.

When she left Sagana towards dusk that evening, she was carrying a quarter of the world on her shoulders.

'For the first time in the history of the world,' wrote Jim Corbett in the Treetops' visitors' book, 'a young girl climbed into a tree one day a Princess, and after having what she described as her most thrilling experience she climbed down from the tree the next day a Queen – God bless her.'

At Nanyuki airstrip the flags were flying at half-mast as she boarded the Dakota that would fly her to Entebbe for the next lap of the journey home. She had been due to visit the township next day.

Understandably, the crowds who came to see her off were quiet and subdued, but the Queen – though unmistakably under strain – gave them a smile as she got out of the car. With scant ceremony the royal plane taxied to the end of the airstrip, turned and took off.

The crowds stayed to watch until it had disappeared from view. Then they slowly dispersed into huddled groups to discuss the day's events. The royal visit was over.

From the point where the plane had left the ground, at least five grass fires were burning within sight of the airfield, defiant reminders that the colony had troubles of its own. Whether Sir Philip Mitchell accepted it or not, there was rebellion in the air, even if he would not be in office to see it. He had had his royal visit. Now it was time for him to retire.

He bowed out in June 1952, insisting to the last that the threat to law and order posed by 'proscribed societies' did not justify the draconian measures being wished on him by his officers in the field. His retirement began with three months' leave on full pay.

Kenya was without a fulltime Governor for that time because the British taxpayer could not be expected to support two at once. It was not until the end of September that his successor, Sir Evelyn Baring, arrived in the colony to set out immediately on a fact-finding tour of the troubled areas.[1]

It took Baring just nine days to decide that an official state of Emergency should be declared in Kenya. His excuse, if he needed one, was the murder of Margaret Wright, found stabbed to death on the veranda of her husband's farm ten miles outside Nairobi. Her murder was followed a few days later by the assassination of Senior Chief Waruhiu, a prominent Kikuyu who was bitterly opposed to Mau Mau and everything it stood for.

Once London had given reluctant approval, Baring required a few more days to finalise his arrangements. Then he was ready. On the evening of 20 October 1952 he signed the proclamation of a state of Emergency.

Just after midnight, the Kenya Police used their new powers of arrest to drag Jomo Kenyatta and eighty-two alleged Mau Mau leaders from their beds to face trial and punishment. The swords were unsheathed at last. Now the killing would begin.

1. On 16 June, just before he left Kenya, Mitchell wrote a letter to Baring which gave no hint of the gathering storm. It concentrated instead on the problem of how an incoming Governor should behave towards divorced Europeans in a colony of cheerful adulterers:

'It is of somewhat unusual complexity especially as we have the amateur champion out here, who has, I think, been divorced by five if not six husbands. The Delamere household is another not very simple one particularly on the occasion of royal visits. The situation in which Lord Mountbatten's sister is technically disqualified from coming to Government House, as her husband is, while Prince Philip is here is not without its difficulties.'

CHAPTER ELEVEN
STATE OF EMERGENCY

All through that first day the arrests continued. By nightfall, almost a hundred prominent Kikuyu suspected of being connected with Mau Mau had been detained. At the same time a spearhead detachment of the Lancashire Fusiliers, airlifted from Egypt under cover of darkness the previous night, made a sudden and dramatic appearance on the streets of Nairobi.

The unfamiliar presence of armed European soldiers served to convince the community that strong measures were being put in hand. This view was confirmed when police reservists and part-time members of the territorial Kenya Regiment received orders to report for duty immediately.

An additional three battalions of the King's African Rifles had already been moved discreetly to Kenya from other parts of East Africa to provide a back-up force for the Kenya Police. The police retained overall command of what was still only a civil, not a military, operation.

The Royal Navy rather failed to grasp this. As soon as the Emergency was declared, it sent a gunboat – the cruiser HMS *Kenya* – steaming across the ocean to drop anchor with an impressive rattle of chains in the peaceful port of Mombasa, some three hundred miles from the troubled area.

As the alleged ring leader of the Mau Mau movement, Jomo Kenyatta was bundled aboard a light aircraft after his arrest and flown up-country to remote Lokitaung in the heart of the Turkana. Lokitaung was about as far away from Kikuyuland as it was possible to go.

There he was kept under heavy guard to await trial. The Government's intention was to destroy the Mau Mau movement at one stroke by locking away its leader as quickly and as quietly as it could. Unfortunately, events took a different turn.

Kenyatta almost certainly did have a connection with Mau Mau, but proving him guilty in a court of law was no easy feat. Foolishly, the authorities charged him with overlording the movement, a claim that was virtually impossible to establish beyond reasonable doubt.

By allowing his case to develop into a show trial, the authorities also provided him with a golden opportunity to present a face of moderation and sweet reasonableness to the world in the teeth of British bigotry. The trial opened on 25 November 1952 and lasted five months.

To defend him Kenyatta chose not a local lawyer but D. N. Pritt, a prominent QC from England. Sharp and quick-witted, Pritt swiftly made mincemeat of the prosecution case. Kenyatta himself argued that far from arresting the leaders of Mau Mau, the Government had picked up the very members of the Kikuyu tribe who by their stature and moderation might have been able to control the movement and prevent its worst excesses.

It was an interesting argument, but not one that the Kenya judge was prepared to entertain. On 8 April 1953 Kenyatta was found guilty and sentenced to the maximum seven years' hard labour.[1] Through crass mismanagement, the British had achieved the opposite of what they had intended. They had turned Kenyatta into a martyr and focal point for his tribe's unrest.

A substantial body of opinion holds that Kenyatta's trial was a disgrace to British justice, and the verdict a mockery that would never have been allowed in an English court. It was certainly true that the atmosphere surrounding the trial was approaching hysteria as the full horror of Mau Mau sank in.

Atrocities were being committed on a daily basis that had no place in a civilised society. The verdict should be seen in the light of the authorities' pressing need to crush the movement and bring the killings to an end as swiftly as they could.

Far from destroying Mau Mau, the arrest of its alleged leaders had, if anything, led to an escalation of violence. Within a few days of Kenyatta's arrest, Mau Mau claimed another white victim in Eric Bowyer, a reclusive bachelor who lived alone on his farm on the north Kinangop. He was found dead in his bath, slashed to bits by pangas.

Outside, his two Kikuyu servants had also been murdered, and the house ransacked. There was no sign of the killers.

This outrage coincided with the arrival from London of two Labour MPs on a nine-day fact-finding visit. The coincidence could not have been more unfortunate. The MPs were Leslie Hale and Fenner Brockway. They had been invited to Kenya at the expense of KAU by Peter Koinange, a close associate of Jomo Kenyatta.

Ever a champion of the black man against the white, Brockway was a leading light in the Movement for Colonial Freedom. He had a reputation among the settlers for unwarranted interference in colonial problems from four thousand miles away in London. With one of their number lying dead in his bath, he was the last man Kenya's Europeans wanted to find poking his nose into their affairs at this particular juncture.

Accordingly, a posse of them trooped out to Eastleigh Airport to meet the MPs' plane with a view to lynching them before they could do any real damage. Right-wing to the core, the settlers were shocked when Leslie Hale emerged from the aeroplane. In a more formal age than now, the fat little socialist – clearly no gentleman - was wearing neither tie nor socks. Hoots of derision and cries of 'poor white' trash thereupon followed him into the terminal building.

The incident caught the public imagination. Back in England, a Tory MP later earned a cheap laugh in the House of Commons by apologising to Brockway for being fully dressed. And when word got around – wrongly as it happened – that Hale and Brockway were staying at the Koinange house in the Kikuyu reserve, a pilot from the Kenya Police Reserve airwing flew overhead and bombed it with a pair of socks.

Brockway later claimed that a Kenya settler also called on him in London with the intention of shooting him. After some discussion, the man decided that he wasn't worth hanging for.

But the situation did not really lend itself to light relief. A month after Bowyer's murder, a retired naval officer named Meiklejohn and his doctor wife, also retired, were sitting in their drawing room after supper when their houseboy led in a gang of five Mau Mau armed with pangas.

Like most Europeans, the Meiklejohns had taken to carrying revolvers since the declaration of the Emergency. Dorothy Meiklejohn's wrist was slashed before she could get her pistol out of her bag. Her ear was half-severed. She took so many cuts on the body that she fainted from loss of blood, whereupon the gang fled, assuming that both its victims were dead.

But Dorothy Meiklejohn later recovered consciousness and with a shattered wrist drove seven miles into Thomson's Falls to fetch help for her husband. Then she allowed herself to be examined by her own doctor, who failed to recognise her, so badly was she cut up. She was lucky to survive. Her husband did not.

New Year's Day 1953 saw a similar assault on a pair of white settlers on the shores of lake Ol Bolossat near Ol Kalou. The victims were Charles Fergusson and his godson Richard Bingley, a young man of 23. They were following the widespread Kenya custom of sitting down to dinner in pyjamas and dressing gown when they were attacked.

While serving the second course, the house staff suddenly pinioned the two men's arms, preventing them from grabbing the revolvers that they kept on the table. A gang of fifteen to thirty Mau Mau then burst in and cut them to pieces with pangas. The bodies were badly mutilated, because it was essential for each of the gang members to take a full share in the crime by adding cuts of his own to ensure complicity.

The house was in darkness when a police patrol arrived later that night to investigate a neighbour's report that something might be wrong at the Fergusson place. Not knowing that the Mau Mau had already made their escape, a young policeman dropped to the ground and crawled into the building on his hands and knees. He expected every moment to hear the sweep of a panga coming down on his head.

Groping through the gloom, he felt something lying on the floor in a patch of sticky wetness. He counted the five stiff fingers of Fergusson's outstretched hand. The rest of Fergusson was slumped on its back in the next room.

The very next night another attack took place on two lady farmers near the fringe of the Aberdare forest north of Mweiga. Mrs Kitty Hesselberger and Mrs Dorothy Raynes Simpson had finished supper and were listening to the wireless when their houseboy and a gang of Mau Mau burst into the drawing room.

Mrs Raynes Simpson always kept her pistol on the arm of her chair facing the door. She used it to drop the leading Kikuyu dead at her feet just as he raised his panga to strike her. Her second shot was aimed at the man attacking Kitty Hesselberger. It killed her boxer dog instead.

By now Mrs Hesselberger had got hold of her shotgun. Between them the two women managed to beat back the gang down the corridor towards the kitchen. Then they returned to the drawing room to seek out a terrorist who had bolted himself into the bathroom next door.

When he declined to come out, they fired their weapons through the thin wooden wall. The man smashed a window and ran for his life, shedding a trail of blood as he went. The rest of the gang had already fled, leaving three dead men behind.

By this time a definite pattern to Mau Mau attacks on European settlers could be discerned. The target would usually be a lonely farmhouse with its back to the forest, giving the gang a chance to escape and be out of sight long before the alarm was raised. They would normally creep up to the farm just after dark and administer a killing oath to the farm servants, who would take it either voluntarily or under duress.

The killing would be done with pangas, because very few Mau Mau possessed a firearm. Such home-made rifles as did exist – made out of elastic bands, old tubing and a firing pin filed down from a doorbolt – were unreliable in the extreme.

The attack would take place around supper time when the target's guard was down. It would be led by the houseboy, because his presence in the building did not arouse suspicion until it was too late.

Despite the initial success of such hit-and-run tactics against the scattered European community, Mau Mau gangs did not invariably have things their own way when they attacked white farms. A courageous handful of Kikuyu squatters and farm labourers proved unwilling or even refused point blank to ally themselves with these strangers against their white bwanas.

The plain fact is that the Emergency tore the tribe apart. As in all civil wars, brother fought brother and families were split asunder as people took opposite viewpoints on whether the pressing need for land justified the shedding of human blood to obtain it.

For many loyal Kikuyu, land-hungry like the rest, the presence of Mau Mau at the door held just as much terror as it did for Europeans. A heavy number paid the supreme price for refusing to lift a hand against their white employers.

Quite a few, pressed into taking the Mau Mau oath, subsequently committed suicide rather than participate in a murder. One teenaged boy who hanged himself left this note for his bwana and memsahib to find: 'It is not your fault, my parents, but only the words of the Kikuyu which has caused me to take this tragic step against myself.'

Isolated cases even arose of loyal Kikuyu witch doctors using their arts to cast a magic spell over a particular settler and his children. They ensured that not so much as a hair of their heads was ever harmed during the sad years of upheaval and distress.

As the Emergency progressed, European settlers often found themselves called away from their farms for perhaps weeks at a time to serve a stint with the security forces elsewhere. They left their womenfolk barricaded alone in the house in the middle of nowhere, nerves strung tauter than a Wakamba bowstring against whatever the dark hours might bring.

If it was going to happen at all, it would happen just as the signature tune *Lilliburlero* heralded the BBC news on the wireless. There would be dogs barking, or cattle screaming, or a lone human being crying through the darkness. The noise would be followed by a frenzied knock at the door and a familiar servant's voice begging the memsahib to come quickly.

Often the memsahib did come, stepping alone into the African night, a gun in one hand and a torch in the other, wondering what new calamity was going to be picked out in the nervous beam of light. Sometimes it was a prize heifer with its udders slashed and its intestines strung around its hamstrung legs, sometimes an old headman naked as Mau Mau left him, with both eyes gouged out.

Sometimes it was a breastless Kikuyu mother still nursing a dead child, sometimes a servant with both hands cut off at the wrist, other times just the left ear. Every gang had its own particular trademark. The Kenya Police soon learned to differentiate between them until they could identify the gang responsible for each attack by the panga slashes left like fingerprints on the bodies.

The culmination of the first wave of Mau Mau attacks against Europeans took place on 24 January 1953, when a family named Ruck was wiped out on the Kinangop in particularly appalling circumstances.

Mbogo the *syce* (groom) and Gitahi the tractor driver lured thirty-eight-year-old Roger Ruck out of his house on a pretext and then butchered him in the darkness. Esme, his young doctor wife, suffered the same fate when she ran to his aid and was then disembowelled.

After hacking the two bodies to shreds, and that of a Kikuyu gardener who tried to intervene, the gang stormed into the drawing room in search of firearms and money.

Half-crazed with bloodlust, Gitahi began to hammer the keys of the piano. Mbogo and the others trooped upstairs and chopped through a locked door to get at six-year-old Michael Ruck, cowering miserably underneath his bed. Jack the Ripper had nothing on the way the gang left Michael Ruck that night.

Perhaps it was the killing of the child, perhaps it was the knowledge that Esme Ruck had devoted her life to running a medical clinic for the local African population, but the Ruck atrocity woke up Kenya's settler population to the fact that Mau Mau wasn't just something that happened to other people.

The Rucks were the very last people to invite such an attack. Plain, honest, hard-working folk, they represented everything that was good in Kenya Europeans. They had been fond of their African servants and had inspired affection in return.

Every African child on the farm received a present at Christmas time. Mbogo the *syce* was known to have been devoted to Michael Ruck. Some days before the murder – and before Mbogo took the Mau Mau oath – Michael had fallen from his horse while riding and had been tenderly carried back to the house by the worried *syce*.

If Mau Mau had once passed itself off as a political movement, then now clearly it had spiralled out of control. Even front-line Mau Mau supporters in Hampstead, reading about the Rucks from the safety of north London, began to wonder if the Kikuyu tribe had not gone off its head.

For many settlers the night of the Ruck killings was the night they first began to hate. Up until then, they had cherished the illusion that while other people's servants might be unreliable, their own Kikuyu would always remain steadfast and loyal.

From that time on, though, the settlers trusted nobody. They began to shoot first and ask questions later. The other side had laid down the rules. Now it would be war to the death, fire fought with fire, no mercy given and none expected.

Many British soldiers in Kenya felt the same way. Some regiments began to keep score boards and organise competitions with cash prizes for the company or platoon that could kill the most Mau Mau. Whenever they shot a prominent gang leader, they dumped his bullet-riddled body in the marketplace of his home location, to show the local populace that he was really dead.

The Public Works Department also built a mobile gallows designed to travel easily around Kikuyuland. It was erected in a condemned man's home area the day before his execution to show the watching Africans that retribution was inevitable. Screened by sheets of corrugated iron, men were hanged on Nyeri golf course.

There were unofficial reprisals too. One settler organised a squad of Nandi warriors to carry out a night raid on a Kikuyu village and teach the bastards a lesson they would never forget. The Nandi whipped the men and viciously raped three women.

What the settler did not bother to find out was that the village was composed exclusively of Kikuyu loyal to the Government. They had been grouped together to protect them from Mau Mau.

From around the time of the Ruck murders dated the mass exodus back to the native reserves of Kikuyu squatters from the white farms of the Rift Valley. They either left voluntarily or were evicted as the settlers sought to replace their labour with men from other tribes. Many of these Kikuyu had lived all their lives on European land and had never even seen the reserves which were in theory their home.

Their families did not welcome these extra mouths to feed. Overcrowded and unwanted, a high proportion of the younger men stayed only a few weeks in the reserves before pushing on to the recently prohibited forests of the Aberdares and Mount Kenya. The forest was the traditional Kikuyu refuge in times of strife. Thousands of discontented souls gathered there, banding together in the name of Mau Mau.

Shock waves from the Ruck killings travelled far and wide. As always, it was the civilian population that bore the brunt. The Kikuyu had initiated the violence, but they were also the ones who suffered most from it. Every Mau Mau atrocity against a European over the next few years was noisily trumpeted abroad by a sensation-seeking press, but the final total of white victims turned out to be surprisingly small.

By the end of 1956, just thirty-two European civilians had been killed by Mau Mau and twenty-six wounded. Against this, perhaps 1,826 Africans – mostly loyalist Kikuyu – had been murdered by their own kind. A further 918 had been brutally wounded.

Far the worst atrocity of all by black against black took place at Lari, a predominantly loyalist settlement near Uplands, close to the edge of the Kikuyu Escarpment. On the night of 26 March 1953 upwards of one thousand Mau Mau fell on Lari with orders to massacre all the inhabitants loyal to the Government.

The terrorists set fire to the thatched roofs of the huts and cut down the occupants as they ran out. The killing was ruthless, demented and brutal. Dazed policemen sifting through the charred wreckage afterwards put the official death toll at eighty-four, two thirds of them women and children. The true figure was almost certainly much higher, because many of the bodies were impossible to recover, let alone piece together for identification.

Bill Howard Williams, who visited the scene of the massacre next day, described it thus: 'I saw the trunk of a child, all its arms and legs gone, and came upon one of the legs and an arm six yards away with teeth marks in it... A pretty girl of about twelve, had been most vilely used, her nature gaping: she had been slit open. I think this was, if anything, the most horrible sight of all; stark and staring bestiality in its most blatant form.'

Bestial and repugnant beyond belief. Nobody realised it more than the Kikuyu. For all the horror of that awful night, for all that it was the high-water mark of Mau Mau's power and reach, the Lari raid proved ultimately to be the movement's undoing. It tipped the scales of moderate Kikuyu opinion against the wild men of the tribe.

Mau Mau won the battle at Lari but lost the war. It was against the background of that atrocity that Jomo Kenyatta was found guilty less than a fortnight later.

Originally Mau Mau had been divided into active and passive wings. The active wing were the fighters, quite a few of them women. They had been formed into an elaborate forest-based army to mount raids against the European and loyalist populations.

The passive wing consisted of Kikuyu in the native reserves and Nairobi who took no part in the actual fighting. They supported the activists instead with a continual flow of supplies, information and whatever logistical help they could offer.

Any guerrilla movement that employs hit-and-run tactics with the support of at least part of the local populace is bound to hold the initiative in the short term. Such movements are extremely difficult to defeat. Yet the key to victory lay in the hearts and minds of the bulk of the population, and their hearts were not with Mau Mau.

Once the shock of Lari had sunk in, Mau Mau began to lose the propaganda war. The hard men were forced onto the defensive as the passive wing turned increasingly against them.

Lari was the turning point. After the massacre, the moderate Kikuyu who formed the majority of the tribe sided with the British against the terrorists. They rushed to join the Kikuyu Guard to defend their homes against terrorist attack. They denied food and shelter to the forest fighters, and they informed on them at every opportunity.

Moreover, those who had been bullied into taking the Mau Mau oath were now able to relieve themselves of their burden, because the Government had found a way of breaking the spell. It had cannily employed a body of Kikuyu wise men, Her Majesty's Witch Doctors, to administer a counter-oath purging the initiates of any allegiance to Mau Mau.

Many Kikuyu hurried to take the counter-oath. Many also took the precaution of being oathed regularly by both camps, just to be on the safe side. By backing both horses, they increased their chances of staying alive. Who could blame them for that?

The death blow to the offensive phase of Mau Mau was dealt in April 1954, when Government forces mounted Operation Anvil, a mammoth internal security drive to arrest and interrogate half the Kikuyu population of Nairobi. The aim was to destroy once and for all the forest army's communication links with sympathisers in the capital city.

The operation began at dawn on 24 April. Police and military units sealed off the escape routes from Nairobi and swooped on the Kikuyu trapped inside the net. By the end of phase one, about 30,000 Africans living and working in Nairobi had been screened by intelligence officers. More than 16,500 had been taken away and detained in concentration camps.

The intention of these camps was to rehabilitate the inmates over a number of years, cleanse them of their Mau Mau impurities, and eventually release them when they were no longer a danger to anyone. The reality was sometimes rather different. One or two of the camps were run so badly that they earned comparison with the concentration camps of Nazi Germany.

The worst one of all was Hola, a special category camp in the Coast province. In March 1959, almost five years after they had been arrested, eleven Hola detainees were beaten to death by unsupervised African guards after refusing to carry out work that they claimed would violate their Mau Mau oath.

A further twenty-two were injured. Until it was unmasked by the press, the Kenya Government tried to pretend that the men had died of drinking contaminated water on an excessively hot day.

But Hola was an isolated incident. With the native reserves lost to them, and Nairobi too after April 1954, the hard men of the movement were forced to withdraw permanently into the forests of the Aberdares and Mount Kenya.

Unlike later guerrilla fighters in other parts of Africa, they had no friendly border to retreat to after a raid, but the mountains were the next best thing. There were more than nine hundred square miles of forest on Mount Kenya and six hundred on the Aberdares. The forest was as good a place as any to hide from the British.

So active Mau Mau retreated to the Aberdares and Mount Kenya. They sheltered in forest so thick that it was usually impossible to see more than a few yards ahead. The men of Mau Mau knew exactly how to use the cover, particularly the old soldiers who had learned jungle craft from the British in Burma. The task for the British now was to go in there and winkle them out.

1. The judge afterwards received an *ex gratia* payment of £20,000 from the Kenya Government. Officially it was compensation for putting his own life at risk from Mau Mau reprisals

CHAPTER TWELVE

THE HUNT FOR KIMATHI

To the forests, at length, came the British army, having all but won the war on the broader acres outside. The problem now was how to defeat a highly resourceful, of necessity self-sufficient enemy, who knew the ground infinitely better than pink-kneed national servicemen from England. The Mau Mau in the forest were fighting on their own turf. They had no intention of being budged from an almost impregnable position.

The forest fighters were divided into two distinct kinds: hard core and soft core. Soft-core Mau Mau were the weak ones, often teenaged boys. They did as all their friends were doing because they thought a few weeks spent in the Badlands would impress the girls. They were the first to desert when life in the forest became unpleasant.

Hard-core Mau Mau were an entirely different proposition. They were not men to give up easily. Fanatics (according to the British), bravest of the brave (according to the Kikuyu), they believed in the rightness of their cause and were prepared to fight on to the bitter end.

Many of the hard core had committed capital crimes in the past. They knew that surrender or capture by the security forces could only lead to execution by hanging. They had nothing to lose by staying in the forest and defying the army to come in and get them.

Though on the defensive, they were by no means beaten. Discipline among the forest gangs was strict, punishment severe. The will to continue fighting remained as strong as ever, in the early days at least.

Each forest was ruled by a supreme commander whose authority was sacrosanct. On Mount Kenya the commander – until his capture by the

British – was Waruhiu Itote, better known as General China. He was a former lance corporal in the KAR who had seen active service in Burma.

In the Aberdares it was Dedan Kimathi Wachiuri, a powerful personality and charismatic leader. Kimathi was by far the most important of all the generals in the high command of the Land Freedom Army, destined to become a famous name in Kenya history.

Against these hard-core Mau Mau was ranged a rag-tag variety of military units, including a large contingent of troops from Britain who knew nothing of jungle fighting. Some of the British regiments were of very dubious quality. One battalion arrived in Kenya trained and equipped for the desert. They were totally unprepared for the misty, frost-covered ravines of the Aberdares.

Another battalion managed to ambush and kill its own commanding officer. Cases even arose of English troops buying the services of Kikuyu prostitutes with a rifle bullet – a trade originally dreamed up by Mau Mau to appeal to the black soldiers of the KAR.

Far and away the most successful white unit operating against Mau Mau was the Kenya Regiment, a small but highly specialised body of local Europeans who had been born and bred in the colony and understood Africans as far as any white man could.

The men of the Kenya Regiment were practical outdoor types, tough and resourceful, who worked in civilian life as farmers, white hunters and game wardens. They had learned to handle guns almost as soon as they could walk.

By Sandhurst standards they had little sense of discipline – and no one could be an officer in the regiment who had not first served in the ranks. Yet many of them were as much at home in the forest as Mau Mau. They could recognise the alarm call of the *ndete* bird for what it was, and knew how to read the signs when a Sykes monkey began to chatter. Some could follow a Mau Mau trail that was invisible to conscript soldiers from Perth, London or Exeter.

Because of their local knowledge, the men of the Kenya Regiment rarely went into action together as a single unit. Instead, they were allocated in ones and twos to advise and assist the more conventional regiments blundering through the forest in search of an ever-elusive enemy. Since they were local, the men of the regiment were also responsible for more than their share of unauthorised reprisals against the Mau Mau who fell into their hands.

Against the backdrop of the Ruck murders and the Lari massacre, prisoners who stubbornly refused to break their Mau Mau oath were sometimes tortured for information or 'shot while trying to escape'. Such behaviour was the exception rather than the rule, but it should not have happened, even if inevitable in the midst of a brutal war.

The incidents were greatly exaggerated by Mau Mau. Illegal reprisals were quickly investigated by the authorities, so it became a Mau Mau tactic to make false allegations as a way of delaying the British advance. Commanding officers of British units routinely ordered their troops in writing to avoid doing anything that might give rise to an allegation of impropriety, no matter how far-fetched or unreliable.

At first, the war against Mau Mau in the forest had very little sense of direction. The army was, literally, feeling its way. For a long time the RAF dominated military thinking with its theory that the best way to destroy Mau Mau was to bomb their hideouts in the forest. A squadron of Lincoln bombers made regular sorties over the Aberdares to unload a cargo of high explosive onto the unsuspecting wild life below.

The bombs made large holes in the ground and tore huge gaps in the ears of enraged elephants, which became nervous and unpredictable and a danger to Mau Mau, British soldiers and game rangers alike for years to come. Nevertheless, the RAF insisted that the bombing was useful. It emerged later that the air force was making a lot of money out of dropping obsolete bombs while charging the Kenya Government the full cost of new ones.

At ground level, initial attempts to make contact with Mau Mau did not meet with much success. Usually the enemy would disappear long before the clumsy British had thrashed into view. When Mau Mau did stay, it was to inflict casualties.

In one such encounter Major Lord Wavell of the Black Watch, son of the war hero, was killed. His death prompted the British public to sit up for the first time and take notice of this Mau Mau tribe, or whatever it was.

Gradually, however, the army began to get the measure of the situation. By trial and error it decided that the best way to make contact with its shadowy enemy, to get right in among Mau Mau, was to organise what British officers termed a 'grouse drive' – because that is exactly what it was.

A section of forest would be earmarked for the drive. At one end a company of British troops armed with rifles and Bren guns would quietly take up ambush positions in a carefully chosen stop line. From the other end would fan out an army of grouse beaters in a U formation designed to encircle any Mau Mau in the intervening forest and drive them forward onto the waiting line of guns.

At a given signal the beaters would surge ahead, shouting, screaming, banging drums, rattling spears against shields, ready to kill any flushed-out terrorist who attempted to double back between them.

Sometimes the beaters would be other British soldiers. More often, they were chosen from the nearby African population. They might be Wakamba tribesmen with bows and poison-tipped arrows that could bring down an elephant in a quarter-of-a-mile run, or they might be members of the Kikuyu Guard, wearing yellow headbands to distinguish them from the desperate Mau Mau who would try to mingle with them in the forest to avoid destruction. Or they could be women.

For one sweep, the District Officer at Meru organised a line of 70,000 villagers, mostly women with pangas, to cut an enormous swathe through the forest and shred any guerrilla foolish enough to wander into their path. Others recruited Masai warriors for a Government-sanctioned opportunity to attack their traditional Kikuyu enemies in the traditional way, with spears and the short two-edged stabbing sword called *simi*.

The Masai arrived fully got up for war with buffalo-hide shields and tall rippling headdresses of ostrich plume and lion mane. The red ochre of their faces was streaked with blue clay and lime. They carried iron war rattles and wore leggings of black and white colobus-monkey fur.

The night before a grouse drive they held a war dance in the firelight, nerve-jumping themselves into a state of excitement for the first legitimate forays against the Kikuyu since the days of Richard Meinertzhagen half a century before. They were burning to wash their spears in Kikuyu blood the way their forefathers had always done.

In the event, the Masai proved to be of little use in the mountains. Too proud to carry any equipment – that was a porter's job – they disliked the cold at high altitude and felt sorry for themselves when everyone else settled down to sleep under a warm blanket that they had brought with them. The warriors performed much better during anti-terrorist operations on the plains.

It wasn't long before the first of the Mau Mau began to quit. The soft core led the way, the swaggering poseurs with little stomach for the fight. They took advantage of Government surrender pamphlets dropped by air to turn themselves in and suffer a period of detention for their sins.

The soft core abandoned the forest with hardly a backward glance, and were little regretted by their tougher brethren. But hard core, too, were eventually whittled down in numbers.

Some were killed by the army, some by the bomb-happy wild life, some died in gang squabbles and others of privation or disease. Towards the end, Darwin's theory of survival of the fittest ensured that those Kikuyu who remained alive in the forest were the ones best equipped to cope with an existence bordering on the animal.

Latter-day Mau Mau were a far cry from the men who had first entered the forest three or four years previously. Their bodies were lean and hard, scarred all over, their hair shoulder length, matted and ridden with lice. Their machine-made clothes had long since fallen to pieces, to be replaced by animal skins sewn together with ligament or creeper.

These Mau Mau lived off wild honey, nettles, roots and whatever animals they could trap. When they moved through the forest, it was on the sides of their feet to avoid leaving footprints. They were instantly alert to every strange animal noise, every sudden change in the tempo of jungle life.

Few of them, perhaps only one in ten, carried guns. The rest were armed simply with pangas, knives and strangling cord. Continual harassment from the security forces had reduced these tattered remnants of a once numerous army to a desperate state. For all that, though, they were still highly dangerous, still a force to be reckoned with.

Around this time the hard core began to step up the gravity of the Mau Mau oath in a bid to retain discipline among the forest gangs. One or two gangs are reported to have used menstrual blood and semen in their ceremonies, arguing that an oath repugnant is an oath redoubled.

There is evidence too that human sacrifices took place. In October 1954 a gang attacked the Nyeri farm of Arundel Gray Leakey. He was a cousin of L. S. B. Leakey and the father of the first Kenyan to win a (posthumous) VC during the Second World War.

Gray Leakey was a blood brother of the Kikuyu tribe. The gang killed his wife and kidnapped the old man. Months later it transpired that he had been forced to take part in an oathing ceremony and then buried alive as a sacrifice to the Kikuyu god Ngai to bring victory to Mau Mau.

One of the most curious developments of this period of the Emergency was the use of captured Mau Mau as informers against their onetime forest comrades. Nobody knows quite why, but a remarkably high proportion of captured Kikuyu were persuaded to go back into the forest and infiltrate the gangs by pretending that they were still Mau Mau.

The purpose of this infiltration was either to obtain information about the gang's future intentions, or simply to kill them when their defences were relaxed.

This use of pseudo-terrorists was not original. The idea had been tried out before in Palestine and Malaya and was later used in Rhodesia, but never with the success it achieved in Kenya. Opinion varies as to why so many Kikuyu should have agreed to act as pseudo-terrorists. They were not offered any amnesty for their past activities.

Since the Kikuyu are often loyal to a person rather than an abstract idea, they might have been won over by the particularly persuasive white Kenyans who dealt with them. Many had borne the hard life in the forest in the belief that Mau Mau was winning the war outside, only to have their confidence sorely shaken when shown that this was not so. Or maybe they cooperated simply because pseudo-terrorism offered a chance to retain their pride in themselves as fighting men.

Whatever the reason, the use of pseudo-terrorists played a significant part in reducing the numbers of Mau Mau still at large in the forest. As the numbers grew thinner, however, the law of diminishing returns began to apply.

By definition, those who had surrendered and become pseudo-terrorists were weaker than those who had not. After a while, the pseudo teams operating in the Aberdares began to report a distinct falling-off in their rate of success.

The pseudos were not as tough and determined as the genuine article. They were faltering from lack of direction. In short, what they needed was firm, decisive leadership to guide them when they came face to face with the enemy.

Faced with this challenge, several Europeans came up simultaneously with what was beyond question the most imaginative and bizarre idea of the entire Emergency: to disguise themselves as terrorists and accompany their men into the forest to make contact with genuine Mau Mau.

At first glance the idea seems incredible. To a casual observer, the chances of a white man successfully passing himself off as a Kikuyu ought to be remote in the extreme. Yet that is exactly what happened.

The notion of dressing up as a native and sitting round the camp fire to eavesdrop on the enemy's plans may sound like a stunt out of the *Boys' Own Paper*, but it could not have been more serious to the tiny band of young Europeans who undertook just such a series of missions in an attempt to bring the war to a speedy conclusion.

The young men knew perfectly well that if they were discovered they would have no chance of coming out alive. They would suffer dreadfully before the mercy of death overtook them. Better to be torn to bits by wild dogs. They went ahead nevertheless, often vomiting physically from fear or breaking down into a nervous body rash afterwards.

It must have been an incongruous sight. Ten thousand feet up in the Aberdare mountains, young men, some not long out of English public schools – often with fair hair and blue eyes – sleeping alongside Mau Mau terrorists who would have cut them to pieces if they had known they were sharing their camp with a European. But the Mau Mau did not know. Often they could not believe it if they did find out.

To a large extent the success of these operations depended on surprise. Since Mau Mau did not expect to find a white man among them, they did not look for one. Most sorties took place in the dark, with the white man keeping well in the background and all the talking being done by one of his Kikuyu pseudos. The European's role was to stiffen the other's resolve simply by being there.

He was always elaborately disguised. He wore Mau Mau clothing and took care to ensure that his skin was blackened to the exact shade of a Kikuyu.

Since this made his eyes stand out like organ stops, he yellowed them down to an African texture with a watery solution of potassium permanganate. For a hairpiece, he discovered by trial and error that there was no substitute for a wig cut from the head of a dead terrorist.

If the aim of the sortie was to gather information, the pseudo-gang could find out what it wanted and be safely out of the forest by daybreak. If it was a killing expedition, they would lie awake until the small hours and then fall on their hard-core neighbours at the hour just before dawn when resistance would be at its lowest.

Sometimes they killed so many that it proved impossible to carry the bodies down the mountain. In that case they would cut off only the hands and put them in a sack to be identified later by fingerprint experts, leaving the rest of the corpse to be devoured by hyenas.

It was a grisly, unpleasant business. Nobody liked doing it. But they were fighting hard-core Mau Mau on their own terms, and they believed they were doing right. One European pseudo, an old Etonian, felt so badly about it that he adopted a Kikuyu baby orphaned in a forest action and brought it up as his own child.

Since the use of white pseudos was for obvious reasons a closely kept secret, blacked-up Europeans attempting to return to base through the outskirts of the forest frequently found themselves being chased by the Kikuyu Guard or orthodox British army patrols who had mistaken them for Mau Mau.

Not surprisingly, the first thing many of them needed when they changed out of their guerrilla rig and re-entered the outside world was a drink. So they took themselves off in dinner jackets to the Muthaiga Club.

There they could sit quietly in a corner and listen to army officers or beer-gripping Kenya cowboys waving six shooters and expounding noisily about the number of Mickey Mice (the term for Mau Mau when Africans might be listening) they had shot up recently in the Badlands.

In time, Mau Mau grew wise to the ways of the pseudos. They began to lift up the shirts of black strangers in the forest to check out their true colours. Nobody was more pleased than the whites when at length the word was passed for them to stop disguising themselves as Kikuyu.

The forest war was almost over by then. Towards the end of 1955, only one Mau Mau leader of any standing still remained at liberty. He was the supreme commander of the Land Freedom Army in the Aberdare mountains. His name was Field Marshal, later self-styled Prime Minister, Dedan Kimathi.

The legends which had grown up around Kimathi were remarkable. As a boy of eleven he had received the dying blessing of his blind grandmother, who sprinkled a goat's horn of water on his forehead and chose him to be the leader of the family. Kimathi interpreted her blessing as a sign from the god Ngai that he should also assume leadership of the whole Kikuyu tribe.

From the very beginning he had possessed an unusually dominant personality, guaranteeing him a prominent place among the Kikuyu of his age group. After a succession of lacklustre civilian jobs and a brief spell in the British army, he had become local branch secretary of KAU and a leading oath administrator in the Ol Kalou and Thomson's Falls area.

Shortly after the declaration of the Emergency, Kimathi had been arrested in his home location of Tetu, near Nyeri. He had succeeded in escaping from his cell and making his way into the Aberdares, where he was soon followed by thousands of Kikuyu recruits to the forest army.

Among these recruits, Kimathi gained a reputation for invincibility and supernatural powers that put him in a class of his own above the other generals in the forest. It was popularly supposed, for instance, that a huge boulder at the end of a track cut by the Royal Engineers had been placed there by Kimathi to prevent them advancing any further into the forest.

Some people believed that he had administered the Mau Mau oath to the buffalo and rhino of the Treetops salient to turn them against the European soldiers quartering the area. Others asserted that he could change prosperous European ranchland into a desolate swamp. It was well known that a single dark look from Kimathi was enough to turn a brave Kikuyu into a quivering wreck waiting only for death, such was the commanding power of his personality.

Trapped in the Aberdare mountains, prevented from communicating with the outside world by a booby-trapped and well patrolled elephant ditch dug around the forest perimeter, Dedan Kimathi and his ramshackle band of followers no longer posed any kind of military threat to the security forces.

They remained a unique danger, all the same. Kimathi's was the one name that still meant anything to the scattered remnants of Mau Mau.

Until he was killed or captured, he would always be a rallying point for those who still adhered to the Mau Mau oath. He was living proof that the movement was not yet done for. It was imperative therefore that he should be picked up at the earliest opportunity.

As the short rains of November 1955 drew to a close, a top priority order was issued to the security forces from Government House. In essence it consisted of just two words: 'Get Kimathi'.

The man selected for this task was twenty-eight-year-old Ian Henderson, a superintendent in the Kenya Police and a second-generation white highlands settler. His Scots father farmed coffee just outside Nyeri, not more than a few hundred yards from Treetops in the Aberdare forest.

Like Dedan Kimathi, seven years his senior, Ian Henderson had been born and bred in the Nyeri area and knew the Aberdares intimately as his childhood playground. There being few other European children in the neighbourhood, Henderson grew up with African playmates as friends. He was one of only a handful of Britons in Kenya who could speak fluent Kikuyu.

This was not so much lack of application by the British as because Kikuyu is one of the world's most complicated and tortuous languages. Its free use of the double negative and *double entendre* had been a major stumbling block at the trial of Jomo Kenyatta, where it had proved impossible to establish for certain whether speeches made by the accused man were actually for or against Mau Mau.

But Henderson understood Kikuyu. He was an excellent policeman and knew the tribe like few other white men. If anybody could track down Kimathi, he could.

Leaving aside the rights and wrongs of the issue, the story of Ian Henderson's hunt for Kimathi must rank as one of the most fascinating escape and evasion tales ever told. Here were two strong men of indomitable will ranged against each other.

On Henderson's side were deployed all the sophisticated machines and weapons of modern war: aeroplanes, armoured cars, loudspeakers, radio sets, sub-machine guns, trained manpower, a fully staffed ops room, everything.

Working for Kimathi were his natural allies of the forest: difficult terrain, thick bush, neurotic *ndete* birds, angry pachyderms and a host of jungle aids to concealment. The Aberdares consisted of six hundred square miles of mixed forest, bamboo and moorland, most of it penetrable only on foot.

Kimathi consisted of just one man, an expert at bushcraft. He simply had to lose himself in the jungle to evade capture. Even with the vast back-up resources at his disposal, it looked as if Henderson had an impossible job ahead of him.

He began by attempting to make contact with a member of Kimathi's gang. Kimathi had a personal bodyguard of some fifty Kikuyu. Together with his girlfriend Wanjiru, they had been with him in the Aberdares for more than three years.

Henderson's idea was to capture some of these men and persuade them to lead the security forces back to Kimathi before the gang leader noticed they were missing and moved his camp.

The scheme was beset with complications, but Henderson could think of no better way to go about it. Past attempts to ensnare Kimathi had included grouse drives, cordon and search operations, efforts to starve him into the open and a plan to lure him towards an ambushed food supply.

There had even been a psychological operation involving coloured smoke grenades and tape-recorded voices to convince him he was being chased by devils. None had met with success.

To put out feelers towards Kimathi's people, Henderson persuaded a surrendered terrorist to write three identical letters to 'The People in the Forest' calling on them to give themselves up. He arranged for the letters to be left in three separate parts of the forest.

One was to be placed in a disused Mau Mau hideout, another in an abandoned Mau Mau food store. The third was to be left beside the rock with which Kimathi was supposed to have outwitted the Royal Engineers.

Then Henderson tape-recorded a six-second message in Kikuyu giving the whereabouts of the letters, but not their content. The message would be broadcast over the Aberdares by a loudspeaker attached to a light aeroplane. It could not be longer than six seconds, because that was all a listener on the ground would hear while the aircraft was overhead.

Provided his curiosity was aroused by the sky message, it seemed likely that Kimathi or one of his junior commanders would send an expendable guerrilla to one of the three points to collect the letter and find out what it said. When the gang member arrived, Henderson would be waiting for him.

That was the plan, but it did not work. Three bull elephants prevented Henderson from planting one of his three letters. Of the other two, one was eaten by a school of Sykes monkeys and the second was captured by a unit of Royal Engineers who bore it in triumph to the police at Nyeri. Henderson was back to square one. He still had to throw a six before he could start.

To his surprise, somebody threw it for him. Two Mau Mau who had heard the sky message made it their business to get in touch with Henderson. They left a message for him in a cleft stick at the edge of the forest. The message named a time and a place high up the mountain where he could meet them if he wished.

The meeting took place with much hesitation on both sides. Each suspected they were walking into an ambush. Only after Henderson and the two men had talked together in Kikuyu for three hours did they begin to relax and warm to each other.

The men's names were Gati and Hungu. Though not members of his gang, both lived in mortal fear of Kimathi.

A long time ago, Kimathi had sentenced Hungu to eighty lashes with a *kiboko* hide whip for the serious offence of having sex with a female guerrilla when not a privileged leader. Rather than face this punishment, Hungu had chosen to escape. The penalty for escape was death.

Gati's only crime was to be a friend of Hungu, but both knew they would be executed on the spot if Kimathi ever caught up with them. Hence their approach to Henderson.

Using Gati and Hungu as the nucleus of his team, Henderson gradually built up a force of more than one hundred hard-core Mau Mau who, for one reason or another, had fallen out with Kimathi and were willing to go back into the Aberdares to hunt him down. Europeans would not do for this operation. Only poachers turned gamekeepers could hope to get near Kimathi.

Henderson's first step was to re-establish the credibility of Gati and Hungu in the eyes of the forest gangs by building them up into anti-Government heroes. He broadcast a message from his aeroplane that the authorities would pay a reward of £600 to anyone giving information leading to their capture – a ploy he at first kept secret from Gati and Hungu, men of nervous disposition both, for fear of upsetting them.

The effect was magical. Within a few hours Hungu had been transformed from unlicensed fornicator to Mau Mau hero (first class). Kimathi passed the word that he was willing to anoint the two of them with animal fat on their foreheads.

But how to reach Kimathi? No one knew his movements, nor would anyone hazard a guess where he might be found. All that was known for certain was that Kimathi and his gang were now shifting camp virtually every night to avoid discovery.

Henderson's teams of ex-Mau Mau made many sorties into the forest but for a long time drew nothing but a blank. They did not get their first real lead until the long rains of April and May 1956.

The pattern of life in the Aberdare mountains changes abruptly with the onset of rain. Almost overnight the forest seems to shoot towards the sky as the vegetation takes a new hold on life and everything green begins to grow again at a furious rate. From high in the bamboo belt, migratory herds of elephant descend to the lush grazing of the mixed forest, churning the game trails beneath their feet into a squelching slip-sliding morass of deep mud.

Streams overflow their banks, hailstorms cover the earth with a pebbled crust. Warthog and bushbuck rush back and forth trying to avoid the thunder, associated at that time with RAF bombing raids. Familiar noises vanish and nothing can be heard but the rain. To take account of the new conditions, patterns of game behaviour alter considerably. So, too, did the behaviour of Mau Mau.

Knowing that it would be difficult to conceal their tracks on wet ground, Kimathi's gang prepared for the rainy season by collecting as much food as they could and storing it in secret caves and hollow tree trunks. They lifted their game snares and set them up again closer to their hideouts. Such a hideout would never be near a large river, because the rain-swollen torrent would make it impossible to hear the approach of an enemy.

Neither would the hideout be in a part of the forest where rain or hail might flatten the undergrowth, or anywhere near the salt licks and *muondwe* patches frequented by elephant or rhino. Nor would it be near the *magomboki* shrub, because *magomboki* grows so thick and matted during the rainy season that buck and other small animals cannot pass through it, and the trapping will be bad.

A good hideout, on the other hand, would be surrounded by a thick bed of leaves and bark enabling a terrorist to check his traps or visit his food store without leaving footprints. It would also be close to the bamboo belt, because bamboo wet or dry is an ideal firewood that never gives out smoke to alert a nearby enemy.

Using this information, Henderson and his team slowly built up a picture of Kimathi's thought processes. They were able to narrow down the search area to a strip of forest covering about fifty square miles in the eastern part of the Aberdares towards the Treetops salient.

Treetops itself had been burned down by Mau Mau soon after the Queen's visit. Since the Emergency, the area had been prohibited to tourists and all unauthorised personnel. It now became the setting for the last act of the Emergency, a dramatic duelling ground for Henderson and Kimathi in a private battle of wits that could end only in defeat for one of them.

Henderson was beginning to get close. Mingled with the spoor of a buffalo herd on a muddy river bank, his men discovered the tracks of a sizeable gang. One of the gang had been wearing a pair of sandals cut from the tyre of a motor car.

Henderson knew that very few Mau Mau in the forest possessed such sandals. Among the few who did was Wambararia, Kimathi's brother.

A little later, Wambararia himself fell into Henderson's hands. A search of his possessions revealed a second stroke of luck. It was a letter from Kimathi to his brother giving details of a vivid dream he had had:

'As I was sleeping I felt someone hold my hand. I woke up and heard God say to me, "My son, come with me." I stood up, and Ngai took me by my right hand and we walked through a most beautiful forest where there were many red and yellow flowers and big birds with green wings.

'There were also many big rocks out of which clean springs were flowing. And Ngai took me to a *mugumu* tree which was bigger and higher than all the other *mugumu* trees in the forest, a tree which was like the father of all trees. And I rested my hand upon it. When I did that, Ngai spoke to me again and said, "This is my house in the forest, and here I will guard you."

'Then the tree came up out of the ground and went up into the clouds and I did not see it again. Then it rained very hard and I woke up a second time, but I could not remember where I had seen the tree. But from this I know that the house of Ngai is in this forest and it must be found and from now onwards no person shall pass a *mugumu* tree without praying, otherwise he will anger Ngai and be destroyed.'

A *mugumu* tree is a wild fig. It plays a major part in the religion of the Kikuyu tribe. It was under a *mugumu* tree at the foot of Mount Kenya that the nine daughters of Gikuyu and Mumbi — known elsewhere as Adam and Eve — met nine fine young men to father the nine clans of the tribe. A *mugumu* has an important role in the festival of circumcision and is held in wide respect by all Kikuyu. And by no one more than Kimathi.

As a result of his dream, he began to make pilgrimages to certain parts of the Treetops salient where large *mugumus* grew, in order to say his prayers and carry out sacrifices to Ngai.

By the first week of August, Henderson had successfully completed phase one of Operation Wild Fig, which was to plot on a map all the big *mugumu* trees in the Kimathi area of Treetops.

His teams had counted eighteen *mugumus*, of which ten could be ruled out for their purposes because the approaches to them were unsafe. Kimathi was a very cautious man. He would never risk exposing himself unnecessarily, not even for religious reasons. That left just eight.

Although Henderson did not find out until later, one *mugumu* in particular was to become Kimathi's favourite place of prayer. Taller and wider than the others, it must have conformed most closely to the one he had seen in his dream. He spent hours beneath its shelter, arms outstretched towards Mount Kenya, in close communion with Ngai the saviour. At peace with himself and, for a little while, with the world too.

Added to the *mugumus* were a number of Mau Mau letter boxes, natural hiding places used by the forest gangs to leave messages for each other. Henderson had identified one in a hollow beneath the roots of a large tree near Treetops, a second in a derelict beehive and a third in a hole in a rock.

His teams had also discovered a pair of food stores in which it was a safe bet that Kimathi would try to conceal wild honey or game caught in his traps.

In all, Henderson counted fourteen key points in the Treetops area. His ambush teams could lie in wait for their quarry in the certain knowledge that sooner or later Kimathi was bound to show up at one of them.

The final stages of the hunt for Kimathi took place in October 1956 against a backdrop of dark clouds over Mount Kenya heralding the imminent arrival of the short rains. Henderson put an outside time limit of two weeks on the operation. He calculated that after two weeks the forest would be so full of his men's tracks that Kimathi would almost certainly abandon it for ever.

The hunted man might move to another part of the Aberdares, or he might sneak across the Kikuyu reserve to the slopes of Mount Kenya. He might even take refuge in Ethiopia or Tanganyika.

Worse still, he might be driven to commit suicide – something he had often talked about – and so achieve a kind of immortality. It would be disastrous for Government propaganda if Kimathi simply disappeared without trace. His legend would survive him and continue to grow for ever.

Without Kimathi's body, living or dead, there could be no victory for Henderson. So Kimathi would have to be found.

He was found. Having divided his bodyguard into several smaller groups to avoid leaving a large trail, Kimathi spent the last few days of his freedom in the company of just one male Kikuyu, and his girlfriend Wanjiru.

While running away from a surprise attack by Henderson's men, he became separated from even these two, leaving Wanjiru to be taken alive by the enemy. For the first time in the forty months he had spent on the mountain, he was now utterly alone.

His most pressing problem was how to find enough food to keep himself alive. At the start he had possessed seven wire snares for trapping game, but all seven had been found and removed by Henderson's men.

They had cut his lifeline. He could eat wild nettles (removing only the lower leaves of the plant to leave no evidence of his passing) and he could drag a tree hyrax out of its hole by thrusting in a spliced stick and twisting it around the creature's fur, but for how long?

Without a vessel to hold water, he could not even boil and eat his buckskin clothes, as some Mau Mau had been forced to do. The dance was coming to an end. Kimathi could not afford to sit it out.

He turned his eyes towards the only source of supply that remained. He had no choice now but to leave the shelter of the Aberdares to seek food in the Kikuyu reserve.

Henderson and Kimathi both reached this conclusion simultaneously. From his prisoner Wanjiru, Henderson discovered the location of two points at which Kimathi was likely to attempt a crossing of the ditch separating forest from reserve. When the fugitive did indeed make his bid, the security forces were waiting for him.

In the early morning of 21 October 1956, while attempting to slip back into the Aberdares with food stolen from the reserve during the night, he was spotted by a patrol of six Kikuyu tribal police. One of them fired three shots and Kimathi fell, badly wounded in the thigh. The long chase was over at last.

Kimathi was taken in handcuffs to Nyeri prison hospital. There he came face to face for the first time with Ian Henderson, the man who had dominated his thoughts for the past ten months. Later, when his wound had healed, he faced trial by the Supreme Court of Kenya on a charge of unlawfully possessing a revolver.

Chief Justice Sir Kenneth O'Connor and three African assessors unanimously found him guilty. Kimathi was sentenced to death. He appealed, but the appeal was dismissed. In Nairobi prison, on 18 February 1957, Dedan Kimathi was hanged.

He has subsequently become a hero to the Kikuyu people, a martyr to the cause of independence and the most famous of all the freedom fighters who lost their lives in the struggle against colonial rule. Every emerging country needs a warrior figure to give it self-respect. In a country lamentably short of heroes, Kimathi is Kenya's choice.

Prominent streets are named after him in every town. He is the subject of numerous eulogistic books, poems and – to be honest – awful plays, all of them written in English, the language of the oppressor. Kimathi receives so much adulation that black Kenyans sometimes forget that, for all his martyrdom, Kimathi was a ruthless killer. All the people he killed were Kikuyu. He never hurt anyone white.

Part of the Kimathi legend stems from his mystical rapport with the god Ngai. During lengthy prayer sessions in the forest, Kimathi would make an offering of honey at the foot of his favourite *mugumu* tree, the one he had seen in his dream, where he believed Ngai lived.

The *mugumu* was well known to Henderson's men. They were afraid to go near it for fear of evil spirits – as indeed were the rest of Kimathi's Mau Mau. It was an enormous tree with a thick trunk standing imperious and alone, looming over the surrounding foliage like a church tower in a country town.

Ten feet above the ground, the tree's aerial roots splayed outwards into a catacomb of twisted archways of cathedral-like splendour, natural flying buttresses in a wooden frame of slanted sunlight and strong shadows. Truly, if the house of God existed, then this was it.

After Kimathi's capture, Henderson stood down his odd little army and called in the ambush teams which had been lying in wait around the *mugumu* trees and other key points in the Treetops salient. The last team to arrive back at base had a curious story to report.

They had been watching Kimathi's favourite sacrifice tree. According to them, as every Kenya schoolchild now knows, the *mugumu* had crashed to the ground within a few hours of Kimathi being caught.

But did it?

The geography of the Treetops salient has changed slightly since Kimathi's day. A new road has been cut through the forest from the national park gate along an old elephant trail to the Yasabara waterhole – the place of leeches – where The Ark game viewing lodge was opened at the end of 1969 to take the overflow of tourists from the new Treetops hotel.

Every afternoon a busload of chattering sightseers climbs the track, *en route* for a night of game spotting at The Ark, through forest once inhabited by Kimathi and his men. Not one tourist in a hundred notices the solitary *mugumu* tree standing erect and silent in a valley south of the track, less than two kilometres from The Ark. Maybe it fell, or maybe it did not, but of one thing local people are certain: that is the sacrifice tree of Dedan Kimathi.

With Kimathi's capture and execution the war against Mau Mau virtually came to an end. A few wild men remained in scattered pockets throughout the forest, either as fugitives from the British or ordinary criminals masquerading as Mau Mau, but they no longer posed a threat to anyone.

Life in Kenya soon returned to normal for the majority of the population. The Emergency was officially declared at an end in January 1960.

It had been an ugly war. Neither side emerged with much credit. The struggle cost £55,585,424 and the lives of perhaps 13,547 people, fewer than a hundred of them white. During the same period, more Europeans were killed in Nairobi traffic accidents than died at the hands of Mau Mau.

But the war was over and the British had won it, of that there could be no doubt. More than seven years of turmoil could now give way to peace and harmony again. For a while, anyway.

A month after the Emergency was officially brought to a close, the prime minister of Britain, Harold Macmillan, made a historic speech to the South African parliament in Cape Town.

Repeating a phrase he had used earlier in Ghana, he announced: 'The wind of change is blowing through this continent, and whether we like it or not this growth of national consciousness is a political fact – we must accept it and our national policies must take account of it.'

CHAPTER THIRTEEN
WIND OF CHANGE

Then, suddenly, it was all over.

Just over a year after the Emergency came to an end, African politicians were invited to join a multi-racial government. Three years later, they had led Kenya to full independence from Great Britain. Having won the war in the Aberdares, the settlers had lost it for good at the conference table.

The countdown to independence began in October 1959 with a reshuffle of the British cabinet following the Conservative triumph in the general election of that month. All over the white highlands, settlers had gathered around their wireless sets to hear the election results.

They listened with growing satisfaction to the news of a Tory landslide. A Conservative government back in power with a huge majority could only be good news for white Kenyans.

Their enthusiasm was redoubled when it was learned that the new Colonial Secretary was to be Iain Macleod, for Macleod's own brother lived in Kenya. That, the settlers assumed, was as good as having a hot line direct to Downing Street.

Now at last, they had their own man in the government, someone who would understand their particular problems and consider the Kenya question with sympathy. Or so they thought.

How wrong they were. Almost the first thing Macleod did on taking office was to set up a constitutional conference aimed at preparing Kenya for independence as quickly and as decently as possible. Up until then, 1975 had been regarded as the earliest conceivable date for independence.

But Macleod was a radical Tory – a bloody Communist, in the revised opinion of most settlers. He understood that the time had come for Britain to stop playing the imperial game and get out of Africa at top speed.

With the full approval of the cabinet, he tore up a whole sheaf of pledges given to European settlers by previous administrations. He made it clear that the 999-year-leased white highlands were henceforth to be opened to Africans. As for compensation, if anybody was going to reimburse the settlers for all the money they had poured into their farms, it certainly wouldn't be the British taxpayer.

In Westminster's view, a lifetime's endeavour in the highlands counted for nothing. Macleod was adamant about that. If the settlers didn't like his decision, they would just have to lump it.

The news was received by the settlers with incredulity. To them, a pledge was sacrosanct. They could not believe that a Conservative administration was preparing to abandon them without a second thought. The idea was inconceivable. For fifty years they had been screaming betrayal. Now, indeed, they had been betrayed.

The first of two constitutional conferences on the future of Kenya took place in London at Lancaster House during January 1960, just a few weeks before Harold Macmillan dropped his 'wind of change' bombshell in South Africa. It was attended by delegates from all Kenya's racial groups, including a large European contingent convinced that they were fighting for their very lives in the struggle to repel the black hordes.

As usual in Kenya politics, most delegations had the colour of their skin in common, but precious little else. The Africans managed to speak with one voice at the conference table, but in reality were divided into tribal factions: the dominant Kikuyu-Luo bloc was loathed and feared by politicians from other tribes. The Europeans too, at a time when they were isolated and unloved as never before, had split into rival camps.

Sir Michael Blundell led the New Kenya Group, a multi-racial party seeking a compromise solution that would make concessions to Africans while preserving safeguards for Europeans. He was opposed by the overwhelming majority of whites, who still belonged to the no sell-out party. No surrender on any terms was their creed. Their champion, though he did not reveal himself until later, was the Duke of Portland.

The Lancaster House conference got off to the worst possible start when the African delegation boycotted the opening plenary session in a show of strength designed to test the defences of the opposition.

It had been agreed that each delegation should be limited to one constitutional adviser, but the Africans now demanded two. They insisted that the second should be Peter Koinange, a close friend of Jomo Kenyatta, still detained at Lokitaung.

Koinange was widely held to be one of the brains behind Mau Mau. As such he was unacceptable to the other delegations, and also the Christian and loyalist Kikuyu. They cabled their strong disapproval from Nairobi.

A public row followed, during which Fleet Street newspapers commented that if Koinange was free to go anywhere in the United Kingdom, it was certainly odd that he should not be permitted to enter Lancaster House. Eventually a compromise was reached, allowing him into the building but not the conference.

The chief constitutional adviser to the Africans was Dr Thurgood Marshall. He was a black American lawyer, later to become a judge in the US Supreme Court. Before the conference, Marshall had irritated Kenya's white settlers by writing an anti-imperialist article in a Baltimore newspaper. He had accused the settlers of being colonial exploiters who had never even taken the trouble to learn the local language.

At one of the conference sessions therefore, Sir Michael Blundell formally tabled a motion for proceedings to be conducted in Swahili. The language was spoken fluently by all the Kenya Europeans present, but not by Thurgood Marshall.

Once the opening blows of the conference had been exchanged, the delegates quickly got down to the serious business of behind-the-scenes lobbying to secure the best deal possible for their respective interests. The Europeans in particular were seeking an assurance from Britain that settlers evicted from the white highlands would receive adequate compensation for a lifetime's work.

What emerged, after several weeks' hard bargaining, was bitter defeat for the whites and their virtual elimination as a political force in Kenya's affairs. The Africans did not win immediate independence or even full self-government, but they were promised a clear majority of seats in the Legislative Council – anathema to most Europeans.

On the all-important question of the white highlands, there were no concessions. Harold Macmillan refused to commit his government to buying out the settlers. He privately told Blundell that Britain was a poor country. If Kenya farmers felt unsure of their future, then so did the British with the threat of a nuclear war hanging over their heads.

It was an unattractive package that Blundell took back to Kenya to try to sell to the European community. Himself for many years a farmer in the white highlands, he held the view that black majority rule was inevitable and that the best thing to do, therefore, was to come to terms with it. That this opinion was not widely shared, he soon discovered.

The by now traditional riot took place at Nairobi airport when he returned from London. Loudspeakers cursed him for a traitor and emotional settlers swore that he had betrayed them. It looked for a moment as if violence might be done.

One man called him Judas and hurled a bag at his feet containing thirty 50-cent pieces of silver. Fighting a way through the hostile crowd, Blundell got close enough to declare that he would still be in Kenya long after the other man had left.

Worse was to follow. For the next two years Blundell and his family were subjected to a constant campaign of vilification and abuse as the settler population, noted more for their outdoor qualities than their intelligence, made it plain what they thought of any compromise with the Africans.

When he stood up on a platform to speak, Blundell was pelted with eggs and tomatoes. When he entered the Muthaiga Club, old friends pointedly turned their backs. Like homosexuals, he and his wife learned never to make the first advance. They would always wait for someone else to smile before gauging their response accordingly.

Yet independence could not be delayed. It was no use blaming Blundell for the political facts of life. Uganda to the north and Tanganyika to the south, neither of which had a settler community, were both to become independent soon. Kenya in the middle could not avoid going the same way.

The Duke of Portland resigned his neutral position as speaker of the Legislative Council to oppose Blundell, but was never able to mount anything more than a rearguard action. The plain truth was that the mother country was no longer prepared to support the settlers with the force of arms. There were too few of them to fight it out on their own.

Gradually they came to recognise the inevitable – albeit bitterly. Once they had got over the initial shock, they abandoned the idea of an armed uprising and turned their attention to more down-to-earth problems. Chief of these was how to persuade the British Government to underwrite their proposed exodus from the highlands.

Here their hand was strengthened by events in the Congo, which had received its independence from Belgium on 30 June 1960. What had followed was the most savage reign of terror against whites ever seen on the most savage of continents.

Stories were commonplace of massacre, cannibalism and multiple rape of nuns. Of those Belgians lucky enough to escape alive, many found their way to Nairobi as refugees *en route* for Europe. Their presence did nothing to convert the local white population to the merits of black rule.

Indeed, the spectre of an undisciplined African with a gun loomed large over the whole continent during 1960 and had a profound effect on political thinking in Britain. It became accepted at Westminster that if Kenya's whites were to stand aside and let the Africans take charge, they would need cast-iron assurances from the British Government first.

Two more factors undermined settler confidence in the latter half of 1960. The first was the execution by hanging of Peter Poole, a white man who had shot an African in cold blood. Of Poole's guilt there was never any question, although there was some doubt as to his sanity. But he was the first European in Kenya to be executed for killing a black. Local white opinion was appalled.

The other factor was the return to respectability of Jomo Kenyatta. If the settlers had been forced to swallow the idea of African rule, it was another thing entirely to expect them to accept Kenyatta. In their eyes, he was the architect of the Mau Mau movement and all its attendant horror.

The African delegation at the Lancaster House conference had demanded that Kenyatta be released to attend as their leader. Kenya's Governor, Sir Patrick Renison, had refused. When Kenyatta was named president of the newly formed Kenya African Nationalist Union, Renison refused again. He declined to register the political party until Kenyatta's name had been struck off.

He gave his reasons as follows:

'Jomo Kenyatta was the recognised leader of the non co-operation movement which organised Mau Mau. Mau Mau, with its foul oathing and violent aims, had been declared an unlawful society. He was convicted of managing that unlawful society and being a member of it. He appealed to the Supreme Court and the Privy Council. In these three separate courts his guilt was established and confirmed. Here was the African leader to darkness and death.'

The Africans wanted him, nevertheless. The days were coming to an end when white men could tell Africans what was good for them. While still in detention, Kenyatta was permitted to give a press conference. He surprised the settlers by making a moderate speech which stressed the need for all races to live together in harmony.

He had long since served the full term of his prison sentence. In the changing political climate, he could not justifiably be held in custody any longer. On 14 August 1961, nine years after his arrest, Jomo Kenyatta was allowed to go home.

For the more excitable elements among the settler population, Kenyatta's release was the last straw. Making plans to dispose of their farms as best they could, they packed up their belongings and prepared to leave the colony for ever in order to start all over again somewhere else. Australia, maybe or Rhodesia – or Canada or South America.

Some had reason to believe that they would not be welcome in an independent Kenya. Others swore that they would never take orders from a black at any price. Among the first to go were the Afrikaner community from Eldoret, Boers whose grandparents had trekked up to the Uasin Gishu plateau in wagon trains between 1908 and 1912.

Older men and women among the Boers still thought of Eldoret as Sixty Four, the name of the town when it had been no more than a numbered block of land on a Government map. As children, they had climbed the steep western wall of the Rift Valley alongside creaking wagons pulled by oxen which slipped and sank into the mud so frequently that vehicles at the rear of the column had taken four days to cover seven miles.

Sometimes it had proved easier to take the wagons to pieces and carry them bit by bit up the escarpment. When the Afrikaners eventually reached the promised land at the top, they had built houses on the empty highbush from stone quarried by themselves. They had lived by ploughing the land with harrows made out of acacia and olive wood, tied together with thongs cut from strips of dried kongoni skin.

The middle of 1961, however, saw the same trek in reverse. The destination this time was South Africa, almost two thousand miles away. Few of the Afrikaners had ever been there. None thought of it as home, but where else could they go? Holland?

As before, the safari was organised and controlled by the Dutch Reformed Church, whose predikants exercised a Moses-like grip over their congregation. One or two of the ox-carts from the original trip still survived to retrace their journey. Most had given way to a curious assortment of cars, lorries, tractors, trailers and caravans which duly formed up into a column heading south for what was – to date – the last great trek of the Afrikaner people.

Nor were the Boers the only ones to leave. As independence day drew closer (the Swahili word for it was *Uhuru*, accompanied by the two fingers of a V sign), the trickle of Europeans leaving the country broke into a flood. Before long, they were pulling out at the rate of seven hundred a month.

This was nothing short of disastrous. In the whole colony the total population of whites was only forty thousand, of whom one in ten was actively engaged in farming. These white farmers produced eighty per cent of Kenya's exports, paid almost all its taxes, and at 1962 prices distributed £10 million in wages alone to African labour.

In addition, injections of settler capital over the past half century had developed the highlands to the extent that every square mile of European land yielded £4,150 against an African's £1,180. If the settlers continued to evacuate the country in such great numbers, taking their capital and management resources with them, Kenya's economy would fall apart by the day of *Uhuru*. For the good of the country, therefore, it was essential that they be persuaded to stay.

Kenyatta rose to the occasion. Voted in as the country's first prime minister after the elections of May 1963, he immediately set out to woo the European farmers and convince them that they had an assured place in the new Kenya. He pointed out that the white highlands were not going to be taken over wholesale, not all at once.

One million acres was the initial target. The land would be purchased by African farmers with grants of more than £13,500,000 put up by the British Government – which had reluctantly come round to the idea – the World Bank and the Commonwealth Development Corporation.

Africans were not simply going to seize white land. They would pay the proper price for it, independently assessed, all fair, square and above board. Kenyatta stressed that those settlers not immediately affected would be encouraged to stay on their property and carry on farming for the foreseeable future. The country needed them. It was as simple as that.

To get his message across, Kenyatta chose to address a meeting of four hundred settlers in Nakuru, long the unofficial capital of the white highlands. The meeting was chaired by Lord Delamere. His father had many times harangued angry gatherings in the same hall.

When Kenyatta rose to speak, he was faced by a hostile and sceptical audience which would cheerfully have shot him a few years back. The settlers knew full well that his new mood of conciliation was dictated by economic necessity rather than love for them. Kenyatta made the gesture, all the same.

He appealed for both black and white to bury the past, especially the recent past, and turn their eyes to the future. 'We want you to stay and co-operate with us,' he told his audience. 'Let us join hands and work together for the betterment of Kenya.'

When, at length, he sat down, it was the settlers' turn to rise to their feet. To their own amazement as much as anyone else's, they gave this hated leader to darkness and death a standing ovation and heard themselves shouting 'Harambee!', the Swahili for 'Let's all pull together'.

The whites had been won round. Kenya was their country too. The settlers loved the land as much as anyone else. If there was still going to be room for them in the highlands, then they would gladly stay.

After sixty-eight years of British rule, *Uhuru* came to Kenya on 11 December 1963 at a ceremony in Nairobi attended by more than 250,000 people. Chief among the guests was the Duke of Edinburgh, representing the Queen. She was to remain head of state for twelve more months before Kenya declared itself a Commonwealth republic with Kenyatta as president for life.

The streets of Nairobi were fully decked out in bunting for the occasion, especially in the newly renamed Kenyatta Avenue. Earlier in the week, the statue of the colonial leader Lord Delamere had been quietly removed from the former Delamere Avenue and taken away by his family.

Up-country too, independence was celebrated with carnivals and fetes. Settlers ordered sheep and cattle to be slaughtered for a feast. The town of Nakuru was reported to have sold out of footballs as the farmers organised competitions for their workers.

From the Aberdares and Mount Kenya, a band of twenty-five Mau Mau generals travelled to Nairobi to take an honoured part in the *Uhuru* celebrations. They were the vanguard of a guerrilla army that would emerge after independence under the general amnesty of 6 November.

Spruce in British-style officers' uniforms, the former terrorists were invited to Government House for the Governor's last garden party. They mingled uneasily with the recently promoted black officers of the King's African Rifles, now to be renamed the Kenya Rifles.

That night they went to the stadium for the *Uhuru* ceremony and were given prominent seats thirty yards to the left of the Royal Box. When they distracted the attention of the photographers from Prince Philip, the police discreetly headed them off and kept them out of the way. This was not Mau Mau's evening. If their moment was to come, it had not come yet.

The British, though, had had their day. Now that they were going, Kenyatta could afford to be magnanimous. He held no grudge against the British for keeping him in detention. Years later, he admitted to Sir Evelyn Baring that he would have done exactly the same if he had been in the Governor's shoes.

'We do not forget the assistance and guidance we have received through the years from people of British stock,' he declared at the independence ceremony. 'Administrators, businessmen, farmers, missionaries and many others. Our law, our system of government and many other aspects of our daily lives are founded on British principles and justice and the ties between our two countries now that we move into a new relationship as two sovereign countries within the Commonwealth will be strengthened.'

The actual moment of independence was preceded by a parade and three hours of tribal dancing. As midnight drew near, all eyes turned to the Union

Jack being lowered slowly to earth for the last time. When it touched the ground the floodlights went out and for two minutes the stadium lay in complete darkness.

Then the lights flashed back on and a quarter of a million people roared approval as the black, red and green flag of Kenya fluttered into life above the new country. The Africans were free at last. From now on they would be in command of their own destiny.

From that moment too, a new Swahili word entered the vocabulary of the Nairobi memsahibs imperiously ringing silver handbells to summon their servants. The word was *tafadhali*. It meant please.

EPILOGUE

For a moment it looked as if a terrible mistake had been made. For a moment it looked as if the prophets of doom had been justified in forecasting the collapse of law and order and civilised values as soon as the British had gone.

Within days of independence, gangs of Mau Mau came swaggering out of the forest. They revealed themselves to the local populace not so much liberators as bully boys who intended to sit in the bwana's chair and give out the orders from now on.

Ian Henderson, the policeman who had hunted down Dedan Kimathi, was deported at short notice. A state of Emergency was declared in the country's northern region as bandits from Somalia laid siege to the disputed strip of Kenya territory no longer protected by the forces of Great Britain.

The new Kenya army mutinied in an attempt to take over the Government. In the ex-white highlands, the new owners of European land sent their womenfolk to cut down for firewood trees planted by whites forty years earlier as a windbreak against soil erosion.

In time, however, the ship of state rode out this early storm and settled down onto an even keel, albeit at reduced speed. Mau Mau quickly discovered that independent Kenya was not going to be all jam and driving on both sides of the road.

A somewhat theatrical ceremony was staged at Nyeri football stadium, at which the returning freedom fighters were supposed to surrender their weapons and pledge allegiance to the Kenya flag in front of a singing and dancing crowd of fifty thousand Kikuyu. Several hundred armed Mau Mau duly appeared for the ceremony.

On closer inspection, many turned out to be common criminals. Others were shysters who had slipped into the forest a few weeks earlier – just as

Frenchmen had rushed to join the Resistance after the Normandy landings – so as to emerge in triumph and claim their share of the land and cash payments being given out to the conquering heroes.

Many of the real Mau Mau had been living in the forest so long that they found it impossible to revert to a more normal way of life. A hoodlum named Field Marshal Mwariama, whose gang held the area of Meru in thrall, received worldwide publicity when BBC television filmed him throwing his arms around a less than ecstatic Jomo Kenyatta.

Within three months, Mwariama had been sentenced to five years' gaol for intimidation. Soon afterwards his gang retreated back inside the forest after a gun battle with police. If there was to be a special place in Kenya for ex-Mau Mau, they would have to learn to behave first, like anyone else.

Nor would the army have things all its own way. The coup attempted by elements of the Kenya Rifles was swiftly crushed by British troops called in by Kenyatta. On the face of it, the use of white colonial troops to contain his own people looked like a humiliation for Kenyatta, but it was a necessary move. The army kept well out of politics thereafter.

Units of the British army – notably the Special Air Service, who could be seen wandering mysteriously around Nairobi carrying passes signed personally by Kenyatta – also took part in the frontier war against Somali infiltrators, a running battle that continued intermittently until a ceasefire was agreed in October 1967. In the age of Al-Qaeda and Muslim extremism, relations along the Somali border continued to be fraught.

An equally serious problem was the dismemberment of the white highlands into tiny, uneconomical smallholdings as the large European farms were divided up among their new owners. The move was economic lunacy, but politically essential. Every African had to have a patch of ground to call his own. If that meant cutting down rain forests, pulling up fences and dispersing pedigree herds, then so be it.

Under the new regime, one sixty-acre farm on the Kinangop which had produced £8,000 a year under white ownership was shared out among four Kikuyu families. Each family grew enough to feed themselves and show a surplus of £40. The total cash income, one fiftieth of the previous figure, provided no taxable revenue for the Government.

Another example of collective folly must have been repeated a thousand times during the first heady year of independence. White farmers on the Kinangop had irrigated their land with water piped from a spring and sold to each farmer on a meter at three shillings a thousand gallons. Rather than pay this colonial imposition, the Kikuyu cut the meter and left the water flowing free.

So much was wasted that the settlement officer disconnected the supply. The Kikuyu thereupon reverted to ancient custom and sent their women two miles with a pot on their heads to fill up at the stream, just as they always had before the British arrived.

A measure of sanity returned after a while as the Kenya Government stepped in to prevent further disasters. Often, in its treatment of Kikuyu squatters, it proved no less firm than the colonial power. Land grabs by Kikuyu businessmen with political connections were far more rapacious that anything the British had ever done. 'Four legs good, two legs better', as George Orwell observed in *Animal Farm*.

Land continued to be a major concern. Kenya had a population of eight million in 1963, many millions higher than it had been at the beginning of the century, when there had been plenty of spare land for all.

By 2013 however, the population had jumped to 40 million, a five-fold increase in 50 years for which the Africans had only themselves to blame. In a country without a welfare system, far too many of them saw a large family as their best hope for security in their old age.

But the land could never sustain so many on smallholdings. White farmhouses often became home to three or four African families after independence. The new owners cooked indoors on open fires, using the floorboards for firewood, and planted maize across the flowing lawns right up to the windows of the house. The soil was soon exhausted, yet the food was never enough. There were always too many mouths to feed.

The consequent flight to the towns in search of a better life resulted in high unemployment amid some of the worst slums in Africa. Not only that, but the divide between the haves and the have nots seemed to increase, if anything, as the years went by. It was certainly far worse than anything that had ever happened under the British.

There was never any doubt as to who the haves were. To Kenya's traditional tribal groupings – the wa-Kikuyu, the wa-Kamba, the wa-Masai – were added the wa-Benzi after independence. The wa-Benzi were the rich, avaricious businessmen who drove everywhere in Mercedes-Benzes, the transport of choice for the African elite.

The wa-Benzi were matched by Kenya's politicians, as venal as any in a country officially recognised by the United Nations as one of the most corrupt on earth. Kenya's Members of Parliament felt no shame in voting themselves free limousines or a tax-free income higher than the pre-tax earnings of a British MP, in a country with a much lower cost of living. Their self-interest could hardly have been more blatant.

Nor were Kenya's Presidents immune. Half a century after independence, more than one Presidential family counted its fortune in hundreds of millions of pounds, if not billions. The elite lived very well, enjoying the high life and sending their children to expensive schools in Britain, while railway tracks were abandoned in Kenya and back roads reverted to bush for want of any maintenance. As Evelyn Waugh said in *Black Mischief*: 'You might as well be in a British colony.'

Yet all was not lost. Despite its many failings after fifty years of self-government, Kenya had also become an economic power house by African standards. Its young, increasingly sophisticated population was well placed to benefit from the new mood of optimism that swept over Africa as the world order changed and countries in Europe went into decline. Kenya's people had much to look forward to in 2013, fifty years after their independence.

And the British? What had happened to the settlers, those arrogant, unlovely autocrats of strong character and inimitable style, able bodied but rock brained, without whom there would never have been a Kenya of any sort, still less a Kenya that holds a unique place in the history of the English abroad?

A good number left the country in the early 1960s, unable or unwilling to adjust to the new order of things. They took compensation for their farms, sold their businesses and headed for fresh pastures in other parts of the world. There they tried to recreate a lifestyle that, had they but realised it, was already passing into history.

Quite a few returned to England. They had always regarded England as Home, without actually knowing much about it. Parties of *voortrekkers* advancing up the M1 scouted out the English shires and reported back that the land was unsuitable for white settlement. They settled anyway, many of them, buying themselves handkerchief patches to farm, or else drifting into different jobs in which they were never entirely happy.

Deep down, they longed to go back to Kenya. Their hearts were there, and their memories too, troubled from time to time by letters from old servants enclosing photographs of their children and asking how long it would be before the bwana and memsahib would come back again.

Many stayed. Elderly settlers in particular, too old to start again, often chose to remain on the land and oversee the seasonal planting and reaping, just as they had always done. That the land was no longer theirs mattered not a whit. Kenya Africans are famously tolerant. They quickly became accustomed to the sight of an angry old buffer in a Panama hat waving his walking stick and banging on about cattle dips or potato blight.

Frequently the settler remained for a while in the same farmhouse. He was left in peace to drink gin on the veranda, ride horses, mend machinery, chase stock thieves and live the same life he had always led.

When the time came to retire, he went not to England but to Mombasa or Malindi. He lived in a bungalow within earshot of the surf pounding the coral reef half a mile out from the beach, cursing furiously when the vacant plot of land next door was bought up by a hotel company intent on filling it with German tourists.

From the coast he would issue forth three times a year to visit Nairobi for the agricultural show and the races, and to meet his cronies at the Muthaiga Club, just as he had always done. As like as not he would have his children and his grandchildren with him too, because there was still plenty of room in the country for British people prepared to pull their weight.

Fifty years after independence, some settler families could count themselves as seventh generation Kenyans, with passports to match.

Those who returned to Britain in the 1960s went home to a country broadly sympathetic to the British Empire and all it had stood for. As the years passed and the country lost its way, attitudes changed.

Old Kenya hands were disconcerted to find themselves increasingly under attack as the villains of the piece, rather than the heroic pioneers that they had imagined. They were puzzled when their own grandchildren told them with the certainty of youth that the British should never have been in Kenya.

It was hard to know what should have happened instead. There was no Kenya before the British arrived. The slavery along the coast was matched by an interior without reading, writing or the wheel. The British had moved in to forestall the Germans. Critics of the move rarely had a better suggestion.

As the settlers saw it, Kenya had been a Crown colony for 43 years. The British had taken it from nothing at the beginning of that time to a fully-fledged Parliamentary democracy at the end. They had given the country back to the Africans in apple pie order, with roads, railways, schools, hospitals and a vibrant economy flourishing under the rule of law. The settlers wondered what they had done that was so wrong.

They were particularly irritated by newspaper reports that surfaced in December 2008, just after Barack Obama's election as the new President of the United States. According to *The Times* of London, Obama's Luo grandfather (or maybe his father, *The Times* could never decide which) had been imprisoned and tortured by the British in 1949, supposedly for being a member of Mau Mau.

The reports alleged that Hussein Onyango Obama's testicles had been squeezed with pincers by an African gaoler on British orders. The image of Barack Obama's grandfather as a fearless freedom fighter suffering at the hands of brutal imperialists went down very well in the United States, but it did not impress old Kenya hands. They were immediately sceptical at the idea of a Luo being involved with Mau Mau in 1949, let along being tortured by the British.

Further investigation revealed that the story had no credible source. Nor was there any record of Obama's trial or conviction. He had subsequently held jobs that would not have been available to a man who had been in prison.

Settlers who pointed this out to *The Times* were brushed off with the assurance that the story was fact, not hearsay. It wasn't until President

Obama, in an aside about the American prison in Guantanamo Bay, observed that the British don't do torture that *The Times* fell reluctantly silent.

Others remained determined to believe the worst about the British in Kenya. Minds closed to the possibility that the British might have done any good in the country, academic historians wrote books that often read as if the authors had begun with fashionably anti-colonial conclusions and then worked backwards in search of facts to fit their case.

The BBC even ran a photograph of Kikuyu children killed by Mau Mau at Lari with the suggestion that it was the British who had been responsible.

Happily, Kenya's Africans are better informed. The ties between the two countries remain close. Fifty years after independence, British troops continue to train in Kenya and British tourists are always welcome.

White Kenyans of British origin have been elected to Kenya's Parliament. Thousands of others still live and work there, good citizens, playing a full and useful part in developing one of the most wonderful countries in the world. *Harambee*! Long may it continue.

BIBLIOGRAPHY

Anderson, Major G. H., *African safaris*, Nakuru, no date

Baker, Carlos, *Ernest Hemingway, a life story*, London, 1969

Benuzzi, Felice, *No picnic on Mount Kenya*, London, 1952

Blixen, Karen, *Out of Africa*, London, 1937

Blundell, Sir Michael, *So rough a wind*, London, 1964

Boteler, Captain Thomas, *Narrative of a voyage of discovery to Africa and Arabia*, London, 1835

Boyes, J., *King of the wa-Kikuyu*, London, 1911

Brockway, Fenner, *Towards tomorrow*, London, 1977

Chatterton, E. Keble, *The Königsberg adventure*, London, 1932

Churchill, Winston, *My African journey*, London, 1908

Clayton, Anthony, *Counter-insurgency in Kenya 1952–60*, Nairobi, 1976

Cobbold, Lady Evelyn, *Kenya, the land of illusion*, London, 1935

Cohen, Morton, *Rider Haggard, His life and work*, London, 1960

Cole, Lady Eleanor, *Random recollections of a pioneer Kenya settler*, Woodbridge, 1975

Corbett, Jim, *Treetops*, Nairobi, 1955

Coupland, R., *East Africa and its invaders*, Oxford, 1938

Cox, Richard, *Kenyatta's country*, London, 1965

Cranworth, Lord, *A colony in the making*, London, 1912

Davie, Michael, *The diaries of Evelyn Waugh*, London, 1976

Dinesen, Thomas, *My sister, Isak Dinesen*, London, 1975

Douglas-Home, Charles, *Evelyn Baring*, London, 1978

Eliot, Sir Charles, *The East Africa Protectorate*, London, 1905

Furneaux, Rupert, *The murder of Lord Erroll*, London, 1961

Grogan, E. S. and Sharp, A. H., *From the Cape to Cairo*, London, 1902

Haggard, Sir H. R., *The days of my life*, London, 1926

Hardy, Ronald, *The iron snake*, London, 1965

Henderson, Ian and Philip Goodhart, *The Hunt for Kimathi*, London, 1958

Hillcourt, William, *Baden-Powell, the two lives of a hero*, London, 1964

Holman, Dennis, *Bwana Drum*, London, 1964

Howard-Williams, E. L., *Paradise precarious*, Nairobi, no date

Huxley, Elspeth, *White man's country. Lord Delamere and the making of Kenya*, London, 1935

Huxley, Elspeth, *The flame trees of Thika*, London, 1959

Huxley, Elspeth, *Forks and hope*, London, 1964

Kariuki, Josiah Mwangi, *'Mau Mau' detainee*, Oxford, 1963

Kenyatta, Jomo, *Facing Mount Kenya*, London, 1938

Kitson, Frank, *Gangs and Counter-gangs*, London, 1960

Krapf, J. L., *Travels, researches, and missionary labours, during an eighteen years' residence in Eastern Africa*, London, 1860

Leakey, L. S. B., *Kenya*, London, 1936

Lord, John, *Duty, honour, empire – the life and times of Colonel Richard Meinertzhagen*, London, 1971

Macdonald, J. R. L., *Soldiering and surveying in British East Africa*, London, 1897

Majdalany, Fred, *State of Emergency*, London, 1962

Maraniss, David, *Barack Obama*, London, 2012

Marshall MacPhee, A., *Kenya*, London, 1968

Meinertzhagen, Richard, *Kenya diary 1902–6*, London, 1957

Meinertzhagen, Richard, *Army diary 1899–1926*, London, 1960

Meinertzhagen, Richard, *Diary of a black sheep*, London, 1964

Millais, J. G., *Life of Frederick Courtney Selous DSO*, London, 1918

Miller, Charles, *The lunatic express*, London, 1972

Miller, Charles, *Battle for the bundu*, London, 1974

Mosley, Leonard, *Duel for Kilimanjaro*, London, 1963

Moyse-Bartlett, Lt. Col. H., *The King's African Rifles*, Aldershot, 1956

Murray-Brown, Jeremy, *Kenyatta*, London, 1972

Nevill, Ralph, *Light come, light go*, London, 1909

Obama, Barack, *Dreams from my father*, London 2011

Owen, Captain W. F. W., *Narrative of voyages to explore the shores of Africa, Arabia and Madagascar*, London, 1833

Pretorius, P. J., *Jungle man*, London, 1947

Rawcliffe, D. H., *The struggle for Kenya*, London, 1954

Reynolds, E. E., *Baden-Powell, a biography*, London, 1957

Roosevelt, Theodore, *African game trails*, London, 1910

Shankland, Peter, *The phantom flotilla*, London, 1968

Sherbrooke Walker, Eric, *Treetops Hotel*, London, 1962

Sherbrooke Walker, Eric (as James Barbican), *The confessions of a rum runner*, London, 1927

Sibley, Major J. R., *Tanganyikan guerrilla*, London, 1973

Stoneham, C. T., *Out of barbarism*, London, 1955

Svendsen, Clara, *The Life and Destiny of Karen Blixen*, London, 1970

The Times, History of the war, Vols X, XII, XIII, XIX, London, 1919

Thomson, Joseph, *Through Masai Land*, London, 1885

Thomson, Rev. James B., *Joseph Thomson, African explorer*, London, 1897

Wade, E. K., *Twenty-seven years with Baden-Powell*, London, 1957

Wymer, Norman, *The man from the Cape*, London, 1959

Also by Nicholas Best (www.nicholasbest.co.uk):

TENNIS AND THE MASAI

A comic novel about a Kenya prep school, later serialized on BBC Radio 4

'Wickedly funny' – *Daily Mail*
'The funniest book of the year' – *Daily Telegraph*
'The funniest book I have read since David Lodge's *Small World*' – *Sunday Times*
'Less savage than Evelyn Waugh, Best is every bit as sharp... an immensely enjoyable book' – *Evening Standard*
'Very good entertainment' – Sir Alec Guinness (*Sunday Times* book of the year)

WHERE WERE YOU AT WATERLOO?

A comic novel about the British army

'As a satire on military bigotry and shambling officialdom, *Where were you at Waterloo?* is in places as sharp as Waugh and sometimes better' – *Times Literary Supplement*
'Combines military satire with exotic thrills in a book reminiscent at its best of that sublime beast *Black Mischief*' – *Financial Times*
'All good, clean fun and never heavy-handed' – *Daily Telegraph*
'Passages of pure comic pleasure' – *Spectator*

THE GREATEST DAY IN HISTORY

The story of the 1918 Armistice

'Sets an example that will be hard to equal... Reading it is like looking into a photograph album full of vivid snaps of the world taken during a week of high tension, crisis, celebration, tragedy and illusion' – *Daily Mail*
'Scintillating... a miscellany of tragedy mixed with delight' – *Literary Review*

'An enthralling read' – *Glasgow Herald*
'A fascinating book' – *Good Book Guide*

FIVE DAYS THAT SHOCKED THE WORLD

An account of the five days in Europe from the murder of Mussolini to the announcement of Hitler's suicide

'Riveting' – *Daily Mail*
'Fascinating' – *The Times*
'Outstanding' – *Midwest Book Review*
'Utterly absorbing' - *Macleans*

THE PRESIDENT'S VISIT

A collection of four stories, one long-listed for the Sunday Times-EFG Bank £30,000 award:

The President's Visit. A comic account of a US President's visit to the grave of his ancestors in a sleepy East Anglian village.
Point Lenana. A long-form story about love and war in Kenya.
The Souvenir. A comic account of American furniture salesmen shopping for souvenirs during a cruise down the Amazon. Long-listed in 2010 for the Sunday Times-EFG Bank short story award.
The Hangman's Story. A novella about an English hangman's visit to Dublin in the 1950s to execute a murderer. Based on a true story.

Made in the USA
San Bernardino, CA
19 May 2017